Birth Control Politics
in the United States, 1916–1945

BIRTH CONTROL POLITICS IN THE UNITED STATES, 1916–1945

Carole R. McCann

Cornell University Press
Ithaca and London

First published 1994 by Cornell University Press
First printing, Cornell Paperbacks, 1999

Library of Congress Cataloging-in-Publication Data

McCann, Carole R. (Carole Ruth), 1955–
    Birth control politics in the United States, 1916–1945 / Carole R. McCann.
        p.   cm.
    Includes bibliographical references and index.
    ISBN 0-8014-2490-9 (cloth : alk. paper)
    ISBN 0-8014-8612-2 (pbk. : alk. paper)
    1. Birth control—United States—History—20th century.   2. Birth control—Political aspects—United States.   3. United States—Social conditions.   I. Title.
HQ766.5.U5M43   1994
363.9'6'0973—dc20   93-42738

Printed in the United States of America

Cornell University Press strives to use environmentally responsible suppliers and materials to the fullest extent possible in the publishing of its books. Such materials include vegetable-based, low-VOC inks and acid-free papers that are recycled, totally chlorine-free, or partly composed of nonwood fibers.

Cloth printing   10   9   8   7   6   5   4   3   2   1

Paperback printing   10   9   8   7   6   5   4   3   2   1

For Russ

Contents

Acknowledgments

I have many people to thank for their support and encouragement over the years that I worked on this book. Financial support for my research was initially given by a 1986 Feminist ORA Research Award at the University of California, Santa Cruz, and a 1988 DRIF Summer Faculty Fellowship at the University of Maryland, Baltimore County. I also received the 1989–90 J. Franklin Jameson Fellowship in American History sponsored by the American Historical Association and the Library of Congress, and the 1989 Berkshire Summer Fellowship of the Bunting Institute, Radcliffe College, Harvard University. These fellowships defrayed the material expenses of my research.

In the course of the substantive research for this book, I have been fortunate to work with a number of manuscript collections that preserve the materials of the birth control movement. Susan Boone, Dorothy Greene, and Eleanor Lewis gave me valuable guidance through the extensive collections of the Sophia Smith Collection. David Wigdor, assistant chief of the Manuscript Division of the Library of Congress, immeasurably aided my journey through the labyrinth of the Library of Congress. I am also grateful to Margery N. Sly, acting director of the Sophia Smith Collection, for permission to use materials from the Florence Rose Papers and Planned Parenthood Federation Records, and to Richard J. Wolfe, curator of rare books and manuscripts at the Francis Countway Library of Medicine, for permission to use materials from the National Committee on Maternal Health Papers and the Clarence J. Gamble Papers. I particularly wish to thank Alexander C. Sanger for his permission to use materials from the Margaret Sanger Papers in both the Library of Congress and the Sophia Smith Collection.

The idea for this project emerged when I first encountered the demographic couple in Michel Foucault's *History of Sexuality* during my first graduate seminar, in the history of consciousness, at the University of California, Santa Cruz. My dissatisfaction with Foucault's analysis of the discourse on contraception led me to investigate the field further, and the academic community of Santa Cruz provided a fantastic environment for those investigations. Ongoing conversations with my fellow students helped me refine my thinking; in particular, Ruth Frankenberg, Lata Mani, Chela Sandoval, and Gloria Watkins challenged me to consider race more seriously as a fundamental element of birth control politics. Valerie Hartouni, Noel Sturgeon, T. V. Reed, Katie King, Elizabeth Bird, and Deborah Gordon encouraged greater complexity in my thinking about the interconnections of gender, culture, politics, and science. My principal intellectual debt is to my teachers, Donna Haraway and Gwendolyn Mink. They provided invaluable intellectual nurturance in the early stages of this project, and the exceptional examples they set, as both scholars and teachers, have sustained me through its later stages.

I also thank James Reed, Rosalind Petchesky, and Susan Reverby, whose fine scholarship initially inspired my own, and who provided valuable criticism and encouragement along the way. I am especially grateful to my colleagues in American Studies and Women's Studies at the University of Maryland, Baltimore County: JoAnn Argersinger, Linda Blankenship, Rebecca Boehling, Warren Belasco, Carolyn Ferrigno, Marilyn Goldberg, Daphne Harrison, Carolyn Koehler, Wendy Kozol, Leslie Morgan, Patrice McDermott, Barbara Parker, Freda Pyles, Leslie Prosterman, Wendy Saul, Simmona Simmons-Hodo, and Jean Soderlund. They have provided me with a vital intellectual community, invariably helpful comments on my work, and friendship, for which I thank them. The friendship and intellectual support of Wendy Owen and Edward Orser have sustained my work through the years, but I am most indebted to Joan Korenman, who willingly read the entire manuscript in all its various incarnations. Her incisive comments, not to mention her excellent editorial skills, immeasurably improved my work.

My students at both Santa Cruz and UMBC have also been a continuing source of rejuvenation for my commitment to scholarly pursuits. I thank Rachel Roth, Lisa Hutchins, Beth Beck, Claudia Lenhoff, Andriana Pateris, Mona Shah, Jane Bird, and especially Juliette Forstenzer and Lory Davis, who provided superb research and clerical assistance to me in the critical moments of manuscript production.

Finally, I owe an incalculable debt of thanks to my parents, Marjorie and Forbes McCann, my sister, Marjorie McCann, and her life partner, Carole Smith, for their love and confidence in me. They have unfailingly provided me with an emotional and material safety net whenever my delicately balanced system for combining single parenting, teaching, and writing collapsed. Without their generous assistance it would have been impossible for me to complete this book. My greatest appreciation goes to my son, Rustin McCann-Piatetsky, to whom this book is dedicated. He has lived most of his short life in the shadows of this project, and yet he has given it extraordinary support. For that and for his pride in me I will forever be grateful.

C. R. M.

List of Abbreviations

ABCL	American Birth Control League
AES	American Eugenics Society
BCFA	Birth Control Federation of America
BCR	*Birth Control Review*
CJG-CL	Clarence James Gamble Papers, Countway Library
CMH	(National) Committee on Maternal Health
CRB	Birth Control Clinical Research Bureau
DNS	Division of Negro Service, Birth Control Federation of America and Planned Parenthood of America
FRP-SSC	Florence Rose Papers, Sophia Smith Collection
HBBCCRB	Harlem Branch of the Birth Control Clinical Research Bureau
LWV	National League of Women Voters
MMFQ	*Milbank Memorial Fund Quarterly*
MRC	Maternity Research Council
MSP-LC	Margaret Sanger Papers, Library of Congress
MSP-SSC	Margaret Sanger Papers, Sophia Smith Collection
NAWSA	National American Woman Suffrage Association
NCFL	National Committee on Federal Legislation for Birth Control
NCMH-CL	National Committee on Maternal Health Papers, Countway Library
NWP	National Woman's Party
PPFA	Planned Parenthood Federation of America
PPFA-SSC	Planned Parenthood Federation of America Records, Sophia Smith Collection
VPL	Voluntary Parenthood League

Birth Control Politics
in the United States, 1916–1945

CHAPTER ONE

Introduction:
The Politics of Pessaries

The most far reaching social development of modern times is the
revolt of woman against sex servitude. The most important force in
the remaking of the world is a free motherhood.
> —Margaret Sanger, *Woman and the New Race*

People constantly try to bend what they are given to their own needs
and desires, to win a bit of space for themselves, a bit of power over
their own lives and society's future.
> —Lawrence Grossberg, "History, Politics and Postmodernism"

Between 1916 and 1945 the American birth control movement succeeded in legalizing contraception and making it available to women
in more than eight hundred clinics nationwide.[1] As the movement developed, however, its feminist vision of voluntary motherhood was
eclipsed by the apparently gender-neutral (and nonfeminist) goal of
"planned parenthood." Margaret Sanger, who coined the term *birth
control*, maintained that access to contraception was a woman's fundamental right. With pessaries, as diaphragms were often called, a
woman would not be compelled to endure endless childbearing. Instead, she would have the practical ability to "decide how many children she [would] have and when she [should] have them."[2] But by
1945, the rhetoric of the Planned Parenthood Federation justified contraception as necessary to maintain both the integrity of the American
family life and a "sound national and international population policy";

---

[1] PPFA, *Organization, Objectives, Services* (New York, 1942), p. 3, PPFA-SSC. Although
birth control was a subject of public debate a few years earlier, this study begins with
1916 because that was the year in which the first contraceptive clinic was opened.

[2] Margaret Sanger, *Woman*, p. 227.

women's rights were indiscernible in its rhetoric.[3] The birth control movement thus established a nationwide network of clinics in which women could acquire female-controlled contraceptives, but it did not legitimate that access as a basic right of women to reproductive freedom and self-determination. This book seeks to explain the eclipse of feminist claims to birth control in the struggle to establish contraceptive clinics between 1916 and 1945.

In the aftermath of more than two decades of fierce battles over the legal status of abortion since *Roe v. Wade*, the process by which birth control became "planned parenthood" seems especially relevant. The election of a pro-choice President has stalled the national drive to recriminalize abortion, yet women's right to control their own reproductive decisions, which was never fully realized under *Roe*, has been severely undermined.[4] The Supreme Court's 1992 ruling in *Planned Parenthood v. Casey* opened the door to new restrictive state legislation that could effectively deny women reproductive choice.[5] Although the goal of the birth control movement was legalized contraception rather than abortion, underlying both is the issue of women's reproductive freedom. Thus, valuable insights into contemporary reproductive politics can be gained by reexamining the processes by which feminists failed to sustain their claims to reproductive freedom during the last "postfeminist" era.[6]

Although by no means the first examination of the history of birth control, this book takes a distinct approach to the topic.[7] As Linda Gordon perceptively notes in a recent review of the state of women's his-

---

[3] PPFA, *Organization*, p. 6. I have chosen 1945 as an appropriate ending point because that year marks a pivotal change in the political context of reproductive rights. With the close of World War II and the beginnings of international colonial liberation movements, the site of reproductive politics shifted from domestic to international arenas. The implications of that shift are beyond the bounds of this study.

[4] See Rosalind Petchesky, *Abortion and Woman's Choice*, pp. 101–32, about the limitations of *Roe*.

[5] The Center for Reproductive Law and Policy, *An Analysis of "Planned Parenthood v. Casey"* (New York, 1992), pp. 8, 12; and Rhoda Copelon, "What's Missing from the Abortion Debate," pp. 86–87. Copelon makes the point that "with seven votes favoring the imposition of further burdens on access to abortion, *Casey* is only the beginning."

[6] See Nancy Cott, *The Grounding of Modern Feminism*, p. 282, on the use of this phrase in the 1920s.

[7] See David Kennedy, *Birth Control in America;* James Reed, *The Birth Control Movement;* Linda Gordon, *Woman's Body* (unless otherwise indicated, all citations are to the 1976 edition); and Ellen Chesler, *Woman of Valor*. The Chesler book was so recently published that I could not give it thorough consideration, although I have referred to it where relevant.

tory, "Most historiographical progress—perhaps most intellectual progress—proceeds by rearranging relationships within old stories, not by writing new stories."[8] In re-examining the relationship between birth control and feminist politics, I give greater attention to conjoined gender, race, and class politics articulated in the effort to establish contraceptive clinics.[9] That is, the possibility of freeing women from involuntary motherhood was never the *only* thing at stake in ideological debates and practical struggles over contraception. Within the dominant culture of the 1916–45 period, the declining fertility of the white, native-born middle class relative to that of the ethnic immigrant poor provoked great concern about both the nation's future in general and the advisability of contraception in particular. These nativist concerns, as they referred to women, separated birth control and feminist politics on the issue of women's sexuality and, in turn, stymied the feminist impulses of the birth control movement. Thus, contraception was legalized in terms of the need for society to protect maternal and infant health, the need of families to limit their size to their incomes, and the need of the nation to control the size and ethnic character of its population. The needs of women, as sexual beings, to control their fertility to their own ends were muted by these other rationales.

Existing interpretations of birth control history from 1916 to 1945 attribute the muting of feminist claims to Sanger's single-issue focus, autocratic control, and personal commitments to the medical profession and to eugenics. These accounts hinge primarily on questions about the character of the movement's leadership. The question of Sanger's personality was defined by David Kennedy's initial account of birth control movement history. In his analysis of "the relation between Margaret Sanger's character and the nature of the movement she led," Kennedy interprets Sanger's political actions in terms of her personal (usually negative) psychological motives.[10] Although this analysis both overestimates Sanger's personal influence on the course of birth con-

[8] Linda Gordon, "What's New in Women's History," p. 20.

[9] By approaching race politics as a primary category of analysis, I move from an analytic stance common among white feminist scholars, in which racism in women's movements is seen as a regrettable flaw of the past, to an analytic stance in which racism is seen as a constitutive element of American feminist politics. See Michael Omi and Howard Winant, *Racial Formation in the United States*, pp. 57–69.

[10] Kennedy, *Birth Control in America*, pp. ix–x. For example, he attributes Sanger's feminist assessment of male domination of women's sexuality to a deep-seated resentment of her father. This resentment, he argues, grounded Sanger's "willful" and "emotional" leadership of the birth control movement (pp. 2–4).

trol history and derides her political agency, it nonetheless delimits the terms of the subsequent historiography.

Linda Gordon's analysis of the birth control movement focuses on the class and gender politics shaping it, yet her interpretation of the movement's development between 1916 and 1945 concurs with Kennedy's assessment of Sanger's leadership. Gordon sees a transparent linkage between class position and feminist practice. Thus, Sanger's opportunistic efforts to cultivate alliances with physicians and eugenicists necessarily involved an abandonment of working-class and feminist politics. To Gordon, the transformation of birth control into planned parenthood resulted from an easy accommodation by Sanger to the social control impulses of these middle-class professionals.[11] James Reed and Ellen Chesler, also compelled to engage the questions of Sanger's personality, offer more generous appraisals both of Sanger's motives and of the movement's outcomes. Reed, in particular, suggests that the transformation of the movement into planned parenthood was a realistic and necessary step in legitimating contraception.[12]

Such a focus on Sanger tends to represent the development of the birth control movement as a consequence of Sanger's will as an autonomous individual, independent of the historical context in which she was situated. It also tends to underestimate the political struggles in which Sanger and her "Sangerist" compatriots engaged to define their vision of contraceptive practice within contested gender and race politics of the period. In contrast, I suggest that Sanger's politics, constituted in and through her actions and rhetoric, do not flow from a predetermined personality. There is not a straight line connecting a historical subject's intentions and actions, and its effects.[13] Rather, drawing on cultural studies theory, I argue that Sanger's actions and rhetoric derive their meaning from within the political terrain and discursive horizons of her time. This broader cultural-political terrain set the boundaries of meaning expressed in birth control politics.[14] There-

[11] See Gordon, *Woman's Body*, pp. 249–300. My reading of the archival records reveals considerably more resistance by Sanger to the political tendencies of both the medical profession and eugenicists.

[12] In his preface to the Princeton edition of *The Birth Control Movement*, Reed acknowledges that he was not as attuned to "inequality" and "exploitation" as he might have been, but he remains a "defender" of Sanger's effectiveness (pp. xx–xxi).

[13] Stuart Hall, "On Postmodernism and Articulation," pp. 53–57.

[14] Linda Alcoff, "Cultural Feminism versus Poststructuralism," pp. 428–36.

4

fore, this study assesses how Sanger positioned birth control with respect to the gender, race, and economic order inscribed in the institutions and discourses she both contested and participated in. In particular, I argue that the "political inflection" of ideological elements brought together in Sangerist rhetoric were not predetermined. Although these elements were articulated to specific political tendencies, those linkages were historically contingent. The political accents of birth control rhetoric developed as the Sangerists struggled to legitimate contraception within the web of gender and race connotations and codes that defined American politics from the Progressive Era to the New Deal.[15]

This approach shifts the focus from questions about Sanger's personal intentions to questions about the political process by which the movement that she anchored legitimated contraception.[16] Nevertheless, throughout this book I do treat Sanger as the center of the birth control movement. I am by no means claiming that she was the only figure in birth control history. Until the mid-1920s, Mary Ware Dennett led a campaign by the Voluntary Parenthood League to repeal Federal laws prohibiting the distribution of contraceptives, and Eleanor Jones led the American Birth Control League (ABCL) from 1928 to 1935.[17] Still, in the popular consciousness, Sanger's name and persona were synonymous with birth control. Among supporters, "Sangerism" meant the use of contraceptives by women to control their fertility. Among opponents, "Sangerism" referred to the villainous practice of contraception, which they derided.[18] This identification of Sanger with contraception made her symbolically and practically the

[15] See Hall, "On Postmodernism," pp. 53–55; and Lawrence Grossberg, "History, Politics, and Postmodernism," pp. 65–67. On the historical contingency of racial meanings see Omi and Winant, *Racial Formation in The United States*, pp. 68–69, 72–82.

[16] "Political process" is Doug McAdam's phrase. See Doug McAdam, *Political Process*. I have taken analytic cues from McAdam's work in order to identify concrete factors of the movement's development. I also embellish his model with my reading of Antonio Gramsci's and Stuart Hall's theories of hegemony. See Antonio Gramsci, *Selections from the Prison Notebooks*; Anne Showstack Sassoon, ed., *Approaches to Gramsci*; Joseph Femia, *Gramsci's Political Thought*; Hall, "On Postmodernism"; Grossberg, "History, Politics"; and Stuart Hall, "The Toad in the Garden," pp. 35–57.

[17] On Dennett, see Christopher Lasch, "Mary Ware Dennett," pp. 463–65.

[18] See Florence Guy Woolston, "Marriage Customs and Taboo among Early Heterodites," reprinted in full in Judith Schwarz, *Radical Feminists of Heterodoxy*, pp. 107–9, for feminists' use of the term *Sangerism*. For opposition uses see David Goldstein, *Suicide Bent: Sangerizing Mankind*; and Ben E. Decotte, "Six Arguments against Sangerism," pp. 51–54.

fulcrum of the birth control movement, despite divisions within it. Although controversial both then and now, Sanger was the one person most closely associated with birth control throughout the period.[19] Thus, she serves as the best vantage point from which to examine birth control politics in the period.

I will not retell the story of the birth control movement in chronological detail; that has been amply done.[20] Instead, subordinating that detail to an analysis of the processes underlying it, I examine the alliances, rhetorics, and practices formed in the effort to establish contraceptive clinics. Although there were several efforts made between 1916 and 1936 to legalize contraception, these efforts were largely ancillary to the organization and operation of contraceptive clinics.[21] Legislative campaigns, particularly those run by Sangerists, served as a means to publicize contraception and thereby to spur the establishment of clinics nationwide.[22] The key alliances shaping the movement's clinical rhetoric and practices were ones with white laywomen, physicians, and eugenicists all of whom were associated with the movement throughout the period, and with white social workers and African-American professionals who became involved with the movement in the late 1920s.[23] Understanding the transformation of feminist birth control agitation to family planning requires tracing the ideological and practical connections between the movement and each of these groups as they were shaped by larger imperatives of American politics. I will argue that increasingly constricted space for feminist politics coupled with constraints imposed by the threatened racial and class order of

---

[19] Sanger remains controversial. The contemporary debate on both the left and the right hinges on whether or not she was racist. Drawing on the analyses of Kennedy, *Birth Control in America,* and Gordon, *Woman's Body,* anti-choice advocates have misrepresented Sanger's eugenics in attempts to discredit Planned Parenthood. See, for instance, Charles Valenza, "Was Margaret Sanger a Racist?" pp. 44–46, which examines the current debate; and Elasah Drogin, *Margaret Sanger: Father of Modern Society,* as an example of an anti-choice indictment of Sanger.

[20] See chronology at the back of this book and n. 7.

[21] See C. Thomas Dienes, *Law, Politics, and Birth Control,* pp. 104–15, on Federal laws; and pp. 116–47, on state laws.

[22] Letter of Margaret Sanger to Alice Boughton, 11 April 1932, MSP-LC. See also Ronald and Gloria Moore, *Margaret Sanger and the Birth Control Movement.* This bibliography shows that news coverage primarily occurred in conjunction with court cases and legislative hearings.

[23] I use the term *laywomen* as it was often used in the period. Among scientific professionals of the time, women who were involved in voluntary organizations that had some relationship to a professional group were called laywomen. Science surely did supplant religion.

6

America account for the shift from birth control to planned parenthood. The remainder of this chapter delineates the ideological elements brought together in the birth control movement, which served as the common ground for its alliances. Those elements were rooted in Progressive Era politics out of which Sanger and the birth control movement emerged.

Birth Control and Political Process

Movements for change in the existing social-political order do not occur randomly. A favorable conjuncture of practical and ideological factors, which destabilize the legitimacy of the existing order, can produce opportunities for social change.[24] Such a favorable conjuncture existed for the birth control movement's emergence in the 1910s.

The legitimacy of the prevailing hegemony, the doctrine of limited government, fractured in the wake of tremendous social changes precipitated by the growth of industrialism in the United States between 1880 and 1920.[25] In this period, many Americans felt that society was dissolving into chaos. Liberty of contract in a free market and the aggregation of individual self-interest in government no longer adequately protected public health, safety, and morality. Business was consolidating into giant trusts that monopolized the marketplace. The economy was raked by a cycle of booms and busts. Politics seemed to have degenerated into patronage. Cities were growing rapidly and haphazardly and becoming centers of filth and disease. Social unrest in the form of labor movements, strikes, rural revolt, and racial violence was on the increase. The country seemed to be crowded with more and more foreigners, whose habits, languages, and customs were vastly different from native-born Americans. Even the fabric of family life seemed threatened by high rates of infant mortality, child labor, and women's increasing demands for political equality and independence.[26]

[24] For a discussion of the concrete factors see McAdam, *Political Process*, pp. 40–51, 55–59. Gramsci's concept of the war of position likewise assumes that hegemony is never fixed or stable. See Hall, "The Toad," pp. 54–55; and George Lipsitz, *A Life in the Struggle*, pp. 11–13, 234–42.

[25] Gramsci makes a similar argument in his analysis of the development of modern European states. See Sassoon, *Approaches to Gramsci*, pp. 97–105.

[26] On the diverse dynamics of this period see Robert Wiebe, *The Search for Order*, pp. 76–110, 133–95; Samuel Haber, *Efficiency and Uplift*, pp. 99–166; and Paula Baker, "The Domestication of Politics," pp. 634–38.

In response to this growing sense of social malaise, a multifaceted Progressivism sought to reform the social order.[27] According to Progressive ideology, in an increasingly large and complex society many things could go awry, and palliative treatments for social problems were no longer adequate. Rational intervention and management of social processes were needed to ensure the order, stability, and efficiency of society.[28] The competence of such intervention was assured by science: Progressives had an abiding faith in the value of scientific methods to identify and eradicate the root causes of social ills.[29] Espousing collective responsibility for social conditions, Progressives pursued social reforms on such issues as factory conditions, government corruption, immigration, and maternal and infant health. From a variety of political persuasions, reformers endeavored to regulate and control the vagaries of modern society by extending the reach of government to matters of social and economic welfare.[30]

The political crises of the period also provided expanding opportunities for workers and women to contest their fundamental subordination within the polity. In the chaos wrought by industrialism, the legitimacy of traditional relationships between labor and capital were challenged by both craft unionists and Socialists. In strikes and at the polls, the working class sought to reconfigure the labor process. As government extended its reach to issues of social welfare, traditionally the concern of women, the legitimacy of women's continued exclusion from formal politics disintegrated. The woman suffrage movement, which mobilized over a million women and succeeded in getting the Nineteenth Amendment ratified in 1920, was only one instance in

[27] There has been much debate about whether Progressivism was liberal or conservative politically. See Daniel T. Rodgers, "In Search of Progressivism," pp. 113–32.

[28] Originally, *efficiency* was an engineering term, but the popularization of scientific management transformed the concept in political discourse to refer to rationalization of all manner of social processes. Gramsci referred to it as "American Fordism." See Haber, *Efficiency and Uplift*, pp. 20–24, 51–74, 87–89, 104–5; and Wiebe, *The Search for Order*, pp. 140–52, 160–62, 172–73.

[29] Wiebe, ibid., pp. xiv, 147; Baker, "The Domestication of Politics," pp. 636–37. This is the period of American history during which modern statistics were developed, as the collection of vital statistics was given priority. See Petchesky, *Abortion and Woman's Choice*, pp. 72–73, 84–89; and Chapter 4.

[30] Wiebe, *The Search for Order*, pp. 164–95; Haber, *Efficiency and Uplift*, pp. 54–55, 77; and Baker, "The Domestication of Politics," pp. 634–38, 641. In many cases Progressive Era reforms were not instituted until the development of the welfare state during the Great Depression.

8

which women challenged the status quo.[31] Women also organized in movements to lower infant mortality, end child labor, and improve the conditions of working women's lives. The birth control movement coalesced in this context of wide-ranging challenges to the political order.

In both her autobiographies, Sanger attributed the awakening of her commitment to the cause of birth control to the death of Sadie Sachs. As a midwife working in New York's Lower East Side for Lillian Wald's Visiting Nurses' Association, Sanger encountered many women desperate to control their fertility, but she singles out one case as forever altering her perspective on women's reproductive needs. In 1912 Sanger provided extensive nursing care to Sadie Sachs, a poor and devoted mother of three small children, while the woman recovered from a pelvic infection caused by a self-induced abortion. As she was recovering, Sachs asked the doctor who was treating her what she could do to prevent another pregnancy. Sanger recounts that the doctor told the woman that "the only sure thing to do" was to abstain from having sex. In the face of this inadequate response, Sachs begged Sanger to reveal ways to prevent pregnancy. Unable to provide adequate advice at the time, Sanger promised to return with information. She did not return until two months later, when she was again called to nurse Sachs after a self-induced abortion. This time the woman died.[32]

Although some historians claim this story is apocryphal, whether these particular events actually occurred is not as important as the political epiphany that the story represents.[33] Confronted with death from illegal abortions, Sanger suddenly recognized that it was unconscionable for women to be forced to choose between avoiding sex altogether or risking their lives simply because the government prohibited them from having simple, safe, and effective contraceptives. She took issue with the "doctors, nurses and social workers who were brought face to face with this overwhelming truth of women's needs" but who ignored it. In the wake of her experiences as a visiting nurse, it was

[31] This name for the campaign to win the vote for women was how suffragists referred to themselves. See Cott, *The Grounding of Modern Feminism*, pp. 3, 6–7; and Aileen Kraditor, *The Ideas*, pp. 4–7.

[32] Margaret Sanger, *My Fight*, pp. 51–57, esp. 53. See also Sanger, *An Autobiography*, pp. 87–90.

[33] Kennedy dismisses it because there is no historical record of the particular incident. He claims the story was perpetuated by Sanger in order to justify her claim to sole leadership of the movement (*Birth Control in America*, pp. 16–18). Gordon, in *Woman's Body*, does not refer to the story. Reed, in *The Birth Control Movement*, pp. 82–83, and Chesler, in *Woman of Valor*, p. 63, concede that it might well be apocryphal.

incredible to Sanger that well-meaning reformers should refuse to recognize the underlying cause of women's ill-health and of their families' collapse. As long as birth control was neglected as a legitimate part of preventive medicine, all other efforts to improve maternal health were, in her opinion, merely palliative. Declaring that nursing the ailing bodies of women only eased their suffering, Sanger concluded the narrative with her decision to "renounce all palliative work forever." Instead she vowed "to do something to change the destiny" of women by providing them with knowledge of effective contraception.[34]

With this narrative, Sanger positioned birth control as a feminist issue. *Feminism* is a term that has often been applied vaguely to women's history. But Sanger's perspective on birth control fits precisely the criteria recently formulated by Linda Gordon, who defines feminism as "a critique of male supremacy, formed and offered in the light of a will to change it, which in turn assumes a conviction that it is changeable."[35] For Sanger, women had "always been the chief sufferer[s] under this merciless machinery of the statutory law" prohibiting contraceptives. The consequence was that a woman bore "the weight of man-made laws, surrendering to their tyranny even her right over her own body."[36] For Sanger, those bodily rights included being able to engage in heterosexual activity without the fear that an unwanted pregnancy would result. In addition, traditional morality, which banned contraception to protect an outmoded standard of women's chastity, "degraded women" and taught them "to look upon themselves through the eyes of men." Endless childbearing, compelled by that morality, prohibited women from developing their own self-consciousness, which could come "only by the exercise of self-guidance and intelligent self-direction" of their fertility. But the "self-evident domination of man" could be overturned through the voluntary motherhood that birth control empowered. Once women attained this "basic freedom" they would "not stop at patching up the world" but would "remake it."[37]

[34] Sanger, *My Fight*, p. 56; and *An Autobiography*, p. 90.

[35] Gordon, "What's New in Women's History," p. 29. See also Cott, *The Grounding of Modern Feminism*, pp. 4–5 and 13. Cott dates American women's first use of the term *feminist* to 1914.

[36] Margaret Sanger, "Shall We Break This Law?" p. 4.

[37] Margaret Sanger, *Pivot*, pp. 209–10, and *Woman*, pp. 6, 8. See also Gordon, *Woman's Body*, pp. 284–98, who argues that Sanger deserted feminism in the 1920s. In contrast, I argue that Sanger did not abandon her feminist perspective on birth control and voluntary motherhood. The differences in our respective historical locations account in part for the divergence of my interpretation from that of Gordon. Gordon wrote her analysis at a time when feminists had achieved concrete goals and the future was expan-

A social revolution grounded in voluntary motherhood formed the core of Sanger's vision of birth control. But at the same time, by evoking the rhetoric of palliatives in the Sadie Sachs narrative, Sanger inserted birth control into the discourses of Progressive reform. As is frequently the case for all members of subordinate groups, Sanger's consciousness, as expressed in this narrative, was a contradictory mix of the dominant cultural ideology and resistance to it.[38] Even as subordinate groups challenge the legitimacy of the status quo, they do not "completely break away from the imperatives and traditions of . . . [their] . . . society." Such imperatives cannot be entirely abandoned because they form the horizons of cultural common sense.[39] Yet although subordinate groups use elements of the dominant ideology, they can, in the process of contesting their exclusion, reposition themselves with respect to that ideology and transform it. They can, as Sanger's rhetoric did, bend what is culturally available to new ends.[40]

The very name given to the movement—*birth control*—embraced the values of rational, scientific management. Explaining the name, Sanger noted, "Nothing better expresses the idea of purposive, responsible and self-directed guidance of the reproductive powers. . . . The verb 'control' means to exercise a directing, guiding, or restraining influence. . . . It implies intelligence, forethought and responsibility."[41] By referring to the terms of scientific management, in which forethought, guidance, and control of a process increased social efficiency, Sanger represented birth control as a necessary part of progress. Human reproduction became one more process that required conscious intervention. Without conscious control, hospitals, asylums, and graveyards would be crowed by the weak offspring of weakened mothers. Freedom from unending pregnancies would enable women to bear and raise healthier children, who would, in turn, become productive members of society. More important, birth control would enable women to develop

---

sive. I write at a time when feminists have had to fight vigorously simply to halt the erosion of those earlier partial achievements. Thus I give greater weight both to the shifting political spaces within which feminists can articulate their claim to reproductive rights and to the ongoing contest to concretize those rights. In her preface to the revised edition, Gordon indicates that she as well might reassess the 1920–45 period in light of the setbacks of the 1980s (pp. v–ix).

[38] Hall, "The Toad," pp. 44–49; see also Femia, *Gramsci's Political Thought*, p. 45.

[39] Lipsitz, *A Life in The Struggle*, p. 234. Hall refers to these as "the horizon of the taken-for-granted." Hall, "The Toad," p. 44. See also McAdam, *Political Process*, p. 48.

[40] Hall, "On Postmodernism," pp. 53–55; Grossberg, "History, Politics," pp. 62–65; and Lipsitz, *A Life in The Struggle*, pp. 13–14, 232–33.

[41] Sanger, *Pivot*, pp. 12–13.

other skills by which to guide society to greatness.[42] With this rhetoric, Sanger constructed a powerful argument against the tradition that reproduction, as God's will, should not be interfered with.

Reconfigured, science could also benefit the cause practically. Women, schooled by gossip in dangerous and unscientific methods of controlling their fertility, desperately needed safe and reliable contraceptive techniques. Detached, scientific observation was necessary to distinguish safe, reliable, and effective methods from among the plethora of techniques spread through the underground created by "Comstockery."[43] Specifically, science was necessary to find a female method of contraception. An infrequently mentioned aspect of the Sadie Sachs story involved Sanger's realization that effective birth control meant a female-controlled method:

> I tried to explain the only two methods I had ever heard of among the middle classes, both of which were invariably brushed aside as unacceptable. They were of no certain avail to the wife because they placed the burden of responsibility solely upon the husband—a burden he seldom assumed. What she was seeking was self-protection she could herself use, and there was none.[44]

The "only two methods" to which Sanger referred were condoms and withdrawal. Both left women at the mercy of their male sexual partners: the control women could exert over their fertility depended upon their ability to persuade their male sexual partners to use those methods. Such methods meant that women's reproductive lives were dependent upon the actions of men. Their only other alternative was to end unwanted pregnancies at the risk of their lives. "In an ideal society birth control would become the concern of the man as well as the woman." But, "whatever the moral responsibility of the man in this direction may be, he has refused it."[45] For the time being, however, birth control was of concern to women, not only because men refused to take responsibility but because more was at stake for women: "It is her heart that the sight of the deformed, the subnormal, the undernourished, and the overworked child smites first and oftenest and

[42] Sanger, *Woman*, pp. 54–56, 60–61, 203–4.
[43] This common term for the restrictive birth control laws comes from Anthony Comstock, the original author of the 1873 Federal laws prohibiting the distribution of contraceptive information and devices.
[44] Sanger, *An Autobiography*, p. 85.
[45] Sanger, *Woman*, pp. 96, 98.

hardest. It is *her* love life that dies first in the fear of undesired pregnancy. It is her opportunity for self-expression that perishes first and most hopelessly. . . ."[46] Throughout the years, Sangerist organizations sponsored the systematic research that was needed to develop the practical availability of diaphragms that gave women a measure of self-determination in their reproductive lives.[47]

Sanger tried to remold the dominant ideology of science to further the cause of women's reproductive rights. By advocating birth control in this language, her rhetoric underscored how the society as a whole would benefit from recognizing the right of women to use contraception.[48] But in the cases of two key components of dominant ideology incorporated in Sangerist rhetoric, the political tendencies of the elements were tightly linked to the dominant race and class order.

The first element, derived from Thomas Malthus, held that families should not have more children than they could afford to support. This premise amounted to a "moral prescription" against large families. It was, in a sense, an "economic ethic" of fertility. The calculus of having only as many children as one can afford to support assumes a market society in which children, like property, are counted as assets or liabilities. This ethic became especially salient as literacy and scientific knowledge became increasingly vital prerequisites for securing middle-class status. The need for higher levels of education, and thus more years of dependence upon parents, shifted the focus away from the quantity of children and toward their quality.[49] If society would permit women to follow this ethic, families would not be driven to destitution by the effort to nurture and educate their children. Thus, social efficiency would be enhanced. Children would no longer be forced at a young age into factories, crime, and prostitution because their number outstripped their families' resources. Nor would children be deprived of care and nurturance because their mothers died or became invalids from the complications of abortions or repeated pregnancies. Men too

[46] Ibid., p. 97 (emphasis in original).

[47] The movement did not invent any new contraceptive technology. However, because there were no manufacturers or distributors of diaphragms in the United States before the movement started, its efforts helped to assimilate this technology into social practice. See Chapter 3.

[48] Lipsitz, *A Life in The Struggle*, p. 10, points out that to challenge the cultural legitimacy successfully, subordinate groups must make "the interests of their social group appear synonymous with the interests of all of society."

[49] Petchesky, *Abortion and Woman's Choice*, pp. 34–42, esp. pp. 38, 34; and Sanger, *Woman*, pp. 44–45, 74.

would benefit: They would no longer be forced to slave for too-long hours at too-low wages to keep the brood from starving.[50] The Sanger-ist version of this ethic differed from that of Malthus in that Sanger assumed women had a right to have sex and limit their fertility; Malthus prescribed abstinence.

The second element, based in evolutionary social thought, was the ideology of racial betterment. *Race* was a highly flexible term in this period. It could be used in the sense that we would use *society, nation,* or *population* today; or it could refer only to a particular ethnic group. Frequently, in the discourse of the dominant white culture, these two senses of the word were conflated to refer simultaneously to native-born Americans of Western European descent and to the nation as a whole. Racial betterment, regardless of how race was defined, was a key ideological element of the Progressive Era.[51] Chief among the concerns of the period were the effects that cultural and ethnic diversity had on the quality of American (male) citizenship. Because social decay and foreign immigration seemed to coincide, "old-stock" Americans were greatly concerned that the numerical increase of ethnics and people of color would undermine America's democratic institutions. This fear fueled vigorous debates about how to ease the negative consequences of ethnic and racial differences that produced a range of proposals to exclude, contain, and assimilate that diversity. Eugenics—the branch of biology concerned with the genetic basis of racial diversity—figured prominently on all sides of these debates.

Today we tend to equate eugenics with Nazism, but during the Progressive Era eugenics was taken up by all segments of the American political spectrum. As William Robinson, the Socialist physician, noted in 1916, "The word eugenics is on the lips of everyone, people who know what it means and people who have the most fantastic notions as to the purport of eugenics and what the eugenists stand for." Eugenicists, applying the principles of scientific management to human reproduction, argued that racial improvement required controlled breeding.[52] Nonetheless, many popular movements, such as those for

[50] Sanger, ibid., pp. 60, 203–4; and "Shall We."

[51] On the meaning of race see Gwendolyn Mink, *Old Labor*, pp. 124–28; Thomas Gossett, *Race*, pp. 88–122, 310–69; Allan Lichtman, *Prejudice in the Old Politics*; and John Higham, *Strangers in the Land.*

[52] William Robinson, *Birth Control or the Limitation of Offspring*, p. 124; Daniel Kevles, *In the Name of Eugenics*, p. ix; and Mark Haller, *Eugenics*, pp. 5, 77–80.

sex education, sanitation, prenatal culture, prevention of venereal disease, and pure milk for babies, appropriated eugenics to their causes.[53]

Both social reformers and the general public saw in eugenics the promise of a scientific guide to racial betterment, with which the word *eugenics* was often synonymous. The Sangerist ideal of racial betterment used the scientifically legitimate language of eugenics to position birth control as essential to all efforts at racial improvement but especially to the maternal support programs of welfare feminists. Instead of the overused and imprecise term *social feminist*, I use the term *welfare feminist* to refer to those women's groups associated with the Women's and Children's Bureaus. In challenging the masculine hegemony of limited government, these groups focused on creating social support programs to benefit women and children.[54] In their arguments justifying social programs to improve maternal and infant health, welfare feminists linked maternal support to efforts to assimilate ethnic diversity. They argued that supporting mothers in their efforts to raise good children provided the best way to uplift ethnic immigrants. In the logic of this racial maternalism, a virtuous citizenry could be assured by training ethnic women in the dominant culture's standards of good mothering.[55] In turn, Sangerists argued that birth control was central to the racial betterment that could be achieved through these maternal support programs. Because birth control enabled women to space their children, it allowed them to rise above the drudgery of endless pregnancies and provide better mothering to those children. Likewise, if there were fewer infants, society as a whole might value them more and work harder to ensure their survival.[56] However, contraception, which continued to imply a desire to indulge in heterosexual activity without its 'natural' consequences, was incompatible with racial maternalist definitions of virtuous motherhood. Sangerists were unable to win the endorsement of welfare feminists.

As the economic and racial orders in America have historically been

[53] Petchesky, *Abortion and Woman's Choice*, pp. 93–94; Kevles, *In the Name of Eugenics*, pp. 59–63; Haller, *Eugenics*, p. 85; and Kenneth Ludmerer, *Genetics and American Society*, p. 75.

[54] See Nancy Cott, "What's in a Name?" pp. 809–29; and Robyn Muncy, *Creating a Female Dominion*, pp. 37–38, 57–62.

[55] On racial maternalism see Gwendolyn Mink, *Wages of Motherhood*, Chapters 1 and 2; and Mink, "The Lady and the Tramp," pp. 92–122. On the politics of race and motherhood in the infant welfare movement see also Richard Meckel, *Save the Babies*, pp. 99–101, 116–19, 121–22, 131–44.

[56] Sanger, *Woman*, pp. 232–34.

entangled, so too were the economic ethic of fertility and the ideal of racial betterment intertwined. At moments, the economic ethic of fertility dovetailed with the ideal of racial betterment.[57] The economic ethic made the ideal of racial betterment attainable; restricting the quantity of its children would increase the society's ability to raise children well. The possibility of creating an American race that would be capable of leading the world justified following the economic ethic of fertility.[58] At other moments, the economic ethic of fertility clashed with the ideal of racial betterment. Sanger's articulation of the economic ethic of fertility served as a counterargument to the rigid hereditarianism of eugenic ideology and the antifeminist aspects of their proposals.

Eugenicists tended to represent cultural and class differences as the fixed biological characteristics of race. Given this view of difference as irremediable, the social reforms of racial degeneracy offered by many eugenicists—immigration restriction, marriage licensing, and compulsory sterilization—were primarily negative measures aimed at containing the increase of difference.[59] Sanger disputed this eugenic hereditarianism, arguing that environmental differences, such as economic deprivations, were the principal causes of social degeneracy. Racial betterment, or social progress, depended upon an environment that sustained mental and physical health. Application of the economic ethic of fertility would help to support such an environment.[60]

At the same time, Sangerists relied on the economic ethic to resist the antifeminist proposals given voice in eugenicists' one so-called positive program. Race and gender politics intersected in eugenic fears that the lower fertility rates of the "old-stock" middle class would cause them to be swamped by racial "others."[61] Throughout the 1910s and

[57] In fact, many texts from the period employ both ideas simultaneously, and it is somewhat artificial to pull them apart. By treating them separately, however, my analysis, unlike the existing literature on birth control history, can illuminate both the distinctions between race and class politics and the myriad connections between them. See also Petchesky, *Abortion and Woman's Choice*, pp. 41–44.

[58] Sanger, like Teddy Roosevelt, believed in the American "melting pot." On Roosevelt and the melting pot see Mink, *Old Labor*, pp. 221–23.

[59] Kevles, *In the Name of Eugenics*, pp. 85–95; and Haller, *Eugenics*, pp. 40–57, 142–44.

[60] Sanger, *Woman*, pp. 234, 178, *Pivot*, pp. 241, 251–55, and "Birth Control and Racial Betterment," pp. 11–12.

[61] I follow Gwendolyn Mink's usage of this term to refer to those groups of native-born Americans who, as descendants of Western and Northern Europeans, were represented as being members of the Nordic and Teutonic races. See Mink, *Old Labor*, pp. 124–28. See also Gossett, *Race*, pp. 88–122.

1920s Sangerists constantly had to rebut the eugenical invectives that old-stock women should increase their fertility before they committed race suicide. The duty of native-born white women to prevent race suicide was counterposited to demands for women's reproductive independence by a range of political thinkers, most notably the self-proclaimed Progressive, Theodore Roosevelt.[62] Sangerists responded that increased fertility among the old-stock women would only lead to a "cradle competition" between the children of the old stock and those of new immigrants in an already overcrowded world. Such a cradle competition would result in greater rather than less social degeneracy because too many children would be compelled to vie for too few resources. Instead, Sangerists argued, the society would regenerate if women were allowed to adjust their fertility to match their family income. Moreover, individual women were best positioned to evaluate those conditions; externally imposed fertility regulation would be ineffective. That women were already trying to follow the economic ethic of fertility by illegal means was demonstrated in both the declining fertility rates among middle-class women and the high death rates from illegal abortion among poor women.[63]

In Sangerist rhetoric, the economic ethic of fertility and the ideal of racial betterment were positioned to reinforce their feminist claims for women's reproductive self-determination. However, both the racial ideal and the economic ethic of fertility contained conventional gender assumptions that Sangerist rhetoric did not challenge. The Sangerist ideal of racial betterment, while supporting voluntary motherhood, nonetheless raised motherhood to a sacred duty. Birth control in the service of racial progress did not challenge women's primary role as mothers. Like that of welfare feminists, the Sangerist ideal of racial betterment attempted to reinvest motherhood with social power but did not challenge the traditional notion that maternity was the ground of women's greatest social contributions.[64] As well, conventional gender assumptions undergirded the economic calculus of proper family size under the economic ethic of fertility. The standard expressed was that "any more than the mother could look after and the father make

[62] See Theodore Roosevelt, "Race Decadence," pp. 763–68, and *The Foe of Our Own Household*, chapter entitled "Birth Reform."

[63] Sanger frequently argued against the "cradle competition." See, for instance, Sanger, *Pivot*, pp. 25, 104, "Racial Betterment," and "Politicians vs. Birth Control," p. 4.

[64] Sanger, *Woman*, pp. 74, 231–32. See also Cott, *The Grounding of Modern Feminism*, pp. 3–10, 40–50, on similar self-contradictions in feminist thought.

a living for" was too many children.[65] In neither case did Sangerists contest the conventional division of labor within the nuclear family wherein men provided financial support and women provided nurturant care. Sangerist rhetoric challenged only the lack of women's power to control their fertility within the nuclear family, not its division of labor.[66] Thus the economic ethic and ideal of racial betterment constituted self-contradictory elements within Sanger's feminist perspective that eventually undercut her claim to women's independent right to birth control. This racial ideal and economic ethic in Sangerist rhetoric provided the common ideological ground upon which nonfeminist (and even antifeminist) allies entered into the movement's clinical organizations and helped to eclipse Sangerists' feminist vision of birth control.

That birth control would evolve into planned parenthood was, however, not a certainty in 1916. That transformation occurred as the historical meaning of the movement's rhetoric was made concrete, but not univocal, within its organizational practices. These practices were, in turn, constituted in and through the movement's conflicted coalitions with other social groups within the shifting political terrain of the period.

The birth control movement emerged in the pre-1920 period of intense feminist activity. But political backlashes diminished the political opportunities for advancing explicitly feminist agendas after 1920.[67] Chapter 2 considers the movement's connections to white laywomen within the shifting political terrain of the entire period. Most of the women who became involved in the birth control movement were feminists who, as individuals, supported birth control as a tool enabling women to participate in the social and political life of the country on a par with men.[68] But not all feminists agreed. In the 1920s and 1930s, as the political opportunities for feminist activism diminished, other

[65] Sanger, *Woman*, p. 64.

[66] Petchesky, *Abortion and Woman's Choice*, pp. 34–45, argues at length that the economic ethic assumes bourgeois family relations. Cott, *The Grounding of Modern Feminism*, pp. 130–42, 186–90 argues that few feminists challenged the traditional sexual division of labor in her discussion of feminist discourse about married women's labor in the 1920s.

[67] Cott's main thesis in *The Grounding of Modern Feminism* is that the 1920s represented a transition in feminism, not its demise. See also Estelle Freedman, "The New Woman," pp. 21–44.

[68] Crystal Eastman, "Now We Can Begin," pp. 52–57, esp. 56. See also "Birth Control in the Feminist Program," pp. 46–49, which was originally published in *BCR* 2 (January 1918): 3, 15.

organizations in which feminists participated—such as the League of Women Voters, the National Woman's Party, and the Children's Bureau—refused requests to endorse birth control publicly, contending that it was too controversial. Birth control threatened to undermine the ideology of feminine chastity that grounded the political authority of those organizations.

Since other feminist organizations did not take up the banner of birth control, a critical aspect of this book involves assessing where and how organizational support for contraceptive clinics was obtained. The initial state response to the movement's illegal clinics partly defined the limits of support for contraceptive clinics. As I discuss in Chapter 3, court rulings gave to physicians what amounted to a medical hegemony over contraception. This legal sanction of physicians' authority for birth control was only one part of the profession's emerging hegemony over pregnancy and childbearing. Birth control organizations were compelled to ally with the medical profession in order to operate legally sanctioned clinics. This relationship developed discordantly as Sangerists resisted physicians' efforts to restrict contraceptive prescription to cases in which women were actively suffering from some organic disease. Sangerist resistance to the medical hegemony relied heavily on eugenicists, who helped to legitimate social and economic reasons for contraceptive prescription. In the process of struggle with the medical profession, the economic ethic of fertility was transformed into a standard of medical practice in the euphemism of "child spacing."

Chapter 4 details the equally conflicted relationship between Sangerists and eugenicists. Sanger sought to bend eugenics' scientific authority to birth control and, at the same time, resisted its more invidious aspects. Departing from previous interpretations of birth control's connection to eugenics, I argue that there were positive benefits to this otherwise problematic association. Eugenicists were powerful allies against the medical hegemony. The statistical expertise and scientific legitimacy that eugenicists brought to the movement's claims proved to be valuable counterweights to the medical profession's derision. Moreover, eugenic studies of fertility provided the movement with a language that helped dissociate birth control from sexual controversy. Sangerists used this language as they tried to position birth control as essential to the racial betterment goals of both the wider culture and welfare feminism.

Chapter 5 provides a detailed historical account of the racial politics within the coalitions formed between the white Sangerists and African-Americans.[69] The textures of birth control's racial politics are revealed through detailed examination of the interactions between African-American and white birth control advocates in the Harlem branch of Sanger's clinic and in Planned Parenthood's Division of Negro Service. Although white Sangerists approached their clinical projects in the African-American community from a white racial perspective, these activities cannot be explained simply as efforts to impose white cultural practices on that community. African-Americans of both sexes, particularly medical professionals, who were themselves concerned with improving the public health of their community, shared considerable common ideological ground with white birth control advocates. They likewise articulated an economic ethic of fertility in the service of racial betterment, although with racially specific accents.

Sangerists tried to bend the economic ethic of fertility and the ideal of racial betterment to sustain their claims to women's reproductive rights. Within the shifting terrain of their alliances, however, Sangerists failed to transform the political tendencies to which the ethic and ideal were connected. Drawn from the dominant culture, these ideological elements carried with them a set of paternalistic assumptions toward poor immigrants and people of color that assumed that these groups required the guidance of scientific professionals to control their fertility properly. The presence of paternalistic class and race assumptions undermined a feminist vision because, when poor women and women of color are seen as dependent, the general claim to women's right to reproductive self-determination is diminished. The distance between the assumption that *some* women are dependent upon the proper guidance of science and the assumption that *all* women are so dependent is short. As discussed in Chapter 6, that distance was bridged through the process of building coalitions in support of contraceptive clinics during the economic crisis of the Great Depression. In the context of

[69] See also Jessie Rodrique, "The Black Community and the Birth Control Movement," pp. 333–44. She examines African-American support for birth control. However, in treating this support as relatively independent of the birth control movement, she uncritically assumes that the white birth control movement is racist and discounts interactions between the two constituencies, despite the fact that her evidence is overwhelmingly drawn from the movement's archives. This essay modifies an argument that there was a separate birth control movement among African-Americans which she presented at a panel of the Seventh Berkshire Conference of Women Historians, at which I also presented portions of Chapter 5, here.

increasing demand for clinic services and greater difficulty in fund-raising, the movement's feminist claims were overshadowed by the more compelling rhetoric of the economic ethic of fertility in the serv-ice of national recovery.

These two ideological elements also helped undermine women's control of birth control institutions. Once women's specific perspec-tives on birth control were eclipsed, the control by women of "planned parenthood" organizations was no longer imperative. In fact, by 1938 women's control of the organizations was viewed as detrimental to their fundraising capacity. The institutions built out of agitation by the birth control movement silenced feminist perspectives on birth control after 1945, and I would never argue that this was a positive outcome. At the same time, the movement and its later institutions did actually succeed in getting contraception into the hands of many women, enabling them to have a measure of reproductive control. The birth control movement offers a case in which a social movement changed the ex-isting political hegemony enough to get some aspects of its demands recognized as legitimate. As such it offers an opportunity to assess the costs of partial success.

CHAPTER TWO

Birth Control and Feminism

It is true that the granting of the franchise was supposed to emancipate woman in some total and miraculous way. . . . But complete emancipation of woman cannot be affected while unjust laws in regard to her body are on the statutes.
　　　　　　　—Florence Tuttle, "Suffrage and Birth Control"

Society has not yet learned to permit motherhood to stand guard for itself, its children, the common good, and the coming race.
　　　　　　　—Margaret Sanger, *Woman and the New Race*

The issue of contraception erupted into American political discourse between 1914 and 1916 when Margaret Sanger was twice arrested for violations of the Comstock Act. Named for its author, Anthony Comstock, this 1873 amendment to the U.S. Postal Code prohibited the shipping of obscene materials on both public and private freight carriers. All information and devices that could "be used or applied for preventing conception" were included among the obscene materials proscribed under the law.[1]

Sanger's first arrest occurred in August 1914 after the Post Office, acting on Comstock's behest, banned seven issues of her magazine, *The Woman Rebel*. Unprepared for the severity of the charges she faced, Sanger fled the country.[2] She returned in late 1915 after Comstock

[1] Dienes, *Law, Politics, and Birth Control*, pp. 313–15. This law also defined information and devices that could produce abortion as obscene.

[2] The historical literature contains several contradictory accounts about the reason for Sanger's arrest and flight from prosecution. Kennedy, *Birth Control in America*, insisted that the primary charges resulted from an article endorsing assassination as a political tactic (pp. 24–25, 78–79). Gordon, *Woman's Body*, notes only the obscenity charges (p. 222). Reed, *The Birth Control Movement*, correctly points out that her arrest came after the assassination article but the charges included lewd and obscene articles (pp. 87–88). Madeline Gray argues that Sanger, frustrated by the Postmaster General's refusal to name the offending articles when he suppressed *The Woman Rebel*, published the assassination article to force his hand. She did not anticipate the severity of the resulting incitement to murder and riot charge, which carried a twenty-five-year sentence. See Madeline Gray, *Margaret Sanger*, pp. 75–76. See also Chesler, *Woman of Valor*, pp. 99, 103–4.

died.[3] Without Comstock the government's eagerness to prosecute Margaret Sanger was greatly diminished, and in February 1916, after several months' delay, the state declined its right to prosecute. This action left the prohibition of contraception unchallenged, but not for long. Nine months later, on 16 October 1916, in the Brownsville section of Brooklyn, Margaret Sanger opened the first contraceptive clinic in the United States. In the ten days before the police shut down the clinic, Sanger, her sister Ethel Byrne, and Fannie Mindell fitted 488 women with pessaries. The arrest, trial, and imprisonment of all three women brought contraception into public debate for the second time in a year and prompted other radicals within feminist, Socialist, and anarchist networks to organize local birth control leagues.[4] The issue this time, though, was not the right to publish contraceptive information but the right to provide contraceptives to women.

The events surrounding Sanger's prosecutions were not the first occasions on which contraception became the subject of public discussion. Rather, this was the first time birth control was "put into the discourse"[5] from a feminist perspective of women's reproductive rights and responsibilities. This chapter examines the changing position of the birth control movement relative to the networks and discourses of women's rights advocacy from the movement's emergence within the expansive political terrain before World War I through its development within the "return to normalcy" of the twenties.

The standard interpretation of the relationship between the birth control movement and feminism, among feminist scholars, holds that as a result of Sanger's commitments to the medical profession and eugenics, the birth control movement abandoned feminism. This strat-

---

[3] Comstock wanted Sanger found and prosecuted, and entrapped her estranged husband, William, in hopes of forcing him to reveal her whereabouts. William Sanger refused to betray her, and his trial in September 1915 for violating the New York version of Comstock's law created such a sensation that she returned to face her own trial. Comstock is said to have caught a chill at William Sanger's trial and died a few weeks later. See Reed, *The Birth Control Movement*, p. 97; and Kennedy, *Birth Control in America*, pp. 72–73.

[4] Kennedy, ibid., pp. 73–77; and Gordon, *Woman's Body*, pp. 226–30. Most notable among those who took up the issue was Emma Goldman. Although many of Sanger's ideas originated with Goldman, and although Goldman included contraception in her public lectures before 1914, by Goldman's own account Sanger's actions spurred her to give the issue more attention. See Emma Goldman, *Living My Life*, pp. 552–53. On the issue of Sanger's problematic relationship to Goldman, see Kennedy, *Birth Control in America*, pp. 19, 74; Gordon, *Woman's Body*, pp. 215–21; Reed, *The Birth Control Movement*, pp. 49–54; and Chesler, *Woman of Valor*, pp. 85–88.

[5] Michel Foucault uses this phrase in *History of Sexuality*, vol. 1, p. 11.

egy of recruiting scientific professionals is said to have shifted the movement away from its feminist base among working-class women.[6] Contrary to this reading of the history, I argue that the ideological underpinning of birth control rhetoric, the organizing style, and the form of political activity that the movement pursued were characteristic of feminist politics of the 1920s. In particular, the movement's commitments to scientific expertise, its linking of gender-based rights to race betterment, and its turn away from Socialist politics in favor of individualist reform locate it well within the discourse and practices of feminism in the 1920s.

In the first section of the chapter, through discussion of its early rhetoric and practices, I explicate how the movement first articulated women's right to birth control within feminist discourse. The first decades of the twentieth century were a dynamic period of growth in women's political activism. A variety of women's rights advocates, who chafed under the narrow focus of the woman suffrage movement, came together within Socialist, anarchist, and Progressive circles in 1913 and began to formulate a political agenda they called feminist. Their goal was a complete social revolution in which women would gain psychic freedom, economic independence, and sexual gratification. Yet, as historian Nancy Cott has shown, the emerging feminist discourse and the consciousness it engendered were muddled and self-contradictory. Feminists sought to overturn laws and customs that confined women within the bourgeois family. But at the same time, the shared experience of such confinement was the basis of their gender solidarity. In particular, women's position within the family grounded the moral superiority upon which women reformers' political authority was based. Thus, feminists confronted the contradiction of trying to end women's subordination and yet maintain the gender solidarity and authority based within that subordination.[7] This contradiction continued to shape feminist politics throughout the 1920s.

---

[6] Based on a particularly harsh reading of Gordon's analysis of the movement between 1920 and 1945, a common interpretation is that in the 1920s the birth control movement turned away from feminism as well as from Socialist politics. See, for instance, Mari Jo Buhle, *Women and American Socialism*, pp. 272–80; and Dorothy M. Brown, *Setting a Course*, pp. 112–17. Even Cott, who takes the 1920s period as the transformative period in feminism between suffrage and the "second wave," primarily focuses on the equal rights and welfare feminists. The birth control movement is cited only as an example of the professionalism and middle-class focus of twenties feminism. See *The Grounding of Modern Feminism*, pp. 90–91.

[7] Cott, *The Grounding of Modern Feminism*, pp. 14–15, 35–37, 49–50.

If permeable intersections among Socialist, feminist, and Progressive politics characterized the 1910s, balkanization of those politics characterized the political terrain of the twenties. Inchoate in the teens, feminism split into a number of separate, and often divisive, single-issue organizations in the 1920s. This split was based in contradictions within feminist discourse, but was exacerbated by the pressure on women's rights advocates from backlashes against them. The American Birth Control League (ABCL), founded by Sanger in 1921, stood alongside, but separate from, the National Woman's Party (NWP), the League of Women Voters (LWV), and the Children's and Women's Bureaus. In order fully to trace the continuities and discontinuities between the birth control movement and other feminist groups, in the second section of this chapter I construct an account of the efforts made by Sanger and the ABCL to inscribe birth control within women's rights discourse and organizational networks of the 1920s.

The relationship of these other feminist organizations to birth control was uneasy, even chilly, in this period. Repeated efforts to secure endorsements for birth control legalization from the NWP and LWV were rebuffed. Just as "competing conceptions of gender equality and gender difference" fomented a split between supporters of protective legislation and supporters of the Equal Rights Amendment,[8] the NWP and LWV refused to support birth control because it clashed with their conceptions of femininity, maternity, and progress. Instead of characterizing the birth control movement as nonfeminist, I argue that it is a more accurate rendering of the history to characterize the split among feminists as one that occurred between supporters of equal legal rights, supporters of protection for women, and supporters of reproductive rights. The split between supporters of reproductive rights and other feminists resulted from their divergent perspectives on women's sexuality.

For many women's rights advocates, the birth control movement's assertion of women's right to sexual freedom was an ignominious claim to make within the political climate of the 1920s. Advertising might well have used sexuality to sell consumer products in the 1920s, and social scientists might well have heralded sexuality as the basis of companionate marriage; but within the political arena the combination of sex and politics still made for scandal, especially if the combination was constructed in a woman's voice. Moreover, birth control's implied

[8] Ibid., p. 8.

26

sexual license was contrary to the Victorian ideology of feminine moral superiority upon which many women's rights advocates staked their political authority.[9]

Official silence about birth control on the part of other women's rights organizations profoundly influenced the movement's development. Within this silence the economic ethic of fertility and the ideal of racial betterment through birth control were fully articulated and came to dominate gender claims within the movement's rhetoric. In part, the birth control movement articulated the ideal of racial betterment through its efforts to link birth control to programs of maternal and infant protection offered by white welfare feminists. That linkage was built upon each group's racial maternalism. White welfare feminists offered regulation and support for motherhood as the best means to uplift racial "others" and mediate the dangers posed to American institutions by cultural diversity. Supporting ethnic women's efforts at regulating their fertility was, Sangerists contended, also necessary to the project of cultural assimilation.

Progress and Women: Femininity, Sexuality, and Morality

Working in settlement houses and voluntary organizations, women achieved considerable authority to define political solutions to social problems during the Progressive Era.[10] Maintaining social welfare was a traditional feminine occupation, and Progressive women's various activities followed the traditional form of American women's politics. For almost a century women's political activity had been grounded in locally based, voluntary organizations concerned with moral and social reform. These organizations exercised influence through informal channels by getting in touch with the "great men" to offer their proposals for reform. In the nineteenth-century age of limited government, women's "selfless activities in the home and community" ensured the stability of the republic. But women's charity work had "hardly made a dent in the dislocations of industrial society."[11] Progressive women sought to extend the range of women's traditional charity work

[9] On the importance of this ideology to women's politics see Baker, "The Domestication of Politics," pp. 625, 631–33; and Muncy, *Creating a Female Dominion*, pp. 21–22, 148–50.

[10] Kathryn Kish Sklar, "Hull House in the 1890s," pp. 658–77; Estelle Freedman, "Separatism as Strategy," pp. 512–29; and Muncy, *Creating a Female Dominion*, pp. 9–10, 32–37, 62–65.

[11] Baker, "The Domestication of Politics," pp. 630, 641.

beyond voluntary associations by enjoining formal institutions to protect the social welfare. Women like Jane Addams, Lillian Wald, and
Florence Kelley led Progressive efforts to change both working and
living conditions by seeking government inspection and regulation of
housing, employment, food, and education. They conducted campaigns to increase pressure on political leaders through petition drives
and public education, which took the form of revealing social wrongs
through testimonial documentation.[12]

By the turn of the century the testimonial documentation produced
by women's groups expressed great faith in scientific methods. In the
Gilded Age women took up the language and methods of the emerging social sciences to sustain their traditional efforts to correct the in-
justices against women and children. As scientific observation replaced
personal testimony as the method for establishing the truth, women's
groups began both to rely on experts and to produce that documentation themselves. The Children's Bureau and the Women's Bureau,
staffed by women, became the primary agencies through which
women reformers established "the facts" about the lives and deaths of
America's women and children and, with an emphasis on preventive
education, established themselves as the expert custodians of those
conditions.[13] Each generation of women reformers from the Gilded
Age to the Great Depression mocked the sentimentality of earlier reformers as they paid ever-greater homage to the values of disinterested
scientific method.[14]

But securing social stability through state regulation and education
was only one edge of Progressive women's reforms. Women also used
the themes of progress and efficiency to contest the hegemonic terms
of femininity by which women were denied direct participation in politics. From 1890 onward suffragists increasingly argued that women's
special gifts were needed to solve social problems. The capacities with
which domesticity and maternity endowed women were all sorely
needed in government. Extension of their authority beyond the home
and good works would bring order and morality to government. In
particular, municipal government, as Jane Addams argued, was house-

[12] Ibid., pp. 625–31; and Cott, *The Grounding of Modern Feminism*, pp. 96–97.

[13] The Children's Bureau conducted more than ten comprehensive investigations on
the causes of infant and maternal mortality between 1913 and 1925. See Muncy, *Creating
a Female Dominion*, pp. 30–31, 76–77; and Meckel, *Save the Babies*, pp. 178–82. Meckel
notes on p. 203 that maternal and infant welfare were inextricably linked by 1920.

[14] Baker, "The Domestication of Politics," pp. 630–32, 636.

keeping on a large scale, and women by virtue of their domestic duties were best fitted for it. As modern cities contended with issues of safe food, pure milk, clean water, waste disposal, and public health, women, whose daily lives concerned precisely these issues, were best equipped to solve those problems.[15] Women's expertise in running homes and raising children would be invaluable to efficiently regulating social life on a large scale.

Distinct feminine capacities were not the only grounds on which women articulated their political subjectivity in the Progressive Era. The older argument of women's natural right to the vote because they were the same as men coexisted with arguments of women's difference. The natural rights argument held less sway, however, in twentieth-century fights for woman suffrage. By that time most people agreed that women, if different from men, were equally human. Yet suffrage had still not been granted to women, because government was still a masculine activity. In the twentieth century the state began to emerge as the broker of group interests and, in so doing, became responsible for establishing just and moral social policy. As government extended its reach to social and economic policy the distinctions between the separate spheres of masculine and feminine influence diminished. Woman suffrage became less threatening as the distinctions between the masculine realm of government and the feminine realm of community good works dissipated. Gender differences became less of a reason for excluding women from the masculine arena of politics and instead became an increasingly compelling reason to include them as one of the groups whose interests were brokered by the state. In the 1910s, arguments for woman suffrage based on gender equality were often offered in conjunction with arguments based on gender differences. Harriet Burton Laidlaw represented the easy conjoining of equality and difference in her 1912 statement that "insofar as women were like men they ought to have the same rights; insofar as they were different they must represent themselves."[16] Twentieth-century suffragists increasingly argued for equal rights to allow women to make their special contributions to society. They "sought to give women the same capacity as men so they could express their differences."[17] Thus women's rights advocates in the Progressive Era contested the dominant culture's

[15] Ibid., pp. 633–41; Kraditor, *The Ideas*, p. 142; and Mink, "Lady," pp. 101–2, 106–9.
[16] Laidlaw is cited in Kraditor, *The Ideas*, p. 111, and Cott, *The Grounding of Modern Feminism*, p. 21.
[17] Cott, ibid., p. 30.

29

definition of the proper sphere of feminine influence while they simultaneously upheld the notion that masculinity and femininity were distinct. Men were men and women were women, but both should have the same capacity to participate in the political life of the nation.

As it developed, the birth control movement followed this pattern of women's rights advocacy. Between 1914 and 1916 Sanger used direct action tactics to generate public discussion; after 1916 she turned to more conventional strategies of women's politics. Throughout the 1920s the ABCL's political action relied on two major strategies. The first was to organize support for legalized birth control among professionals and organizations concerned with social welfare. It targeted such groups as the National Conference of Social Work, the American Medical Association, the NWP and LWV, and the Children's Bureau as well as social scientists, clergy, and legislators. The second strategy was to generate support within local communities for opening and operating birth control clinics. The birth control movement also reflected the commitment to scientific methods common among women reformers. Throughout its history, Sanger's clinic collected and published data that demonstrated the efficacy of pessaries. Over the years in the *Birth Control Review,* testimonial letters from mothers pleading for contraceptives were replaced by statistical surveys of effective contraceptive practices.[18]

To justify legalizing contraception, Sanger linked it to the Progressive reform agenda through her concept of the feminine spirit. As the "motive power of woman's nature," the feminine spirit was one of the "great driving forces" within humanity, "the action and reaction" of which "give character to civilization." It constituted "the absolute, elemental, inner urge of womanhood," from which "woman's desire for freedom is born." As an aspect of natural law, its impulses could be followed by blind instinct or consciously, but they would be followed. It was futile for society to attempt to restrict women's freedom. "Driven by an irresistible force within them, [women] will always seek wider freedom and greater self-development regardless of the cost."[19] If "given free play" the feminine spirit "asserts itself in beneficent ways;

[18] On the role of publicity in social reforms of this period, and on women reformers' commitment to research and advocacy, see Muncy, *Creating a Female Dominion,* pp. 17, 21, 55–58, 80–82, 111.

[19] Sanger, *Woman,* pp. 10, 9, 27–28. See also Chesler, *Woman of Valor,* pp. 192–94. On similar representations of women's essential nature by women reformers see Mink, "Lady," pp. 97–101.

interfered with, it becomes destructive." Fundamental to the feminine spirit was the impulse to limit fertility to the level of prevailing social conditions. "The chief obstacles to the normal expression" of this impulse were "undesired pregnancy and the burden of unwanted children." Following Progressive logic, by which the only way to ensure efficient social processes and thus progress was to bring human laws into alignment with natural law, the only rational course of action was to give women ready access to contraception by repealing the Comstock law. If women continued to be denied this freedom, society would continue to be inefficient. If reproduction were not brought under rational management, efforts to manage other segments of society efficiently would fail. Thus, according to Sanger, society had two choices: it could either try in vain "to crush that which is uncrushable, or it [could] recognize women's claim to freedom and cease to impose diverting and destructive barriers." The latter course meant legalizing "scientific contraceptives."[20]

Sanger articulated this natural law with a particularly feminist inflection. As she argued it, "The question of bearing and rearing children . . . is the concern of the mother and potential mother." She objected to "the State or the Church which appoints itself as arbiter and dictator in this sphere and attempts to force unwilling women into compulsory maternity."[21] The right to control the processes of one's body was a natural right essential to freedom. According to her, "No woman can call herself free who does not own and control her own body. No woman can call herself free until she can choose consciously whether she will or will not be a mother."[22] This is a classical liberal argument in which self-possession of the body and self-regulation of its processes are the grounds of political autonomy. Property in one's body is the bedrock of individual freedom, delimiting the domain of government authority.[23]

Sanger conjoined gender equality and gender difference in her demands for women's bodily integrity. She argued that insofar as women were like men, they had the same natural right to property in their bodies. To her, the feminine spirit should be no more restricted by social law than was the masculine spirit. However, insofar as women were different from men, their natural property necessarily included

[20] Sanger, *Woman*, pp. 10, 28–29.
[21] Sanger, *Pivot*, p. 197.
[22] Sanger, *Woman*, p. 94. See also Sanger, *Pivot*, p. 259.
[23] Petchesky, *Abortion and Woman's Choice*, pp. 2–8; and Mink, "Lady," pp. 95–96.

their "reproductivity." With this argument, Sanger extended the classical liberal construction of bodily integrity, which referred only to the right of independent manhood to self-preservation and voluntary labor. But, as she pointed out, a woman "goes through the vale of death alone, each time a babe is born." Because it was a matter of life and death, "it is the right neither of man nor the state to coerce her into this ordeal." It was a woman's "right to decide whether she will endure it."[24] The instinct of self-preservation, which grounded the inalienable rights of the individual's bodily integrity, dictated that women had an inalienable right to control their reproductive capacities. Prohibiting birth control violated women's most basic instinct, and according to her reading of it, history showed that the suppression of birth control led women to use "violent means of freeing" themselves: "infanticide, child abandonment and abortion."[25]

Access to and use of contraception would give women the same capacity of self-possession enjoyed by men, eliminating the inequities women faced. Such freedom, Sanger believed, would never be received until women organized to take it for themselves. Yet, although Sanger's rhetoric gave voice to many of the same themes heard today in pro-choice rhetoric, she insisted on recognition of women's bodily integrity primarily to enable women to express their gender difference. Self-possession would enable women to participate in life on a par with men, but with this freedom, Sanger claimed, women must express their unique qualities:

> The woman is not needed to do man's work. She is not needed to think man's thoughts. She need not fear that the masculine mind, almost universally dominant, will fail to take care of its own. Her mission is not to enhance the masculine spirit, but to express the feminine; hers is not to preserve a man-made world, but to create a human world by the infusion of the feminine element into all of its activities.[26]

Thus Sanger's arguments brought equal rights to the service of ex-

[24] Sanger, *Woman*, pp. 11, 100.
[25] Ibid, pp. 11, 10. See pp. 11–28 for Sanger's rendering of human reproductive history. This fear of death was not exaggerated by Sanger; in 1913 the death rates of women in childbirth were second only to tuberculosis. See Meckel, *Save the Babies*, p. 202. On women's great fear of death and disability in childbearing in the period see Judith Walzer Leavitt, *Brought to Bed*, pp. 27–35.
[26] Sanger, *Woman*, pp. 98–99.

pressing gender difference. The feminine element, "manifest most frequently in motherhood, but greater than maternity," infused into society would "for the first time . . . establish a true equilibrium and 'balance of power' in the relation of the sexes."[27] Women, with possession of birth control, would not be "compelled to give lavishly of their physical and spiritual strength in bearing and rearing large families." Such women would work to ensure that all children would have a "similar opportunity . . . [to] work out their own destinies."[28] These women would be able to direct their previously "dormant qualities of strength, courage and vigor" to contribute "directly to the progress of [their] times or the betterment of social conditions." Expression of the feminine spirit would correct the "impoverishment" of all areas of human endeavor.[29]

Sanger's rhetoric used Progressive ideology to construct women as autonomous, independent, although uniquely feminine political agents. Reiterating gestures of feminist discourse, her feminine subject would ensure social progress through rational control of her reproductivity. But for Sanger social progress was not the only reason for contraception; the nature of women's sexuality required access to contraception as well. Sanger's articulation of women's right to birth control also drew on and helped to constitute a new sexuality that was blossoming among feminists, Socialists, and anarchists.

In Greenwich Village in the 1910s the intersections of Socialist, anarchist, and women's rights organizations constituted the terrain in which a group of younger bohemian intellectuals began to formulate an analysis of society that questioned both class and sex hierarchies. Located primarily in and around the Socialist Party but heavily influenced by the IWW, their analysis brought together the Socialist critique of capitalism's oppression of the working class with a critique of bourgeois culture's repression of the individual.[30] Based on their particularly American misreading of the "repression hypothesis," these intellectuals rebelled against the constraints on self-development and self-expression imposed by bourgeois values.[31] Against Victorian sexual ethics the intellectuals offered a "new morality" based on the

---

[27] Ibid., p. 10; Sanger, *Pivot*, p. 275.

[28] Sanger, *Woman*, p. 54, and *Pivot*, pp. 273–74.

[29] Sanger, *Pivot*, p. 272, and *Woman*, pp. 54, 99.

[30] Buhle, *Women and American Socialism*, pp. 258–59; Cott, *The Grounding of Modern Feminism*, p. 35.

[31] The misreading of the repression hypothesis saw repression as bad rather than as necessary to the progress of human history.

teachings of Krafft-Ebing, Havelock Ellis, Ellen Key, and Edward Carpenter. In these works, American leftist intellectuals found an argument for the elimination of sexual repression that became the basis of their rebellion against bourgeois cultural institutions. The new psychology posited sexual desire as the motor behind the evolution of both individual psyches and civilization, and thus the expression of sexual desire was central to individual self-development and social progress. Blurring the boundaries of culture and politics, the new morality added the dimension of sexual love to the "cooperative commonwealth" envisioned by American Socialists.[32]

The new psychology provided a scientific theory of sexuality that recognized that women as well as men experienced erotic desire. Women within the Socialist and women's rights networks of Greenwich Village gave greater weight to (hetero)sexuality than did other women's rights advocates. They were committed to transforming the conventional ideas of submissive femininity, and they used the new psychology's articulation of female desire to push against the Victorian femininity of "nurturant service and moral uplift." One group of women whose "central aim" was to explore the dimensions of "individual psychic freedom" joined together into a Saturday luncheon club. They called the club Heterodoxy and themselves heterodites. The club's purpose was to afford members of the opportunity to create "a new consciousness in women" that depended on the "will to vote, desire for economic self-support and the social revaluation of outgrown customs and standards," especially sexual standards. Women, in their view, were "preparing to reject all forms of subservience."[33] A "joyfully self-important motive to flout convention" characterized the "spirit of rebellion" to which heterodites were committed. According to their reading of the new psychology, the sex drive was as strong in women as in men; thus sexual love was healthy, natural for women, and should "be allowed to flourish without restriction."[34] The spirit of rebellion and cultural blasphemy engendered by the new psychology was not unique to these women; it was common among radical male intellectuals of the period, for whom Socialism redressed the insufficiencies of bourgeois

[32] Buhle, *Women and American Socialism*, pp. 24–25, 257.

[33] Cott, *The Grounding of Modern Feminism*, pp. 37, 39; Buhle, *Women and American Socialism*, p. 291.

[34] Cott, *The Grounding of Modern Feminism*, p. 36; Buhle, *Women and American Socialism*, p. 260.

Progressivism.[35] However, as Nancy Cott argues, among women it represented the most radical edge of nascent feminist consciousness, because it challenged the terms of Victorian femininity, which equated virtue with chastity.

Within this spirit of rebellion and cultural blasphemy Sanger first articulated women's right to control their fertility as a necessary condition for freely expressing their sexuality. In *The Woman Rebel* Sanger condemned marriage as a degenerate institution and proclaimed that woman's duty was "to look the whole world in the face with a go-to-hell look in the eyes, to have an ideal, to speak and act in defiance of convention."[36] In its pages women's rights included "the Right to be an Unmarried Mother, the Right to Destroy," and "the Right to Create."[37] Sanger's rhetorical and organizational bases for this venture were solidly grounded in Socialist-anarchist circles. Sanger had been an organizer for the Socialist Party and often gave lectures on sexual hygiene to Party locals. Socialist Party and IWW locals distributed Sanger's pamphlet, *Family Limitation*, which she released as she fled the country after her first arrest in 1914. But, although a member of the Socialist Party, she was always closer to the IWW anarchists from whom she derived her direct-action tactics.[38]

The support that Sanger received during her prosecutions came from the middle-class, leftist intellectuals of Greenwich Village who were most familiar with the new morality.[39] Individual feminists flocked to Sanger's call for support during her prosecutions.[40] Such people as Emma Goldman, Rose Pastor Stokes, Elizabeth Gurley Flynn, Jessie Ashley, Caroline Nelson and others wrote and spoke in defense of Sanger and worked in local birth control leagues.[41] These women

[35] See Ellen Kay Trimberger, "Feminism, Men, and Love," pp. 131–52.
[36] Quoted in Gray, *Margaret Sanger*, p. 70. The first issue of *The Woman Rebel* included, among other things, Emma Goldman's now-classic article "On Marriage and Love."
[37] Ibid., p. 72. The April–May issue carried an article about the dangers of abortion. The mere presence of the word was enough to cause the Post Office to ban the issue.
[38] She also wrote articles on sexuality in 1912 for the *New York Call* and spoke to a meeting of Heterodoxy. See Gordon, *Woman's Body*, pp. 213–25; Buhle, *Women and American Socialism*, pp. 272–80; Schwarz, *Radical Feminists*, pp. 81–82; and Sanger, *Autobiography*, pp. 105–6 and *My Fight*, p. 132. On her tactics see Buhle, *Women and American Socialism*, pp. 274–77.
[39] This source of support has been used as evidence that Sanger abandoned Socialist politics before the Great War and Red Scare. See Gordon, *Woman's Body*, pp. 215, 220–21; and Buhle, *Women and American Socialism*, pp. 278–79.
[40] Several Heterodoxy members, including Elsie Clews Parsons, Mary Ware Dennett, and Fannie Hurst, were among them.
[41] Gordon, *Woman's Body*, pp. 212–30.

grounded their support for legalized contraception in a political analysis that linked economic and sexual oppression. Sanger made this connection as well. Until the Red Scare, she focused on the links between class conflict and gender conflict. Many Socialist-feminist birth control supporters, including Sanger, saw themselves as disrupting the capitalist conspiracy to keep the working class poor and multiplying by instructing working-class women in the secrets of the rich.

The introduction to the 1915 edition of *Family Limitation,* which was the major source of contraceptive information throughout the period, presented birth control as necessary to class struggle and women's liberation.[42] The pamphlet began with this disclaimer: "There is no need for any one to explain to the working-class men and women in America what this pamphlet is written for or why it is necessary that they should have this information. They know better than I could tell them, so I shall not try." It continued: "The working class can use direct action by refusing to supply the market with children to be exploited by refusing to populate the earth with slaves. It is also the one most direct method for you working women to help yourselves *today*."[43] These passages explicitly link class struggle to women's liberation from unwanted pregnancy. Elsewhere Sanger argued that "sex morals" had "been fixed by agencies which have sought to keep women enslaved; . . . to use woman solely as an asset to the church, the state and the man."[44] The asset to "male-dominated civilization" gained by sexual oppression of women had "been numbers"[45]—numbers to feed the cannon, the machine, and the priesthood.

But Sanger's critique of traditional sexual morality went farther than criticism of social institutions. Included within Sanger's assertion of women's right to the same bodily integrity that men enjoyed was the assertion of women's right to sexual expression, a right that necessi-

[42] Prior to 1924 Sanger's pamphlet was the best source of information available. It contained more concrete, reliable information than any article published in a medical journal since the Comstock law passed in 1873. Reed, *The Birth Control Movement,* pp. 83 and 397, n. 39.

[43] Margaret Sanger, *Family Limitation* (1915), pp. 2–3, emphasis in original, MSP-SSC. For an analysis of the change in tone of *Family Limitation* before and after the First World War see Joan Jensen, "The Evolution of Margaret Sanger's 'Family Limitation' Pamphlet, 1914–1921," pp. 548–55. Jensen's analysis examines only the shift from what she calls a left-wing rhetoric to a liberal rhetoric. She does not discuss the sexual rhetoric in the pamphlet.

[44] Sanger, *Woman,* p. 179. The title of the chapter from which this quotation was taken is "The New Morality."

[45] Ibid., p. 227.

tated access to contraception. Drawing on the rhetoric of the new morality, Sanger insisted that the sex drive was as strong in women as in men, and, as with men, its expression was healthy and natural. In fact, "a mutual and satisfied sexual act is of great benefit to the average woman, the magnetism of it is health giving, and acts as a beautifier and tonic."[46] However, "sex morals" had, for women, "been one-sided; they [had] been purely negative, inhibitory and repressive." They had "nothing to do with the basic sex rights of the woman, but enforce[d], rather, the assumed property rights of the man to the body and the services of his wife . . . their vital factor, as they apply to woman, is submission to the man."[47] In contrast, Sanger argued that bodily integrity for women, as for men, included the right to refuse sex when they did not desire it and the right to engage in pleasurable sex without the risk of pregnancy, if they so desired. Women's sexuality should not be subject to any more restriction than was men's; such restrictions were abuses of male domination.[48]

Throughout the years it was published, *Family Limitation* gave contraceptive instructions that were framed in terms of women's right to sexual pleasure. The pamphlet's assessment of the various contraceptive methods was phrased in terms of a woman's right to enjoy sex without the fear of pregnancy. Sanger condemned the practice of withdrawal, not because of any assessment of its contraceptive effectiveness but because of its "evil effect upon woman's nervous condition." Withdrawal occurs, Sanger notes, at a moment before a woman has "completed her desire, she is under a highly nervous tension, her whole being is, perhaps, on the verge of satisfaction. She is then left in this dissatisfied state, which is far from humane. This does her injury."[49] In discussing condoms, Sanger remarks that they had "another value quite apart from prevention." This value is not, as one might expect today, that condoms prevent sexual transmission of disease. Rather, condoms decrease "the tendency in the male to arrive at the climax in the sexual act before the female." In so doing it helped solve the common sexual problem of female "sexual coldness," which Sanger attributed to men's "ignorance, selfishness and inconsiderateness." As she argued,

it is usual for the male to arrive at this stage earlier than the female,

[46] Sanger, *Family Limitation* (1915), p. 6.
[47] Sanger, *Woman*, pp. 179, 169.
[48] Ibid., pp. 167–85, especially 178–79. See also Sanger, *Pivot*, pp. 209–14.
[49] Sanger, *Family Limitation* (1915), p. 6.

with the consequence that he is further incapacitated to satisfy her desire for some time after. During this time the woman is in a highly nervous condition, and it is the opinion of the best medical authorities that a continuous condition of this unsatisfied state brings on or causes disease of her generative organs, besides giving her a perfect horror and repulsion for the sexual act.[50]

Such an explicit discussion of women's sexuality was uncommon even among sex radicals in Greenwich Village. Even Sanger's supporters were critical of her explicitness and her tactics. From both Socialists and suffragists she received advice to abandon birth control, or at least tone down her tactics. This criticism referred both to illegal direct-action tactics and to sexual politics. That criticism within the circles from which Sanger had most expected to get support spoke of the limits of rebellion and blasphemy to which even the radicals held.

The Limits of Blasphemy: Suffragists, Socialists, and Chastity

There were limits to the support women's rights advocates would give to birth control because of its sexual implications. Although feminists were committed to being frank about sexuality, their commitment primarily translated into frank acknowledgment of women's erotic desires. In espousing sex rights for women, many feminists were ambivalent about the form and content of such rights beyond observing that women had erotic drives that bourgeois marriage smothered. How those erotic drives might be expressed was unspecified. Also, most feminists were unwilling to be frank in public about their sexual practices. When Elsie Clew Parsons suggested that twenty-five prominent women stand up in court at Sanger's 1916 trial and plead guilty to using birth control only one woman agreed.[51] Despite the ambiguity over the content of women's sex rights, most feminists did agree that this issue should be kept separate from suffrage and would not pursue the issue in public if it endangered that movement. Mainstream suffragists were quick to disavow frank discussion of female sexuality; it was too reminiscent of the free-love scandal that had stymied suffrage

[50] Ibid., pp. 10–11. Other passages of this pamphlet were revised over time. These passages remained the same throughout the thirteen years, 1915–28, in which the pamphlet was distributed.

[51] Sanger, *My Fight*, p. 137. The woman who agreed went unnamed.

efforts a generation earlier.[52] Frankly, many older suffragists disagreed with the premises of the new psychology. Charlotte Perkins Gilman characterized Freud's doctrine as morbid and called the "suppressed desires" theory a "bugaboo."[53]

Sanger decried repeated advice that nothing could be accomplished until the right to vote was secured. For her, "the foundation of the Feminist or Woman's Movement should be how to augment the efficiency of woman, how to release her sexual bondage of childbearing and place it on the plane of a voluntary and conscious undertaking [that she may] be approximately equal to man. Upon this foundation only can she strive for equal rights."[54] Sanger was angered by suffragists who sought to "inspire women" to find "a deeper meaning in their lives" but did not support birth control. To Sanger, "it seemed unbelievable they could be serious in occupying themselves with what I regarded as trivialities when mothers within a stone's throw of their meetings were dying shocking deaths."[55] Sanger attributed feminist reluctance to support birth control to their "inherited prejudices about sex." In her estimation, their attitude, in which "sex as such was akin to sin, shame, and only the bearing of a child sanctioned its expression," continued to be "subject to the age-old, masculine atmosphere compounded of protection and dominance."[56]

Mainstream suffragist attitudes toward sex, although not exactly prejudice, consisted of a complex response to that "masculine atmosphere," which made support for the birth control movement problematic. Much of the political influence that women held derived from the ideology of separate spheres in which women were more moral than men. The moral superiority of women was grounded in the home and maternity. From the 1830s onward women's political activities had been directed against the unjust consequences of men's immorality for women and children. Prostitution, vice, and intemperance were recurring political concerns for women; men's moral inferiority was the cause. The end of legal barriers in education and employment and the entrance of government into social policy blurred the distinctions

---

[52] Suffragist supporters of birth control were also likely to be Woman's Party members rather than NAWSA members.

[53] Charlotte Perkins Gilman, "Back of Birth Control," p. 31.

[54] Margaret Sanger, draft of speech on feminism and birth control, Untitled Early Speeches file, MSP-SSC, p. 1. The text that appears in brackets was handwritten in the original.

[55] Sanger, *An Autobiography*, p. 105.

[56] Sanger, feminism and birth control speech, p. 2, and *An Autobiography*, p. 106.

between the masculine and feminine spheres. Yet, suffragists still staked their claims to women's political authority in the moral superiority of domesticity. As the home, community, and government blurred, women's special moral nature continued to be a primary legitimating rhetoric for their equal participation. The rhetoric of social housekeeping rested not only on women's domestic expertise but upon their naturally greater, maternally based concern for social justice. Woman suffrage was meant to extend women's traditional authority, not abandon it.[57]

Suffragists did not dispute Sanger's claim that women had the same right of bodily integrity that men had, nor did they dispute that women should consciously choose motherhood. The notion of voluntary motherhood had a long history in the women's movement.[58] What they did dispute was Sanger's perspective on women's sexuality. Since the late nineteenth century, opponents of woman suffrage accused its supporters of also supporting free love. This accusation derived from the perspective that woman suffrage threatened the basis of family life and, with it, the moral control of sexuality. Invested in the claim of women's moral superiority, suffragists worked hard to disprove this charge and shunned any issues that smacked of promiscuity.[59] Moreover, many suffragists agreed with Charlotte Perkins Gilman's contention that the sexual function in men, and some unfortunate women, had become overdeveloped. From within this perspective the chief concern in ensuring voluntary motherhood was the elimination of the double standard of sexuality, which held women to chastity and permitted male depravity. What finally distinguished Sanger from mainstream suffragists was not her rhetoric linking scientific control of fertility to social efficiency (defined as racial or economic well-being); it was that she explicitly linked voluntary motherhood to heterosexual gratification. Demands for legalized birth control, which many middle-class women used in private, appeared to validate charges that suffragists were selfish supporters of free love. Contraceptives implied the ability and desire to engage in sex without its "natural" procreative consequences and thus implied the freest love. Sanger's rhetoric

[57] On women reformer's historical claim to moral superiority see Baker, "The Domestication of Politics," pp. 633–35, 639–40; and Mink, "Lady," pp. 101–2, 106–8.

[58] Gordon, *Woman's Body*, pp. 95–116; and Linda Gordon, "Why Nineteenth-Century Feminists Did Not Support 'Birth Control,'" pp. 40–53.

[59] Gordon, *Woman's Body*, p. 243.

seemed to resolve the double standard in favor of masculine excess. Such implications threatened the sexual-political system, which both confined desire and pleasure to marriage and simultaneously under-girded suffragists' claims to women's moral superiority. Thus, distance from the birth control issue was the official stance of suffrage organizations before 1920 and their offshoots after 1920.

At the same time, the influence of bohemian intellectuals who articulated a new morality in the Socialist Party was largely confined to their own circles. By 1914 interparty conflict had led the Socialist Party to a purge of the IWW as revolutionary "disloyalists." That purge and the defeat of the 1913 Paterson strike caused the IWW to withdraw from the East Coast.[60] These changes left bohemian intellectuals and their new morality without a wide base of support within the Socialist Party. The majority of the Socialist Party continued to support the principles of social purity, developed within the national hysteria over the white-slave trade.

Always a chimera, hysteria about the white-slave trade asserted that young women nationwide were being abducted into prostitution at epidemic rates. Providing an explanation for the apparent increase in prostitution found by municipal vice commissions, the white slavery discourse confirmed Victorian ethics, by which no woman would willingly enter into a sexual liaison. The white slave trade, characterized in Progressive terms as "vice trusts," focused national anxiety about female sexuality between 1907 and 1911, leading to the 1910 passage of the Mann Act prohibiting interstate transport of women for immoral purposes.[61] In the Socialist Party view, white slavery served as an example of capitalism's degradation of women. The problem was that low wages and insecure employment forced families (read: fathers) to send innocent daughters out into a dangerous world of abductors and con men. Party policy constructed female sexuality within a perspective of masculine paternalism. Protecting young women from the dangers posed to them by their sexuality was the mainstay of the Party's anti–white slave trade policy. This stance usefully put the Party into the center of bourgeois respectability and served as evidence against the frequent charge by opponents that the Party endorsed free love. The extent of the Party's engagement on the question of women's sexuality

[60] Buhle, *Women and American Socialism*, pp. 274–75.
[61] Allan Brandt, *No Magic Bullet*, pp. 33–34.

was to counter the delegitimating charge of free love by vigilant protection against the white-slave bugaboo.[62]

Distaste for sexual radicalism and direct-action tactics limited the support that Sanger and the birth control movement received from both Socialists and feminists during her prosecutions. Socialist stalwarts were not eager to support her law-breaking activities; the Party's organizing style did not "condone the conscious violation of laws." Kate Richards O'Hare refused to send *Family Limitation* to people who wrote to her paper. Instead she suggested that they write to Congress to demand a repeal of the laws. Because birth control was illegal the Socialist Party was "not in a position to wage this battle at present." In early 1915 Caroline Nelson, a longtime Socialist organizer, urged Sanger to follow a more subdued course and eschew publicity. This, Nelson felt, was necessary to garner working-class women's support. She also suggested that Sanger use less-provocative rhetoric and instead articulate contraceptive information within a construct of morality familiar to the social purity background of the Party rank and file.[63]

The National Birth Control League (NBCL), formed in Sanger's absence in March 1915, also eschewed Sanger's law-defying tactics. Mary Ware Dennett, who went on to form the Voluntary Parenthood League in 1919, Anita Block, Clara Stillman, and Otto Bobsein were the officers of the League, which was formed to seek repeal of the New York State and Federal Comstock laws. When Sanger requested their support in anticipation of her *Woman Rebel* trial the League responded that "a law-abiding organization, formed primarily to change the laws, could not logically support a person who had broken those laws."[64] Dennett later agreed to serve on the editorial board of the *Birth Control Review*. However, in January 1920 she resigned because the "militantly feminist policy" and "terminology of the labor struggle" within the *Review* were a "menace" to the efforts of her Voluntary Parenthood League.[65]

After her 1916 trial the tone of Sanger's rhetoric about women's sexuality and class struggle changed, as evidenced in the *Birth Control Review*. The changes involved a refinement of her rhetoric to fit the

[62] On the Socialist Party social purity campaign see Buhle, *Women and American Socialism*, pp. 249–57.
[63] Ibid., pp. 268, 277. Floyd Dell and Max Eastman also supported a legislative campaign as the best course of action for birth control agitation.
[64] Sanger, *My Fight*, p. 125.
[65] Letter of Mary Ware Dennett to Margaret Sanger, 20 January 1920, MSP-LC.

discursive horizons of class-conscious and feminist politics, rather than an abandonment of those politics. When it first appeared the *Review*, more "staid in contrast to the *Woman Rebel*," garnered a good deal of support among Socialist Party regulars and women's rights advocates.[66] Eugene Debs gave it heartfelt endorsement and contributed an article to it in praise of Sanger. Anita Block of the *New York Call* urged her readers to subscribe. Two members of Heterodoxy, Mary Ware Dennett and Lou Rogers, contributed to it.[67]

Sanger did abandon the rhetoric of class warfare that appeared in the *Woman Rebel*, but the *Review* continued until 1920 to characterize Comstockery as an effort to compel the working classes to produce factory and cannon fodder. Thereafter, invectives urging working-class women to seize the means of reproduction were replaced with pleas for education of these women about birth control methods. Such pleas were still phrased in terms of working-class self-determination, but the specter of capitalist conspiracy had largely evaporated. This alteration honed the focus on contraception. The tone of class warfare was questioned even by Socialists and would have deflected from Sanger's challenges of the Comstock law. Within the context of the United States' impending entrance into World War I in June 1917 and the passage of the Espionage Act in July, distance from even implicitly radical language was essential to keep the *Review* from being banned.[68]

Also absent from the *Review* were proclamations of the rights to unmarried motherhood and the right to destroy (read: abortion).[69] Proclaiming such rights gave the *Woman Rebel* an inflection that keyed into the heart of cultural anxiety over the heterosexually independent woman. Legalized abortion was not supported by any groups within the American political spectrum. In the discourse of the time, despite the physician exemption for therapeutic abortion in some states, the

---

[66] Buhle, *Women and American Socialism*, p. 278.

[67] Ibid. See Eugene Debs, "Freedom Is the Goal," p. 7. Lou Rogers was listed as an associate and art editor from 1919 to 1921.

[68] Sangerists did continue to use radical tactics through early 1917. Upon her imprisonment in January, Ethel Byrne went on a hunger strike, as British suffragists were doing and the Woman's Party pickets would soon begin to do. Sanger, unable to undergo the physical trauma of a hunger strike because of her tubercular condition, offered passive resistance to authorities during her confinement to prison in February and early March.

[69] Gray claims that Ellis convinced Sanger to abandon the right to abortion. William Robinson advised Sanger to restrict her Brownsville clinic service to married women as the suggestion that she was giving unmarried women contraceptives would bring the full weight of the law down on her. See *Margaret Sanger*, pp. 126–27.

word *abortion* denoted a back-alley, life-threatening crime of the desperate. The challenge to the Comstock laws would be deflected if the birth control movement seemed to support a criminal offense that accounted for 25–30 percent of the annual maternal death rate.[70] Birth control was offered to end this "social scourge," not to abet it.

Representing the right to contraception for unmarried as well as married women would have mired the issue within the cultural anxiety over the "decaying morality of American youth."[71] In the first decade of the century recognition of women's heterosexual desire fed anxiety about adolescent female sexuality. The "girl problem" of the immediate pre-and postwar period assimilated the psychoanalytic discovery of female sexual desire into the newly discovered problem of female delinquency, defining it almost entirely as sexual precocity. Throughout the 1910s, and particularly during the war, police powers were brought to bear on young women through active surveillance of their sexual activity. During the war an adolescent girl could be arrested for public flirting or consorting with military personnel. All young women who were arrested for any reason were given a medical examination; if they were found to have a veneral disease they were charged with prostitution and could be incarcerated without a trial for the war's duration.[72] The fact that the criminal justice system could see sexually active young women only as innocent dupes of white slavers or incorrigibly delinquent prostitutes speaks to the strength of the cultural anxiety that women might escape traditional patriarchal control. Both white slavery and the girl problem essentially denied that women might express their sexual desire to their own ends, apart from the proprieties of marriage. Only when sexuality was assimilated into companionate marriage was it acceptable.[73] This was not a cultural context that would allow the legalization of contraception if there were any hint that unmarried women would have access to it. In fact, Mary Ware Dennett complained bitterly that the most frequent objection raised

[70] Joyce Antler and Daniel Fox, "The Movement toward a Safe Maternity," pp. 577, 581.

[71] The 1873 ban on birth control was part of an obscenity law designed to protect the nation's youth from vice.

[72] Brandt, *No Magic Bullet*, pp. 81–92. See also Ruth Alexander, "Psychology, Prostitution, and the Female Adolescent, 1900–1930," a paper presented at the American Studies Association meeting, Miami, Florida, 1988. The Woman's Party White House picketers were charged with blocking a public walkway—a charge used to control street prostitution.

[73] Scharf and Jensen, *Decades of Discontent*, pp. 12–13.

by Congressmen to amending the Comstock Act was that without the fear of pregnancy nothing would keep women chaste.[74] If women now had desire, it was even more dangerous to allow them to have the means to express it without bearing the consequences.

Abandoning the right to abortion and single women's right to contraceptives was not merely a matter of political shrewdness. Throughout its history, the birth control movement's advocates were repeatedly charged with threatening the morality of young women and with being murderers.[75] These charges were particularly potent for delegitimating birth control, because the discursive boundaries of sexual politics precluded support for nonmarital sexuality or for abortion. The particular changes in rhetoric after the war defended birth control against opponents' outright attempts to delegitimate it, but they were also a strategy to invigorate supportive networks.

Even in the pretwenties period of permeable boundaries between women's rights advocates, Socialists, and Progressives birth control was marginalized. From the beginning birth control pushed the limits of what constituted acceptable politics among even the radical edges of feminist and Socialist networks. In linking women's sexual freedom to reproductive control, birth control heightened existing cultural anxiety that women's erotic and reproductive behavior might escape the masculine control inherent in the standards of bourgeois respectability. That cultural anxiety limited support for birth control even among the networks that supported rebellion and blasphemy.

Wartime repression of dissent was directed, in the name of national security and patriotism, at the antiwar left. As a result, the linkages between the left and women's rights advocates were disrupted. Suffrage organizations, whose political opportunities continued to expand during the war, protected themselves by purging leftists.[76] The NAWSA was not alone in this purge; shedding a Socialist identity for an individualist reform identity was common for women's groups in

[74] Mary Ware Dennett, *Birth Control Laws*, pp. 173–89.

[75] As a precursor to the common refrain of anti-choice rhetoric, Roman Catholic clerics referred to Sangerists as murderers. In 1935, for instance, a New York City archbishop compared Birth Control Leagues to "Dillinger Mobs," saying both were "organized to commit murder." See "Birth Control Leagues Called Dillinger Mob," *New York Herald-Tribune*, 18 August 1935; and in response NCFL, "Press Release," n.d., MSP-LC.

[76] Cott, *The Grounding of Modern Feminism*, pp. 60–61, suggests that the Woman's Party grew in part because purged leftists flocked to it because of its opposition to the NAWSA. On the Children's Bureau's response to wartime repression see Muncy, *Creating a Female Dominion*, pp. 94–96.

the 1920s.[77] Nor were women's groups alone in their actions; the AFL did the same thing to protect its growing acceptance by national political elites.[78] When the organizational and discursive boundaries between Progressive, Socialist, and feminist politics resolidified after the war the grounds for support of birth control within those organizations dissolved.

Discontinuities and Continuities in the 1920s: Equal Rights, Welfare Feminism, and Birth Control

Even as suffrage was won, the alliances among feminists that made solidarity possible across "all shades of political, religious, and social opinion" were strained.[79] With the goal achieved, women's common experience of exclusion from public life, the old basis for gender solidarity, disappeared. The question of what to do next posed a problem for revitalizing gender solidarity as much as it posed a question of policy. The retreat from reform and growing fears of diversity during the "return to normalcy" strained gender alliances even more. The 1920s was a decade in which tolerance of dissent and difference was at a low ebb. Space for political opposition was constricting, and within this the basis for gender solidarity narrowed. International peace activists and isolationists squared off over military funding and the League of Nations. Socialists and nationalists squared off in the Red Scare hysteria over Bolshevism. Assimilationists and white supremacists squared off over immigration restriction as the means to securing America's democratic institutions against the "rising tide of color."[80] Jim Crow moved North, and the Klan reemerged in the South.

The National Woman's Party, successor to the Woman's Party, struggled to hold women "of all shades of opinion" together by developing the single-issue focus on equal legal rights. The League of Women Voters, successor to the NAWSA, also struggled to find a common ground. In the early 1920s the League developed the single-issue focus on non-partisan voter education but maintained close ties to the Children's

---

[77] Joan Jensen, "All Pink Sisters," p. 205. The birth control movement's jettison of a Socialist identity occurred in the 1920s, not before.

[78] These efforts failed. The political positions of both women's groups and the AFL were disrupted after World War I because of the taint of Socialism. See ibid., pp. 211–14; and Mink, *Old Labor*, pp. 200–202, 259.

[79] Editorial from *Equal Rights*, 20 August 1927, quoted in *BCR* 12 (January 1928): 21.

[80] Lothrap Stoddard, *The Rising Tide of Color*. This book title also served as a platitude in the 1920s.

Bureau. In its campaign for the Sheppard-Towner Act of 1921, the Children's Bureau focused on infant and maternal health as the issue to unite women. These organizations squelched the discussion of divisive issues. In particular they avoided the taint of sexual promiscuity implied by birth control and the racial division posed by African-American women's requests for inclusion.[81]

Within this balkanized political terrain the belief of some feminists that sexuality already received too much attention curbed support for birth control. In a 1922 *Birth Control Review* article Charlotte Perkins Gilman identified this belief as the primary reason behind the lack of general support for the movement. Gilman readily agreed that "the advantages of a balanced population are plain" and that "no woman should have more children than she desires, or than she thinks wise; she should at least be a free agent in the matter." But although she also agreed that a woman's "abuse in this function is a frequent cause of injury to her and to her crowding little ones, with resultant neglect, poverty and often vice," she argued that "there are two good reasons" why "many free-minded wellwishers to mankind" did not support the movement with enthusiasm. "The first, and most conspicuous [was] this: Among the many evils which beset the world none is more injurious than that sum of vice and disease, shame, crime and common unhappiness, which springs from excessive sex–indulgence."[82]

The second reason she gave was that this "misuse of the sex function" has submerged the "dignity, freedom and vast potential power of motherhood." Birth control on the face of it seemed to seek "to eliminate a consequence while leaving the cause untouched." Greater sexual restraint was the ultimate answer. "The purpose of mating is clear, the accompanying pleasure is not the purpose." Sex was something, according to Gilman, that should only be engaged in for the purpose of reproduction. Birth control, which allowed one to experience the accompanying pleasure without the procreative consequence, was not then in the best interests of conscious social evolution. Gilman gave grudging support to birth control only because centuries of misuse could not be overturned in one generation. In the meantime birth control was "a step in the right direction" toward "directed" social evolution. Birth control at least could reduce the size of the surplus

[81] Cott, *The Grounding of Modern Feminism*, pp. 68–70, on Paul's efforts to keep African-American women's voting rights out of the 1921 NWP convention.

[82] Gilman, "Back of Birth Control," p. 31. The abuse to which she refers is excessive sexuality.

population produced by the misuse of sex until humans learned self-restraint.[83] To Sanger the purpose of mating was the "accompanying pleasure," whether or not offspring were intended. Women's freedom was constrained because they were submerged by the weight of excessive childbearing. But for organized feminism, sexually wary themselves, the sexual license that birth control suggested was too controversial, especially in a time when cohesion of their programs was delicate.

At the February 1921 NWP convention, which was to celebrate the suffrage victory and formulate the future agenda, Alice Paul tried to prevent the topic of birth control from being introduced at all. Pressure from the VPL and ABCL was brought to bear on Paul, who partially relented. Both Mary Ware Dennett and Margaret Sanger were given the chance to speak to the resolutions committee, but birth control was not adopted by the committee and was not raised at the convention. Paul felt that both birth control and black women's voting rights were divisive issues and wished that those supporting such issues would direct their attention to the relevant authorities, leaving the NWP out of it.[84] Repeatedly between 1920 and 1930 Sanger and the ABCL attempted to persuade the NWP to put birth control on its agenda. In May 1923, the ABCL met with the leaders of the NWP at the Party's headquarters in Washington, D.C., in the hopes of convincing them to include birth control in their program for equal rights. The meeting began with Dr. Cora King's statement, made at Paul's request, that the NWP could "take up no line of work except that which it had made its own—the securing of equal rights in every respect for women and men." The various League speakers pointed out that it was "absurd to suppose that women had equal rights with men so long as they did not possess the right to control their own bodies, both as regards sex relationship with their husbands and the use of their body for maternity."[85] Although the League praised the Party's work they suggested as well that "they were neglecting the laws affecting the far more primary right of a woman to own herself." The League's speakers received a polite response, but the NWP was not persuaded to take up the birth control cause.[86] The harshest exchange

[83] Ibid., pp. 32–33.

[84] Cott, *The Grounding of Modern Feminism*, p. 71. See also "Editorial," *BCR* 5 (April 1921): 3–4; and Winnafred Corwin Robinson, "One Way to Run," pp. 13–14.

[85] "Editorial," *BCR* 7 (June 1923): 141.

[86] Ibid., p. 142.

between the two came in the midtwenties. At the time, the NWP was working to reform women's custody rights. The League could not understand how the NWP could consistently appear at legislative hearings regarding women's custody rights and yet ignore birth control. How the NWP could publicly support a woman's right to children after they were born but not her right to decide if they would be born was incomprehensible to Sanger and the ABCL. They concluded that the NWP had fallen victim to "complacent middle-class self-satisfaction."[87] The Party members, the League argued, could be politically active only by virtue of their access to contraception. It was unconscionable that they would not help to gain access to contraception for all women. The NWP countered by reiterating that theirs was "a program of common justice on which women of all shades of opinion [could] unite."[88] Birth control was too controversial for the NWP to support. Also, the NWP reiterated its belief that "singleness of purpose makes for strength and for the speedy achievement of the purpose of any organization." The NWP suggested that it was no more appropriate for the League to expect it to support birth control than for it to expect the League to work for equal rights.[89]

The League made no headway in persuading the NWP to accept birth control as essential to equal rights. As historian Nancy Cott has noted, within the NWP's narrow focus on the Equal Rights Amendment the feminist connection between equal economic rights, sex rights, and social revolution was ruptured. The NWP constructed the rationale for their equal rights program in terms of a liberal individualism; they tended to see both the political and economic sphere in pluralist terms in which atomized individuals competed by choice among equal opportunities. Women, strong vital individuals, were wrongly restrained by outmoded laws from equal opportunities in politics and employment. The Equal Rights Amendment was designed to remove those outmoded barriers. However, the NWP agenda referred primarily to gender relationships in the public realm.[90] It did not overly concern itself with the gender inequality within marriage. For instance, the legal requirements in which a woman's services were

[87] "Editorial," *BCR* 5 (April 1921): 3.
[88] "Editorial," *BCR* 12 (January 1928): 6.
[89] "Editorial," *Equal Rights*, 20 August 1927. Doris Stevens and Edith Hooker supported birth control personally, but they followed the NWP position and kept their distance from the ABCL.
[90] See Cott, *The Grounding of Modern Feminism*, pp. 81, 120–28, 134–42, especially 140.

49

her husband's property went unchallenged.[91] The NWP did not want a woman's social or political status to be determined by her husband's, but it did not see women's traditional responsibilities within marriage as barriers to women's participation in the public life of the nation. Once barriers to the public sphere were removed, women would no longer be forced to depend on marriage. It became one more choice. With regard to employment, the NWP position coincided with wider social codes. A woman was free to work or to be sexual but not both; marriage was the determinant of what women should do. Single women were free to work but were not free to be sexual, as sexuality was proper only within the confines of marriage. Married women could be sexual but could not control the conditions of their work, as women's work was properly subordinated to their families' needs.[92] Within such an ideological construction of women as either single working women or married mothers there was no room for the woman who both had sex and earned wages. Nor was there room for contraceptives, which would facilitate combining the two activities. However, the controversy that birth control entailed also kept the NWP at a distance. From early in the decade, the specter of both Bolshevism and immorality was raised by opponents of various women's rights measures. Any connection with birth control could easily fuel opponents' arguments that feminist agendas promoted immorality.

The National League of Women Voters also failed to include birth control in its agenda at its 1920 organizing convention. Carrie Chapman Catt personally disclaimed it as "narrow" and "sordid." While it might bring some good, overall birth control would, in her opinion, lead to "degeneracy" through "over-sexualization."[93] The March 1920 *Review* criticized the emerging LWV by arguing that suffrage itself was never the goal but rather a tool by which women could reconstruct the nation. The editorial charged that "even those [women] who are most active in politics seem[ed] to have forgotten this promise," and efforts to get birth control included in the program of the LWV failed throughout the 1920s.[94] The LWV saw itself as a "middle-of-the-road organization in which persons of widely differing political views might work." Its own journal, the *Woman Citizen*, characterized its members

[91] Ibid., pp. 138, 185–87.
[92] Ibid., and Scharf and Jensen, *Decades of Discontent*, p. 13.
[93] Letter of Carrie Chapman Catt to Margaret Sanger, 24 November 1920, MSP-LC as quoted in Joan Gaulard, "Woman Rebel," p. 20.
[94] "Has Suffrage Reached Its Goal?" unsigned editorial, *BCR* 4 (March 1920): 3.

in 1924 as "well and tastefully dressed," with no signs of "queerness." Members were "not afraid of new ideas nor eager for them merely because they [were] new."[95] Reorganization of LWV procedures in the midtwenties made it increasingly difficult to introduce new items to its program. New items first had to be approved for a two-year period of study before they could even be considered as an item in the action program. Also, new items could only be introduced through the sub-committees, not from the convention floor. In 1924 Sangerists tried unsuccessfully to introduce a pro–birth control measure before the LWV citizenship program. That committee was deciding whether or not to study sterilization of the unfit as a measure to reduce degeneracy among the citizenry. The sterilization question was adopted for study, but opponents successfully argued that the citizenship program should not be "crowd[ed] with another social subject, of so controversial a nature" as birth control. The convention report suggested that birth control was not a subject that belonged "among women citizens' concerns."[96]

In 1926 and 1928 the ABCL tried to introduce birth control into the LWV's Child Welfare and Social Hygiene Committees. However, in neither committee did the measure "receive the 3/4 majority necessary" to add a new item to the study agenda.[97] National officers attended the committee hearings in 1926 and urged the committees to vote against the resolutions, saying that birth control would disrupt the organization altogether.[98] Birth control posed too great a threat to the delicate cohesion of the LWV to warrant even general discussion on the convention floor. The fear was that Roman Catholic members would resign in protest over a resolution supporting contraceptive legalization. As early as 1921 the National Council of Catholic Women pledged to fight any efforts made anywhere in the United States to repeal laws prohibiting the "addiction" and "sin" of birth control.[99] Because the members of the leadership were themselves ambivalent

---

[95] "What Women Voters Want," p. 10.

[96] Ibid., p. 11.

[97] "Editorial," *BCR* 12 (July 1928): 200.

[98] Defeat of the resolution precluded LWV support for the ABCL legislative program for at least four more years. See "The League of Women Voters and Birth Control," *BCR* 10 (May 1926): 177.

[99] *National Catholic Welfare Council Bulletin* 2 (January 1921): 21, quoted in Sanger, *Pivot*, pp. 191–94. In 1921 Catholic women supported the Sheppard-Towner Act. But by 1926, the Roman Catholic clergy opposed its renewal, linking it to birth control. See Muncy, *Creating a Female Dominion*, p. 105; and Meckel, *Save the Babies*, p. 215.

about the sexual freedom implied by birth control, the LWV sought to avoid such a conflict.

The League of Women Voters was closely tied into the networks of welfare feminism around the Children's Bureau. Among its first legislative efforts were support for the Sheppard-Towner Act, and the Anti–Child Labor Amendment. The official stance of the Children's Bureau toward birth control extended to its close allies.[100] Although the Bureau's charge granted it considerable latitude in the field of infant and maternal welfare, the Bureau would not refer to contraception, even obliquely. The Bureau, which annually answered thousands of mothers' requests for infant and maternal health care information, refused to give any information to women who wrote requesting contraceptive advice. The Bureau would either ignore that section of a letter or state that it had no information; it would not refer women to the ABCL.[101]

Opponents of the Sheppard-Towner Act had successfully endangered its initial passage in 1921 and its extension in 1926, relying in part on the claim that it would provide birth control.[102] The Children's Bureau did not want to provide fuel to the opposition and followed a "hands-off" policy dictated by Grace Abbott's and Julia Lathrop's perception that "it was too early . . . to sustain the principle of public money for birth control." Grace Abbott reported that "there were States where it was not 'good form' to speak of the pre-natal period" or the causes of death in maternity because of the risk of raising the specter of Bolshevik-backed birth control and abortion.[103] Thus, amid the hostility of the medical profession to maternal and infant health programs in general, opposition from Roman Catholic groups, the moral conservatism of social workers, and the heritage of women's po-

[100] In addition to the LWV, the Children's Bureau influenced the agendas of the General Federation of Women's Clubs, the National Conference of Social Work, and the Visiting Nurses' Association. See Muncy, *Creating a Female Dominion*, pp. 57–61, 92, 102–8.

[101] Muncy, *Creating a Female Dominion*, pp. 47–49, 98, 162. Molly Ladd-Taylor, *Raising a Baby*, pp. 2–3, 9, 179–80.

[102] Lela Costin, *Two Sisters for Social Justice: A Biography of Grace and Edith Abbott*, p. 176.

[103] Ibid.; Ladd-Taylor, *Raising a Baby*, pp. 179–80; and Meckel, *Save the Babies*, p. 195. This official hands-off policy remained in place until 1940 when Katherine Lenroot gave begrudging support to the principle that birth control was a "state's right" in New Deal maternal health programs. However, the Bureau did not encourage states to utilize that right. See Letter of Katherine Lenroot to Thomas Eliot, 9 January 1940, MSP-LC; and Chapter 6.

litical influence grounded in maternalism, birth control could not find its way onto the welfare feminist agenda in the twenties.

Sanger and the ABCL were frustrated by what they saw as timidity and obdurateness of welfare feminists. Sanger's 1922 book, *The Pivot of Civilization,* railed against their silence. She characterized their position as a "*laissez-faire* policy of parenthood or marriage, with an indiscriminating paternalism concerning maternity." She said the protectors of infants and mothers offered a program in which the state would care for children when they were born while denying women the right to choose to bear those children. Such a policy left women as the "passive victims of blind instinct." Throughout the book, Sanger repeatedly drew from the Bureau's own studies of infant and maternal conditions to argue against the Bureau's policy.[104] In 1928, when Grace Abbott publicly reiterated that the Bureau had no hand in birth control activities, the ABCL similarly used the Bureau's own statistics to argue that maternal mortality rates would not fall until the reason for illegal abortions was eliminated by legal contraception.[105] In fact, much of Sanger's rhetoric was directed at persuading welfare feminists to include birth control in their programs.

Against the Equal Rights positions of the NWP, welfare feminists argued for ongoing recognition of women's special needs. Barriers to equal participation by women were not as pressing a concern, in their view, as the need to protect women from exploitation within a heartless industrial order. Protective legislation, which welfare feminists continued to support vigorously in the twenties, was originally legitimated by the argument that women's reproductive capacities limited their right of contract. The Brandeis brief in the 1908 *Muller v. Oregon* case argued that women's right to make labor contracts should be restricted to protect their reproductive capacities from harm. Such protection was warranted by the state's interest in the propagation of healthy citizens. The women most in need of protection were the poor, helpless, and overburdened wives of men who could not make an adequate living. This view of women emphasized their differences from and dependence on male breadwinners. While ERA advocates saw women as robust (middle-class, white) individuals, welfare feminists saw women as overburdened members of (poor, ethnic) families who, by virtue of

---

[104] Sanger, *Pivot*, pp. 49, 52. On Sanger's use of Children's Bureau studies see pp. 54–79, 251–52. For a contemporary analysis of these studies see Meckel, *Save the Babies*, pp. 178–88.

[105] "Editorial," *BCR* 12 (March 1928): 74.

maternity, were economically dependent. To welfare feminists a married woman worked only because of "failure on the part of the husband" to provide adequate support. This perspective maintained the critique of class relations of nascent feminism but lost sight of gender critiques.[106]

Nancy Cott and others rightly argue that married women's work was the rock upon which feminism foundered in the twenties. Cott claims that Sanger held more firmly to maternalism than other feminists. However, it was the ideology of maternalism undergirding welfare feminism that made married women's work so problematic.[107] For welfare feminists, working mothers were the focus, not childless working women. In the 1920s women's maternal duty within marriage and with regard to citizenship was the focus of welfare feminist proposals. Here again, women's rights advocates did not question the sexual division of labor; women bore children and rightly provided the moral rearing of those children, whereas men provided economic support. The subordination of women's work to family need assumed that childrearing was that which was lost to the family when women went out to work. Marriage led naturally and inevitably to children; the presence of young children in need of care dictated the restrictions on women's work. The tragedy of wage-working women was represented by the levels of infant mortality. Deprivation to the little ones and the blows to maternal feeling were the consequences of women's employment. The solution offered by welfare feminists to high rates of infant mortality was to raise male wages so mothers could quit.[108] Thus, both the NWP and welfare feminists, while seeing women differently as either individuals or as family members, made similar assumptions about women, work, and sexuality. Women on their own were free to work but were nonsexual; women in families were mothers whose individual desire or need for wage work was subordinate to the family's need for their domestic work.

Within this representation of women, Sanger offered birth control

---

[106] As quoted in Cott, *The Grounding of Modern Feminism*, p. 206; see also p. 128; and Mink, "Lady," p. 108.

[107] Cott, *The Grounding of Modern Feminism*, pp. 179–211, 120–42, 46–50; Scharf and Jensen, *Decades of Discontent*, pp. 10–15. On Republican use of maternalism see Sonya Michel and Robyn Rosen, "The Paradox of Maternalism," pp. 364–85.

[108] Cott, *The Grounding of Modern Feminism*, p. 206; Meckel, *Save the Babies*, pp. 194–95; Muncy, *Creating a Female Dominion*, pp. 122, 162; and Mink, "Lady," pp. 100–101.

as a solution to the problem of married women's work.[109] If women had access to contraceptives they could then limit their family size to the level of male wages. Thus, mothers would not be compelled by economic need to go out to work. They could provide full-time care and nurturance to their children if endless pregnancies did not outstrip their husbands' ability to support the family. However, among welfare feminists the threat of birth control to the ideology of chastity outweighed its potential to improve maternal and infant well-being. Chastity was central to welfare feminists, because it undergirded not only the ideology of women's moral superiority on which their political identity rested but also their racial consciousness upon which much of their political authority rested.

In her forthcoming book, *Wages of Motherhood*, Gwendolyn Mink persuasively argues that racial maternalism was the basis of welfare feminists' political ascent. She traces their articulation of racial maternalism to the Progressive Era, during which there was a "seemingly indelible association of poverty with ethnic diversity." Most of the wage-earners that Progressives sought to provide with aid were foreigners. Poverty and, by association, "unmediated diversity" were, for Progressive reformers, "irreconcilable with good citizenship." Thus assimilation of dominant culture values was established as the "fundamental solution to social problems." Political allegiances to Progressive social reform were confounded after 1920 with the increasing fear that ethnic diversity would undermine American democracy. Revelations of the low scores on Army I.Q. tests and the poor physical condition of ethnic and African-American Army recruits heightened fears that these groups could not be assimilated into American political and cultural institutions.[110]

Welfare feminist programs of maternal support were "welded" to Americanizing ethnic immigrants before the war and to 100 percent Americanism after the war. The goal under both standards was "uplift to a common moral, physical and mental standard established by the dominant culture." The ideology of maternalism used by welfare feminists made gender "the solvent of diversity." That is, women's common experience of maternity provided the basis for assimilating differ-

[109] Throughout the 1920s clinics offered contraceptive services to married women only, but were, nonetheless, accused repeatedly of giving single women birth control. See Chapter 3.

[110] Mink, *Wages*, chapter 1, and "Lady," pp. 95–96; Meckel, *Save the Babies*, pp. 102–3, 116–17, 193, 200–201.

ence.[111] By educating ethnic mothers in "scientific standards of care," maternal support programs could mold women's "natural" ambition to raise "good children" toward rearing Americanized children.[112] According to Mink, this stance amounts to racial maternalism because it "bind[s] race consciousness with gendered remedies" in offering programs directed at women but defined by anxious desires to mediate racial difference. These programs defined the remedies needed by poor, ethnic women in terms of the dominant culture's standards of mental, moral, and physical health and well-being. The racial maternalist programs first required assimilation of the dominant culture's standards and then fostered equal opportunity. Also, racial maternalism, defining the woman citizen's greatest contribution to the American polity in terms of her contribution to cultural homogenization, reinforced traditional political common sense. Motherhood had always been the significant aspect of women's political contribution.[113]

Sangerists used the language of racial maternalists as they tried to insinuate birth control into the welfare feminist agenda. In her 1920 book, *Woman and the New Race*, Sanger asked if these problems of ethnic diversity could be solved by giving the immigrant "low wages, a home in the slums and those pseudo-patriotic preachments which constitute our machine made 'Americanization'" instead of an "opportunity to develop his own culture." Her answer was no. Instead, intoning the rhetoric of racial maternalists, she declared, "We know that in each of these submerged and semisubmerged elements of the population there are rich factors of racial culture. Motherhood is the channel through which these cultures flow." Arguing that "the rising generation is always the material of progress, and motherhood is the agency for the improvement and the strengthening and guiding of that generation," Sanger positioned herself with the welfare feminists who "helped forge political space for racial liberalism" by opening access to American culture. For welfare feminists, uplifting immigrants to higher standards (their own) of domestic and civic life would alleviate the dangers of diversity and allow its riches to blossom. Sanger concurred. For her, the amalgam of "precious metals of racial culture" with "physical perfection, mental strength and spiritual progress"

[111] Mink, *Wages*, chapter 2. See also "Lady," pp. 97–108; Meckel, *Save the Babies*, pp. 121, 130–31.

[112] Ibid. See also Meckel, *Save the Babies*, pp. 119–20, 150, 220–21.

[113] Mink, *Wages*, chapter 1 and Muncy, *Creating a Female Dominion*, pp. 112–14, 122, 162–63.

(old-stock standards) would produce "an American race, containing the best of all racial elements, [that] could give the world a vision and a leadership beyond our present imagination."[114]

However, Sanger was also critical of welfare feminist Americanization because it ignored birth control. Unless "reproduction beyond our capacity to assimilate our numbers" was held in check, the "melting pot" would not "refine"; it would not "make the coming generation into such physically fit, mentally capable, socially alert individuals as are the ideal of democracy." With this argument Sanger articulated a racial maternalist logic for legalized birth control. If ethnic mothers had birth control they could rise to the scientific standards of motherhood and prevent disease, delinquency, and dependency among their children. For motherhood to succeed in guiding progress, "we must popularize birth control thinking. . . . We must set motherhood free. We must give the foreign and submerged mother knowledge that will enable her to prevent bringing to birth children she does not want."[115] A free motherhood "instinctively . . . avoids all those things which multiply racial handicaps." Like that of welfare feminists, birth control rhetoric reinforced the belief that motherhood was the significant contribution of the woman citizen. Sanger's formulation of better mothering required women's reproductive and sexual freedom, yet it also raised motherhood to a sacred duty: "Free womanhood turns of its own desire to a free and happy motherhood, a motherhood which does not submerge the woman, but which is enriched because she is unsubmerged."[116]

Birth control was not easily fit into welfare feminists' version of racial maternalism, though. Throughout the 1920s Sanger and the ABCL tried to cultivate support for birth control among feminists and women's rights organizations. They were unsuccessful, and the movement remained distinct from other feminist organizations. Among welfare feminists, even though Sanger espoused racial maternalism, birth control remained an inappropriate issue. Because Sanger framed contraception in terms of women's right to sexual pleasure, birth control was inimical to the welfare feminist conceptualization of maternal virtue. "Injudicious sexuality and ignorance in the domestic arts were the chief justifications" for the "quality control of mothers"

---

[114] Sanger, *Woman*, pp. 43, 74, 45–46; Mink, *Wages*, chapter 1.
[115] Sanger, ibid., pp. 44–46. On the melting pot see Mink, *Old Labor*, pp. 221–23.
[116] Ibid., pp. 45, 231.

offered by welfare feminists.[117] Clean houses and well-groomed children were indices of good mothering, but sexual propriety remained the preeminent yardstick by which to measure maternal virtue. For welfare feminists, only chaste mothers could produce civic-minded sons and daughters. Celibate widowhood was the principal legal criterion upon which states distinguished those mothers who deserved public support from those who did not.

What finally distinguished Sanger and the birth control movement from welfare feminism was not her racial consciousness or her reliance on expertise. Welfare feminists likewise welded maternal support to America's racial order through the languages of the social sciences. What distinguished Sanger and her organizations was that she explicitly insisted that good mothers had a natural right to heterosexual gratification.[118] This sexual perspective could not be reconciled with the moral posture of welfare feminism. Their programs and political authority depended on women's chastity, and thus birth control could not find its way into the welfare feminist agenda in the twenties.

Yet Sangerists utilized the discourse of maternalism to sustain their claim that birth control was a social right, and they used racial maternalism to assert the value of birth control to the nation. By taking up racial maternalism, the movement positioned itself well within the ideology of early feminism, with all its pitfalls. However, without support from organized feminism the movement was left to find allies among other groups for whom gender equity (by any definition) was unimportant. In the next chapters I will turn to consider two such alliances, those between the movement and physicians and eugenicists. Physicians were key because early state responses to Sanger's direct action solidified state policy giving the medical profession hegemony over contraception. Eugenicists were important because they provided a sexually neutral language with which to speak publicly about reproduction. The pitfalls of racial maternalism were accentuated in the birth control movement through its alliances with both physicians and eugenicists.

[117] Mink, *Wages*, chapter 2 and "Lady," p. 108. Evidence of a woman's moral character was required by most states before she could qualify for a mother's pension.

[118] Cott, *The Grounding of Modern Feminism*, p. 48, argues, based primarily on Kennedy and Gordon, that Sanger defined the essence of the feminine element to be maternity. I argue that sexuality is the elemental force about which Sanger writes. Maternity comes to the foreground in Sanger's rhetoric when sexual radicalism lost favor.

CHAPTER THREE

Birth Control and the Medical Profession

No longer could I look upon birth control knowledge as primarily a free speech fight. I realized now that it involved much more than talk, much more than books or pamphlets.
— Margaret Sanger, *My Fight for Birth Control*

We as a profession should take hold of this matter and not let it go to the radicals, and not let it receive harm by being pushed in any undignified or improper manner.
— Robert Dickinson, *Surgery, Gynecology, and Obstetrics*

Initially Sanger envisioned birth control as a free speech issue and focused on getting repressive laws repealed. But her goals changed while she was in Europe, and she returned to the United States in 1915 determined to organize contraceptive clinics nationwide. She attributed her changed vision to her experiences with Dutch birth control clinics. Sanger was drawn to Holland because of its low infant and maternal mortality rates. There she found Johannes Rutgers, who trained doctors, midwives, and nurses to work in clinics throughout Holland giving women contraceptive advice, an individually fitted pessary, and instruction in its care and use. While studying Rutgers's technique, Sanger became convinced that pessaries were the best female contraceptive method available and that "personal instruction, personal advice, and personal examination were absolutely essential in order to guarantee" their effectiveness.[1]

If women's reproductive self-determination was to depend on pessaries, clinics were essential. The effectiveness of the pessary, or "occlusive diaphragm" as it is now called, depends greatly on the physical

[1] Sanger, *My Fight*, p. 144.

condition of the vagina and cervix by which it is held in place. Repeated pregnancies, whether aborted or carried to term, tend to soften the cervix, which can cause a diaphragm to slip out of place unless it is carefully fitted.[2] During the 1910s and 1920s there were fifteen known varieties and fourteen sizes of pessaries. Personal fittings were required for each woman to find the best device for her particular physical condition from among the many choices. Also, successful use of any pessary requires a woman to be intimately familiar with her internal anatomy so that she can insert it correctly. A setting was needed where trained practitioners could screen women for existing health problems, fit devices, and teach women to insert the device themselves. A setting in which to evaluate the safety and effectiveness of the various types of pessaries was needed as well because none of them had ever been systematically tested.[3] Thus, the next logical step for the birth control movement was to organize clinics, specially dedicated to birth control, as a place to instruct women and evaluate devices.[4]

Sanger's shift in emphasis from free speech to clinics repositioned the movement for legalized contraception. State repression of knowledge and devices was no longer the only issue; new concerns and relationships materialized because clinics were ambitious undertakings that required money and medical skill. Dr. Rutgers had convinced Sanger that personal instruction depended upon medical supervision because only medical practitioners had the requisite knowledge of human physiology. Sanger herself believed nurses and midwives were, with training, expert enough to fit contraceptives because the "means of prevention were simple enough to guarantee safety in the average case and very seldom needed the skill of a gynecologist."[5] U.S. laws, however, gave physicians sole authority for contraception, and the birth control movement had to secure physicians' support to operate any clinic legally. As a whole, the medical profession was hostile both to birth control and to "specialty" clinics in general. Moreover, no medical

[2] In addition, injuries commonly sustained in childbirth also affected the condition of the vagina and cervix. See Leavitt, *Brought to Bed*, pp. 28–32, 142, 203–4.

[3] Sanger, *My Fight*, p. 110, on the variety of devices; and p. 144, on clinics. On clinical testing of devices see also James Reed, "Doctors, Birth Control, and Social Values: 1830–1970," p. 114; and Merriley Borell, "Biologists and the Promotion of Birth Control Research, 1918–1938," p. 58.

[4] Gordon, *Woman's Body*, p. 230, likewise concluded that clinics were the next logical step. She suggests that the move to clinics helped separate the birth control movement from the left, which was not organizationally equipped to deliver such services (p. 245).

[5] Sanger, *My Fight*, p. 111.

schools provided training in contraceptive techniques, and when Sanger's clinic opened there was a dearth of knowledge even among physicians. Opening contraceptive clinics thus required the movement to cultivate (educate) supportive practitioners from a hostile and self-protective medical profession.

Beyond medical support, a stable source of funds was needed to pay the staff and to purchase supplies.[6] Funding for her clinic, the Birth Control Clinical Research Bureau (CRB), was an ongoing struggle for Sanger throughout the twenties and the thirties. The clinic, providing its services regardless of a woman's ability to pay, always incurred large budgetary deficits.[7] On the whole, outside funding came from or through wealthy women whom Sanger enlisted into the movement.[8] Sanger tried to get institutional support for both the CRB and the ABCL, but her status as a laywoman and agitator always undercut her ability to garner corporate foundation dollars. She was repeatedly faced with the difficulty of demonstrating that her organizations were sufficiently professional to warrant foundation support. In fact she succeeded in obtaining philanthropic dollars only when she had the support of medical and scientific professionals. The effort to secure stable funding to keep clinics open pushed Sanger and the movement to accentuate the scientific professionalism already encoded in American law and in birth control rhetoric and strategy.

The first section of this chapter examines the judicially established medical hegemony over birth control and considers the consequent feasibility of the two historical strategies for legalizing contraception. The remainder of the chapter details the discordant relationship between the medical profession and Sangerists as they contested the terms of proper procedure for birth control clinics. Sanger did not

---

[6] Initially these supplies were smuggled into the country, often by the Three-in-One Oil Company, which was owned by J. Noah Slee, Sanger's second husband. In 1925 Herbert Simmonds, an admirer of Sanger's, founded the Holland-Rantos Company with financing from Slee and began manufacturing pessaries in the United States. Once Simmonds demonstrated that the business could be run legally and ethically, other pharmaceutical companies followed suit. See J. Noah Slee, letter of 25 November 1925; and of Percy Clark to Margaret Sanger, 24 March 1930, MSP-LC; and on Holland-Rantos, see Reed, *The Birth Control Movement*, pp. 114–15.

[7] Reed, ibid., p. 116. By 1930 the Bureau budget was $35,000, only $10,000 of which came from patient fees. Slee was the single largest contributor to the ABCL and CRB.

[8] Reliance on the patronage of wealthy women in a constant search for funding was typical of women's reform groups. See Muncy, *Creating a Female Dominion*, pp. 17–20, 24. On the movement's membership, see Kennedy, *Birth Control in America*, p. 100; and Francis Vreeland, "The Process of Reform with Especial Reference to Reform Groups in the Field of Population," pp. 154ff.

simply relinquish birth control to doctors; she tried to win the endorsement of the medical profession but evade its dominance. Sangerists
and the medical profession, both white and middle-class, largely concurred on questions of racial betterment. Their disagreements turned
on questions of whether women would define the scope of contraceptive practice for themselves within a matrix of public health reform
or if a male-dominated medical profession would define it within the
matrix of medicine for profit. Disconnected from the network of
women reformers who were also concerned with infant and maternal
health, Sangerists' resistance to medical dominance of clinics relied
heavily on eugenicists. Although it accentuated the movement's race-
conscious rhetoric, this alliance with eugenicists provided the movement with scientific legitimacy that was independent of the medical
profession. Eugenics' language and data strengthened Sangerists' ability to contest the medical profession's narrow definitions of acceptable
contraceptive practice. In this contest over contraceptive practice,
women's sexual and reproductive self-determination was eventually
supplanted by the economic ethic of fertility, which was installed as a
standard of medical practice through the euphemism of child spacing.

Medicine and the Law

Defining all sexually explicit materials as obscene, the Comstock Act
prohibited the distribution of all contraceptive information and devices. In the years following their passage, U.S. courts held that the
Comstock Act did not violate the First Amendment guarantee to freedom of speech. The courts reasoned that the police powers of the state
legitimately included protecting the community's moral health from
obscenity. By disconnecting sex from procreation, the existing barrier
methods of contraception were judged to be inherently obscene; de-
bauchery was the only possible purpose of such devices. This judicial
interpretation did not even provide a medical exemption for physicians; no redeeming use for contraceptive information and devices was
recognized.[9] However, in response to the Progressive Era discovery of
an epidemic of venereal insontium (infection of the innocent), New
York and several other states' laws were revised, allowing physicians to
prescribe condoms to prevent the spread of venereal disease. While
physicians continued to prefer continence as the best means of con-

[9] Dienes, *Law, Politics, and Birth Control*, pp. 49–65.

taining venereal diseases, they did begin to prescribe condoms to infected men. Condoms remained illegal as a "means of preventing conception," but their ability to block the epidemic of venereal disease among innocent women and children provided one "decent" use for these otherwise obscene devices.[10] Within this perspective, pessaries, a female-controlled contraceptive, seemed not to protect women's virtue; rather, they facilitated women's corruption.

The tension between disease control and obscenity was rearticulated in court decisions regarding Sanger's Brownsville clinic. In January of 1919, the U.S. Supreme Court declined to hear an appeal of Sanger's conviction for illegally distributing contraceptive information to women, thus affirming the New York State Appeals Court's 1918 decision. Although the Appeals Court upheld her conviction, it also extended the existing interpretation of the law, providing the grounds upon which clinics could operate. Sanger's lawyer had argued that Section 1142 of the New York State Penal Code, which prohibited oral communication of contraceptive information, was an unreasonable use of the state's police power. Her lawyer conceded that it was "within the police power of the legislature, for the benefit of the morals and health of the community, to make such a law as this applicable to unmarried persons." But, if the law was "broad enough to prevent a duly licensed physician from giving advice and help to his married patients in a proper case, it [was] an unreasonable police regulation and therefore unconstitutional."[11]

Judge Crane, writing for the Court, had a twofold response to this argument. First, he noted that the appellant, Sanger, was not a physician, and thus she had no standing before the Court on the constitutional question. Second, he pointed out that Section 1145 of the State Penal Code, enacted for venereal disease control, excepted physicians from the provisions of Section 1142 when their actions cured or prevented disease. Even though Sanger had no standing on the question, Judge Crane rendered an interpretation of this section:

> This exception in behalf of physicians does not permit advertisements regarding such matters, nor promiscuous advice to patients irrespective of their condition, but it is broad enough to protect the

---

[10] See Brandt, *No Magic Bullet*, pp. 14–31, on the Progressive Era "discovery" of this epidemic.

[11] Quotations are taken from a typescript of Judge Crane's decision, MSP-SSC, p. 1. The case is *People v. Sanger*, 222 N.Y. 193, 118 N.E. 637 (1918).

physician who in good faith gives such help or advice to a married person to cure or prevent disease. "Disease," by Webster's International Dictionary, is defined to be, "an alteration in the state of the body, or of some of its organs, interrupting or disturbing the performance of the vital functions, and causing or threatening pain and sickness; illness; sickness; disorder."[12]

By reaffirming physicians' exclusive right to prescribe contraceptive devices, Judge Crane's decision defined the terms of the medical hegemony over contraception that subsequently developed.[13] In effect, this decision delineated the birth control movement's future options. The Court rejected any nonmedical justifications for birth control and limited acceptable medical practice to those cases in which contraception was given for the "cure and prevention of disease." But by defining disease broadly as any alteration of vital function that threatened pain and sickness, Crane's decision effectively widened the scope of legal contraceptive prescription. In the 1910s and 1920s, pregnancy itself was increasingly defined as a potentially pathological condition, and Crane's decision could be read as legitimating the prescription of contraception to prevent its inherent risks to women's health.

Sangerists read Crane's decision as a partial victory. All they needed to operate a birth control clinic legally was a doctor in charge who would identify some health reason for each prescription. However, to achieve the goal of giving all women access to contraception regardless of their medical condition, the movement was left with two major options. One option was to convince physicians to prescribe birth control within the broadest construction of "cure and prevention." The other option was to pursue legislative changes to allow birth control for nonmedical reasons. Both options were pursued and pushed the movement farther from its roots in direct action and closer to the more traditional strategy of cultivating the support of those with institutional power. But persuading the medical profession to utilize contraception as a means of treating reproductive pathology was not an easy task. To insist that physicians prescribe contraception for social reasons was to suggest apostasy. In the 1910s and 1920s the medical profession was consolidating its newly achieved authority into a private, hospital-

[12] Crane, ibid., p. 2, concluded that the sociological reasoning for contraception presented in evidence by Sanger's lawyer was a matter for the legislature, not the courts.

[13] In effect, by ruling that Sanger, a nurse, had no standing on the constitutional question, the decision denied nurses and midwives any right to distribute contraceptives.

based medical care system. Allopathic physicians, or "regulars" as they were called, had achieved dominance over the practice of medicine through licensing laws that gave them control of state medical examinations. With this control, regular physicians were able to surmount their sectarian competitors and secure professional independence. Their new authority was legitimated in the therapeutic revolution occasioned by "germ theory," which added effective treatments to the profession's assets. Homogenizing the profession through licensure enabled physicians to standardize fees, securing the financial stability that had eluded them in the nineteenth century.

Committed to an ideology and practice of private medicine on a "fee-for-service" basis, the profession resisted any attempt to provide publicly funded medical care.[14] The threat posed by public health care, whether financed by the state or by voluntary agencies, was twofold: it intruded social reform concerns into the profession's newly independent domain, and it undercut the profession's newly achieved financial security. These two threats were inextricably linked for physicians. The intrusion of social reforms into medical practice might lead to public provision of medical care. As William Allen Pusey noted in his presidential address to the American Medical Association in 1924, "There is an evident tendency now to appropriate medicine in the social movement; to make the treatment of the sick a function of society as a whole; to take it away from the individual's responsibilities and to transfer it to the state; to turn it over to organized movements." Such appropriations threatened the medical profession's authority, independence, and economic base. In general, the profession opposed any kind of non–hospital-based, or extramural, clinics because they were administered by laypersons and provided free treatment. The profession insisted that public health should be maintained by the wisdom of private practitioners.[15]

The emerging authority of obstetricians and gynecologists, the physicians most responsible for women's reproductive health, was even more vulnerable than that of other physicians. Although asepsis and antisepsis served as a strong basis for moving surgery out of dirty kitch-

---

[14] Meckel, *Save The Babies*, pp. 127, 190–98; and William Arney, *Power and the Profession of Obstetrics*, pp. 45–46.

[15] William Pusey, 1924, as quoted in Jane Pacht Brickman, "Public Health, Midwives, and Nurses," p. 76. On the medical profession's opposition to public funding for maternal and infant health programs in particular, see Muncy, *Creating a Female Dominion*, pp. 137–38; and Meckel, *Save The Babies*, pp. 189–93.

ens and into clean hospitals and the sterile hands of licensed surgeons, obstetricians were still seen primarily as the "potboilers of the profession." Thought to require little skill, obstetrics was the least esteemed specialty of medicine. Although doctors entered America's birth rooms in the nineteenth century, their authority over childbirth was limited. In home births physicians had to share control of the process with the birthing woman and her attending friends and relatives. Moreover, until the midtwenties the majority of births were attended by midwives and general practitioners. Before obstetricians could wrest childbirth from general practitioners and midwives they first had to convince women that the expert services obstetricians offered were indispensable.[16]

In the 1910s obstetricians rather abruptly began to describe pregnancy and childbirth as pathological. Although they agreed that childbirth was a natural process, obstetricians began to argue that the potential for pathology existed in every pregnancy. Thus, they argued, prevention of the inherent risks of childbirth, primarily hemorrhage and infection, required the expert prenatal care of scientific specialists and the sterile environment of hospitals for childbirth. Wrapped in the mantle of science, these specialists attacked general practitioners and midwives as incompetent and assailed home birth as dangerous to women and newborns.[17] With the promise, but not the reality, of greater safety, obstetricians drew American women into their domain; by 1940 a majority of American births took place in the hospital. Once there, isolated from women's networks of support, physicians appropriated control of childbirth from women as well. But in the 1910s, obstetricians still "stood on the brink" of power. They did not yet have the control over childbirth that they thought possible, and they reacted belligerently to any efforts by laywomen and other practitioners that could prevent the specialty from achieving its due.[18]

Although contraception might have been incorporated into medical

[16] Brickman, "Public Health, Midwives, and Nurses," p. 68; on the limits of obstetricians' authority, see Arney, *Power and The Profession of Obstetrics*, pp. 41–42, 44–47, 52–53; and Leavitt, *Brought to Bed*, pp. 59–60, 62, 98–106, 179.

[17] On the role of "potential pathology" in the development of prenatal care and hospital birth see Leavitt, ibid., pp. 160, 169, 179–80; Arney, *Power and The Profession of Obstetrics*, pp. 44, 51–57; and Meckel, *Save The Babies*, pp. 163–65, 170–72.

[18] Leavitt, *Brought to Bed*, p. 138. Maternal mortality rates actually increased, and puerperal infection rates remained steady in the 1920s and early 1930s. If hospitals were indeed safer, these rates should have declined as more women gave birth in hospitals. See ibid., pp. 153–54, 164, 170–79, and esp. 182–90. On physicians' increasing control over birth, see ibid., pp. 189–95.

practice as one more tool for preventing the potential pathology of pregnancy, the birth control movement, espousing freestanding clinics controlled by a laywomen's voluntary association, drew the enmity of the medical profession. Birth control advocates not only sought to legalize contraception, they also encouraged women to demand contraception from their physicians. The movement's claim that women had a right to make such decisions for themselves, based on their social and economic conditions, threatened the profession's growing authority. Physicians wanted exclusive authority to decide proper medical therapy; patients, especially women, were not supposed to presume to tell them what and how to practice.[19] Moreover, this male-dominated profession sought to cure women's desire to avoid pregnancy, not to facilitate it. In the wisdom of physicians, like most other "respectable" people, the legal equation of contraception and vice was proper. In the estimate of many physicians, the birth control movement's intrinsic criticism of civilized morality threatened stable family life; the profession would do harm not to denounce it.[20]

Beyond the immediate issues of power in the doctor-patient relationship and protection of public morals, any social and economic reasons for using contraception, if legitimated, could undermine obstetricians' and gynecologists' authority over human reproductive processes. If there were legitimate nonmedical reasons for birth control, perhaps there should also be nonmedical authority for it. As Louise Bryant, executive secretary of the Committee on Maternal Health, noted, "You can't imagine how fearful the medical profession is of any suggestion of economics or sociology—it instantly conjures up for them 'State Medicine,' 'medical socialism' and what not."[21] Birth control clinics posed a direct financial threat as well. If women could get inexpensive gynecological care on demand from a lay clinic, they would not utilize specialists. Thus, even to physicians who supported contraceptive practice, Sanger's organization was "an anathema."[22]

The medical profession's enmity limited birth control advocates' efforts to legalize contraception. The AMA's active opposition prevented

[19] See Leavitt, ibid., pp. 130–40, on the profession's vehement resistance to the "twilight sleep" movement, which, like birth control, emerged among women's groups in 1914. "Twilight sleep" refers to the use of the anesthetic scopolamine in labor and delivery.
[20] See Reed, "Doctors," pp. 111–12, 119–22, on objections to birth control by the profession's leaders during the 1920s.
[21] Reed, *The Birth Control Movement*, p. 176.
[22] Secretary's report, CMH, 17 March 1924, NCMH-CL.

any policy that approximated a national health program from becoming law. Even the Sheppard-Towner Act—which provided, on a voluntary basis, only information and not actual medical care to pregnant women and new mothers—was derailed by the AMA. Initially passed over objections from the AMA that it posed a "stumbling block to the progress of medicine," the Sheppard-Towner Act was repealed in 1929.[23] The birth control movement, without great support among welfare feminists, had little chance of changing the Comstock laws without some accommodation of physicians' interests.

Throughout the 1920s, two approaches to legislative change were pursued. The first approach, labeled the open bill, was Mary Ware Dennett's fight for a straight repeal of the Comstock laws. The second approach, the Sangerist-supported legislation, labeled the doctors-only bill, would have amended the law to allow only physicians to prescribe contraceptives. A comparison of the open bill and the doctors-only bill illuminates the political positions available to the birth control movement with respect to medicine and, further, illuminates why, in the long run, the movement was unable effectively to resist the medical hegemony over birth control.

The first open bill was introduced into the New York State legislature in 1917 by Dennett and the National Birth Control League (NBCL). This bill would have stricken the words "for the prevention of conception" from Section 1142 of the State Penal Code. Thereby, birth control would no longer be classified as obscene. Unsuccessful in getting this bill out of committee, the NBCL disbanded in 1919. Dennett immediately formed the Voluntary Parenthood League to concentrate on amending the Federal law by striking the same phrase from all five Postal Code sections dealing with obscenity. The VPL attempted to enter this open bill in each Congress until 1926.[24] The doctors-only bill was first proposed in 1916 by the New York Birth Control League. However, no action was taken until 1921, when the ABCL endeavored to change the New York State physician exemption, Section 1145, by striking the phrase "for the cure and prevention of disease" from it. Physicians would thereby be permitted to prescribe birth control for any reason, but the general topic of birth control would not have been

[23] George Kosmak, testimony before the House of Representatives on the Sheppard-Towner Act, 1921, as quoted in Brickman, "Public Health, Midwives, and Nurses," p. 76. See also Meckel, *Save The Babies*, pp. 206–11, 214–19; and Muncy, *Creating a Female Dominion*, pp. 124–25, 132–42.

[24] Dennett, *Birth Control Laws*, pp. 72–93 for the New York State repeal effort; pp. 94–122 for the Federal effort.

removed from the obscenity statutes. Each year from 1921 to 1925 the ABCL sought passage of its bill. Each time it failed. The first attempt at a Federal doctors-only bill was made by the ABCL in 1924. It would have amended the U.S. Postal Code so that birth control information could be legally mailed between physicians and patients or pharmacists. In 1926 the ABCL could not even get sponsors for the bill and abandoned further efforts. In the 1930s, the National Committee on Federal Legislation for Birth Control (NCFL), which Sanger chaired, tried again to secure an exemption from the Federal laws for physicians.[25] These efforts failed as well.

All attempts at legislative change were unqualified failures. None of the bills was ever positively reported out of committee. Yet the rhetoric articulated by each bill's advocates represented the two positions the birth control movement held in relation to medicine. At first glance, these bills seem very different. One would completely remove birth control from its legal connection with obscenity; the other would remove only medically sanctioned practices from the classification of obscenity. There is considerable common ground between the two bills, however. Examining the common ground between them illuminates why the open bill, or free-speech approach, was a weak challenge both to the Sangerist approach and to the medical hegemony over birth control that was eventually established by the Federal courts.[26]

Mary Ware Dennett's arguments justified the open bill as a matter of free speech but nonetheless articulated birth control as a scientific topic. According to Dennett, because it was scientific, birth control should be neither classified as obscene nor restricted in any way: "Information when scientifically sound, should be readily available. Such knowledge is of immediate and positive individual and social benefit. All laws which hamper the free and responsible diffusion of this knowledge among the people are in the highest degree pernicious and opposed to the best and most permanent interests of society."[27] Within this rhetoric, scientific knowledge was pure knowledge, and it, above all else, deserved First Amendment protection. The advocates of the doctors-only bill also appealed to science as the justification for their

---

[25] In the 1926 version of the bill, medical publishers and importers were included in the exemption. Kennedy, *Birth Control in America*, p. 91; Dennett, *Birth Control Laws*, pp. 80, 98, 200–216.

[26] The Voluntary Parenthood League was never able to command as much support as the ABCL and disbanded in 1926 for lack of funds.

[27] Dennett, *Birth Control Laws*, p. 68.

proposed amendment. In fact, the Federal doctors-only bill was proposed in 1924 precisely to make possible the free exchange of the CRB's scientific data between the CRB and the emerging network of contraceptive clinics:

> To meet this new situation, which is developing out of the establishment of clinics in various States, it [the ABCL] has secured the drawing up of a bill which, while not opening the mails to the commercial exploitation of Birth Control, would free the hands of the medical profession and enable the clinical data to be passed from one group of doctors to another.
>
> It would facilitate the establishment and working of Birth Control clinics, and it would aid the doctors in assuming the new duty of giving Birth Control advice and prescriptions.[28]

The main difference between the two strategies was that the doctors-only bill would have legislated a medical monopoly over contraceptive information. Yet, even though the open bill did not legislate a monopoly to doctors, it did uphold their sole authority over contraceptive knowledge. Dennett argued that the repeal of the Comstock laws would simply allow physicians to exercise this authority unhindered: "We make it plain that the question of methods is the sphere of the medical scientists, that it is not for us laymen to presume to teach, and much less is it possible for the laws to determine methods. . . . And all we ask is the opportunity to help make the knowledge of the scientists accessible to all who need it."[29] The difference between the two bills derives from the role each articulated for the state in regulating the market. Rhetoric supporting each bill assumed that capitalist market relations provided the context for the distribution of birth control; neither rhetoric questioned these relations. However, the two bills represented the effect of these market relations on women's access to birth control differently, and thereby they argued in support of different roles for the state to play.

Dennett argued that an open market of knowledge was the only democratic market of knowledge. The open bill attempted to reestablish the free market in birth control that had existed prior to the Comstock law's enactment. In this way, individuals would have the most freedom to choose how and when to control their fertility. Contracep-

[28] Ibid., p. 209, quoted from a *BCR* editorial (volume and date not cited).
[29] Ibid., p. 77.

tion was an entirely private matter; the government had no business interfering with individuals' free exercise of their private rights. Rhetoric in support of the doctors-only bill recognized the danger of capitalist market relations; it was the onus of these relations that justified the bill's restrictions. From the position of the bill's advocates, a perfectly free market would leave consumers at the mercy of birth control peddlers; women would have no guarantee that the birth control devices they bought were either safe or effective.[30] As Sanger argued it, "No one had sufficient knowledge of the possible consequences of some contraceptives to permit them to be manufactured or distributed without guidance or direction. They might kill the birth control movement as well as some of the women who used them."[31]

The patent medicine trade, or "medical commercialism" as the AMA referred to it, was not a minor issue. It had run rampant in the United States prior to the passage of the Comstock Act. It was a contemporary problem in England, where there was no Comstock law. After a 1930 court decision loosened the Comstock Act, as discussed below, there was an immediate flood of patent contraceptives onto the U.S. market. Among these patent medicines were the myriad dangerous douching agents discreetly advertised as "feminine hygiene" products that would end the "calendar fear." During the depression these products did a booming business. By the midthirties, Americans spent almost $200 million dollars a year for patent douching agents—like Lysol— and for contraceptive jellies and foams. This situation was the direct result of physicians' reluctance to enter into the public discourse on contraception. British and American patent medicine distributors created a lucrative trade in the vacuum left by the silence of doctors.[32]

Like others involved in public health movements, Sanger was concerned about quality control. She feared that a straight repeal of the

[30] Ibid., pp. 20, 57–59, 152, 233–35. In 1925 the VPL added to the open bill a provision requiring medical certification of contraceptive devices by five licensed physicians. This was Dennett's only concession to the arguments for quality control. She never liked this addition and did not feel it was needed. The only protection necessary was against fraudulent advertisements, which she felt were covered by the existing Food and Drug Act. At the time, however, the FDA did not consider contraceptives to fall within its purview. See Edna Rankin McKinnon, field report, 5 February 1937, MSP-LC.

[31] Sanger, *Autobiography*, p. 405.

[32] On the widespread use and disastrous consequences of caustic douching agents like Lysol, see Eric Matsner, "Contraceptives and the Consumer," pp. 9–10; and Rachel Palmer and Sarah Greenberg, *Facts and Frauds in Woman's Hygiene*, pp. 128–57. On the magnitude of the patent contraceptive industry, see Reed, "Doctors," pp. 122, 110; and Angus McLaren, *Birth Control in Nineteenth-Century England*, pp. 116–40, 231–50.

Comstock Act would let loose a flood of quack remedies to victimize women. In an open market, the motives of profit would far outweigh considerations of health and safety:

> The removal of the Federal restrictions would almost certainly be followed by a flood of widespread advertising, of hastily written and probably misleading books and pamphlets purporting to give Birth Control information, and of supposed preventatives which might or might not prevent and which certainly could not meet the needs of the numerous women who require personal physical examinations and personal prescriptions to suit their individual idiosyncrasies.[33]

Sanger's personal distrust of the commercial contraceptives resulted from her experiences with contraceptive manufacturers who used variations on her name for commercial profit.[34] Her solution, like those of others in public health, relied on the expertise of medical science to ensure quality of the public health.[35] Bowing to the mystique of expertise, she believed that with medical control of contraception people would be guaranteed that the devices they bought were safe, effective, and appropriate to their needs.

The doctors-only bill was an attempt both to open the market and to provide some measure of quality control. Yet in relying on the monopolization of knowledge in the hands of experts as its main lever, the bill instituted privileged access to and control of contraceptive knowledge. Dennett reacted strongly to the class privilege called for by the doctors-only bill. Her position, framed in the ideology of the self-regulating market, recognized no legitimate need for a medical monopoly. From this perspective quackery could thrive only in darkness. The light of science and free speech would destroy it: "But on the whole would it not be best to have the laws simply provide an open field, and let the dignified authoritative scientists compete with the quacks and the spurious folk, with faith that eventually the best would win, very much as the increased public knowledge of general hygiene is steadily putting quackery into the background?"[36] In a free market, good sci-

[33] Dennett, *Birth Control Laws*, p. 206, quoted from a *BCR* editorial signed by Sanger (volume and date not cited). See also letter of Margaret Sanger to Annie Porritt of 16 December 1925, MSP-LC.

[34] Contraceptive manufacturers file, MSP-LC. Two such products were Sangyne and Santrol. See also Elizabeth Garrett, "Birth Control's Business Baby," pp. 269–72.

[35] On quality control in health reform, see Meckel, *Save The Babies*, pp. 62–91, 197–98; and Muncy, *Creating Female Dominion*, pp. 96–102.

[36] Dennett, *Birth Control Laws*, pp. 255, 81, 252.

entific knowledge would defeat and displace the bad birth control. Whereas Sangerists might have agreed that good scientific knowledge would defeat quackery in the end, the potential costs in terms of women's health and safety were too great.[37]

From Dennett's perspective, removing birth control from legal obscenity would be sufficient to place it firmly in the realm of cultural decency. Often equating birth control to dental and dietary hygiene, Dennett discounted the culturally embarrassing connection of birth control to sex that was central to Congressional timidity in dealing with her open bill. The authority of science, she believed, would be sufficient to remove cultural embarrassment from birth control. She assumed the medical profession was reluctant to deal with birth control *only* because it was illegal. She represented the profession as waiting at the gates, ready to flood the market with good information the moment birth control was legalized. Thus, she argued, "All the laws can do is to give freedom to the scientists to give the world the knowledge that has been locked in their brains and only given out surreptitiously on occasions."[38]

Even as late as 1930 Dennett's assumptions were questionable. Sangerists had the greatest knowledge about the safety and effectiveness of various contraceptive methods, and the medical profession shunned their data. Few medical societies had yet been persuaded to endorse any change in the Comstock law.[39] The American Medical Association avoided dealing with the issue at all before 1935 when exponential growth of the feminine hygiene business led it to condemn all contraception. In England, where there was no Comstock law, the medical profession had repeatedly condemned birth control morally and scientifically. The ability of quacks to operate in the field of birth control depended on public ignorance and lack of access, regardless of whether it resulted from law or taboo on public discussion of sexual matters.

---

[37] Sanger's assessment of the cost in women's lives reflected the trends in maternal mortality, which increased in the twenties and thirties. About 25 percent of these deaths resulted from illegal abortion. See Helena Huntington Smith, "Wasting Women's Lives," pp. 178–80; Antler and Fox, "The Movement," p. 577; and Leavitt, *Brought to Bed*, pp. 182–88.

[38] Dennett, *Birth Control Laws*, pp. 77, 253. On Congressional timidity about the sexual connotations of birth control, see also ibid., pp. 173–89, 253; and Chesler, *Woman of Valor*, pp. 328–29. Sanger attributed Dennett's mistaken notion that perfect birth control already existed to Dennett's lack of practical clinical experience. Sanger, *My Fight*, p. 199.

[39] Dennett, *Birth Control Laws*, pp. 228–32.

The open bill, framed in terms of free speech, largely ignored the issue of market regulation. In this sense it was ideologically outdated; it was much more appropriate to the liberal, laissez-faire state than to the emerging welfare state. Moreover, by appealing to science and medical expertise for justification, it gave the medical profession authority over birth control by default. The doctors-only bill, framed in terms of social welfare, addressed the issue of social management of the market; if passed it would have added contraception to the solidifying authority of physicians for pregnancy and childbirth. As such the Sangerist strategy was more appropriate to the emerging welfare state as it had been codified in the Sheppard-Towner Act, which relied upon the ideology of expertise to guarantee quality health care.[40] Also, because it seemed to demonstrate Sanger's deference to medical authority, the doctors-only bill was politically useful for another reason: it diffused opposition within the medical profession.

In the end the medical hegemony over contraception was accomplished by judicial interpretation, not legislative reform. Crane's 1918 decision regarding Sanger's Brownsville clinic set the stage for a series of decisions between 1930 and 1936 that removed the onus of obscenity from contraceptive information and devices. A 1930 trademark infringement case raised, within judicial circles, a logic for reinterpreting the Comstock Act. This case involved two condom manufacturers. The defense argued that it could not be charged with trademark infringement because the trademarks of an unlawful business were not entitled to legal protection. The judge in the case argued in dicta that there was a need to reevaluate the legislative intent underlying the Comstock laws. Noting that Federal law prohibited neither the manufacture nor the use of contraceptives, he suggested for the first time that obscenity was constituted not in the information and devices but in the intent of those using them.[41] If this interpretation was accepted, then the basis of Comstockery would be changed. The first use of the new interpretation came in a 1933 case of a medical supplier who had been arrested for including contraceptive devices in his products catalog. In overturning the conviction, the U.S. Court of Appeals ruled that the lower courts must consider a defendant's intent, saying, "Intent that the arti-

[40] Meckel, *Save the Babies*, pp. 170–72, notes that the infant welfare movement likewise privileged good medical care as the primary mechanism for improving infant health.

[41] *Young's Rubber Co. v. C.I. Lee and Co.*, 45 F.2d 103 (2d Cir. 1930). See Dienes, *Law, Politics, and Birth Control*, pp. 110–12. Sanger's case served as a precedent for the case. The court ruled that the trademark was protected.

74

cles . . . were to be used for condemned purposes is a prerequisite to conviction."[42] However, the Court did not go on to delineate what the legitimate purposes of contraceptives might be.

With the 1933 ruling Sangerists pursued a clear interpretation of legitimate contraceptive practice. In the 1936 *One Package* case brought by Sangerists, the U.S. Appeals Court explicitly ruled that medical prescription of contraception for the purpose of saving life or promoting the patient's well-being was not a "condemned purpose" under the Comstock law. This decision, arising from the confiscation by customs officials of a package of Japanese pessaries sent to Dr. Hannah Stone at Sanger's clinic, effectively legalized birth control because it did not require the presence of disease to legitimate contraceptive prescription. It opened the mails and interstate commerce to birth control information as long as that information passed through the hands of physicians.[43] One year later, the AMA tentatively endorsed birth control as proper medical practice, reluctantly accepting their position as mediators of American women's fertility control practices.

Sangerists supported this exemption from the laws for doctors only and hailed the *One Package* decision as a complete victory. But it would be unfair to characterize Sanger's efforts as simply deferring to medical authority. She was not willing merely to turn birth control over to established medicine.[44] Throughout the 1920s she had struggled to persuade the medical profession to endorse birth control but had continually contested the profession's ideological framing of contraceptive practices. In particular she resisted efforts made by Robert Dickinson and his Committee on Maternal Health to dictate her clinic's practices.

Resistance to Medical Hegemony

Although she thought the 1918 Crane decision was "inadequate" and its "limitation" was "silly," Sanger decided to "take advantage of it" by opening a second clinic.[45] After two years of effort, on 2 January

---

[42] *Davis v. United States*, 62 F.2d 473 (6th Cir. 1933). See Dienes, *Law, Politics, and Birth Control*, pp. 111–15.

[43] *United States v. One Package of Japanese Pessaries*, 13 F. Supp. 334 (E.D. N.Y. 1936), aff'd 86 F.2d 737 (2d Cir. 1936). See Dienes, *Law, Politics, and Birth Control*, pp. 108–15. After this decision Sanger ceased efforts to obtain legislative reform.

[44] Even as late as 1942 Sanger believed that if she had simply turned the CRB over to physicians it would have been abolished. See Margaret Sanger, handwritten note, of 29 September 1942, MSP-LC.

[45] Sanger, *My Fight*, p. 312.

1923, the Birth Control Clinical Research Bureau (CRB) opened its doors at 104 Fifth Avenue in New York. In accord with the court ruling, Sanger hired a doctor, Dorothy Bocker, to direct the clinic. The clinic was not racially segregated; all (unpregnant married) women who presented themselves at the clinic were admitted, regardless of their race or their ability to pay. The women received a cursory general physical and a complete gynecological examination, and those women for whom health reasons for doing so could be found were then fitted for pessaries. If no health reason could be found then the woman was referred to the private offices of a physician working in the clinic where, away from public scrutiny, she would be given contraceptives. The average cost of the clinic's services was $6.50 per patient. Women paid only what they felt they could afford, however, and never paid more than $5.00.[46] Thus all (unpregnant married) women who sought contraception from the ABCL received it, one way or another. Most of the 1,208 women who were given contraceptives in the first year were referred from the ABCL office across the hall.[47]

In addition to the walk-in clinic, a full-time secretary was employed to answer the thousands of letters the ABCL received requesting contraceptive information. The secretary either recommended a local clinic or physician from which birth control could be obtained or, if there was none in the writer's area, sent a copy of *Family Limitation.* These activities provided women from across the country with practical advice and were meant to exert public pressure on the medical profession. The women who wrote in were asked to send the name of their physicians, to whom the ABCL would then offer information and training.[48]

When Sanger had first rented rooms for the Bureau in 1921 she was notified by the State Board of Charities, the agency responsible for

---

[46] Patients who could afford physicians' standard fees were referred to the private practice of clinic physicians, as a supplement to the latter's low clinic salaries. In this way, the more successful the clinic was the larger its deficits grew. See Reed, *The Birth Control Movement,* p. 116; and Gordon, *Woman's Body,* p. 271.

[47] Penelope Huse, confidential report to the Executive Committee, ABCL, December 1929, MSP-SSC, also indicates that from at least 1926 to 1929, pregnant women who came to the ABCL offices desperate for help were frequently referred to abortionists.

[48] Ibid.; and Sanger, *My Fight,* p. 317. Information about contraceptives and "bringing on blocked menses" in these letters were copied from prepared samples written by Sanger. All these activities of the secretary were technically illegal under Section 211 of the Federal Postal Code. But the Federal government did not interfere before 1928, when in the course of the tax-evasion case against J. Noah Slee it investigated the letter-writing practices of the ABCL.

licensing and inspecting medical dispensaries in New York, that the ABCL could not operate a clinic without a license from the Board. Applications by the ABCL for a license were subsequently denied. The Board ruled that the ABCL was not properly incorporated to run a dispensary.[49] There were a large number of medical services offered in New York City at this time that were not licensed by the State Board of Charities. The Board, influenced by the medical profession, opposed extramural, specialty-care clinics.[50] Unlicensed medical services could be offered as long as these agencies were not called clinics; use of the word *clinic* was strictly limited to Board-approved agencies.[51] But physicians in private practice could dispense medicines, even in research, without specific state approval. Throughout the twenties and thirties the clinic operated as a research project in a physician's private practice, first under Dorothy Bocker and then under Hannah Stone. The clinic was called a research bureau in conformity with these legal restraints.[52]

In opening the CRB, Sanger envisioned it as a two-year pilot clinic. Pilot clinics were a common device used by public health reformers to demonstrate the efficacy of a variety of new techniques. They expected either state agencies or private medical practitioners to take over after a few years.[53] In Sanger's vision this pilot clinic was the first step in an effort to construct a comprehensive contraceptive service, one that would be not "an isolated agency, but . . . an integral factor of public and racial health, forming an integral part of all pre-natal and post-natal agencies for maternal and child welfare."[54] From the beginning,

[49] The clinic was never opened in 1921 because Lydia DeVilbiss, the physician who tentatively agreed to run the clinic, backed out. See Kennedy, *Birth Control in America*, pp. 181–82. The ABCL application was denied in 1922 and in 1924. Letters of Charles Johnson, secretary, State Board of Charities, to Margaret Sanger, 17 November 1921; of of Richard Wallace, assistant secretary, State Board of Charities, to Anne Kennedy, 16 May 1922; of Charles Johnson to Margaret Sanger, 15 January 1924; and of Richard Wallace to Margaret Sanger, 14 August 1924, MSP-LC.

[50] "Historical News on Proposed Maternity Research Council," pp. 5–6, MSP-SSC; and letter of Charles Johnson, State Board of Charities, to Robert Dickinson, 29 October 1926, NCMH-CL.

[51] *The Law in Relation to Dispensaries*, MSP-LC, on New York Law. Licensed dispensaries could utilize nurses instead of physicians to provide patient care.

[52] Robert Dickinson, "Report of Visit to Sanger Clinic," 4 January 1924, NCMH-CL. Hannah Stone first came to the clinic in 1923 as a volunteer.

[53] On the use of pilot projects in infant welfare reform see Meckel, *Save The Babies*, pp. 124–48; Muncy, *Creating a Female Dominion*, pp. 17–18, 56, 99, 111; and Brickman, "Public Health, Midwives, and Nurses," pp. 77–79.

[54] Sanger, *My Fight*, p. 310.

Sangerists hoped the clinic's practices would be assimilated by the maternal health care system emerging in the wake of the Sheppard-Towner Act. The CRB's records served as the data demonstrating contraceptive efficacy by which Sangerists sought to legitimate birth control. Over the years, the safety and effectiveness of various pessary models and jelly formulas were tested in the clinic.[55] Patient records were used to show the effectiveness of contraception in preventing pregnancy-related disease and mortality.[56]

While Sanger bowed to the authority of physicians to prescribe pessaries, she actively resisted the profession's narrow ideological framing of contraception. Committed to defining contraception as a technique of preventative medicine to which every (married) woman was entitled, the CRB interpreted "the cure and prevention of disease" to include illegal abortion, breast-feeding, and a living child younger than age two as acceptable indications for contraception.[57] However, mainstream medical wisdom regarded all mechanical contraceptives as ineffective at best and morally and physically dangerous at worst. Since the physicians' crusade against abortion in the 1870s the medical profession had represented itself as the gatekeepers of women's virtue. The medical profession disdained birth control, not only because it was illegal but because indiscriminate prescription of contraception to women would cause "harm to the sexual morality of the community."[58] Even physicians who were sympathetic to birth control adhered publicly to a strict construction of the "cure and prevention of disease" as the acceptable medical conditions warranting contraception. Members of the New York Obstetrical Society responding to a 1923 survey identified only the presence of disease that "endangers life" and disease caused by excessive childbearing as conditions warranting contraceptive pre-

[55] CRB activities were primarily responsible for the improvements made in the spring-loaded diaphragm in the 1920s. See Reed, "Doctors," pp. 110, 114. Lactic acid jelly, which served as the basic spermicidal jelly through the forties, was initially developed by Stone and Cooper at the CRB in 1925. See Hannah Stone, "Therapeutic Contraception," pp. 1–18 (reprint in CJG-CL).

[56] Marie Kopp, *Birth Control in Practice;* Raymond Pearl, "Second Progress Report on Family Limitation," pp. 248–69; and Regine Stix and Frank Notestein, "Effectiveness of Birth Control," pp. 57–68.

[57] Advisory Council meeting, minutes, ABCL, January 1925, MSP-LC.

[58] Letter of Robert Dickinson to Margaret Sanger, 20 October 1925, MSP-LC. See also Kristin Luker, *Abortion and the Politics of Motherhood,* pp. 20–35; Petchesky, *Abortion and Woman's Choice,* pp. 78–84; and Reed, "Doctors," pp. 111–12, 119–22.

scription. They also indicated that no uniform method was known.[59] Physicians who disapproved of birth control on moral grounds were not inclined to investigate its medical consequences.

To achieve wider access, Sangerists had to persuade the medical profession both to accept that pessaries were safe and effective and to prescribe them in cases of social and economic indications. The profession's moral posture and professional defensiveness against lay intrusions made it hostile to such persuasion. The medical profession, especially gynecologists, spurned Sanger's clinic and its practices, suspecting that it treated healthy women.[60] Professional medical journals refused to publish the CRB's data because the data were tainted by association with a lay organization. This created an absurd situation in which the medical profession continually refused to endorse birth control because it was not proven to be safe and effective, while suppressing the only existing clinical data offering such proof. When in 1928 Hannah Stone did succeed in publishing her case studies of pessaries, the article contained an explicit disclaimer that all women who received contraception at the CRB "presented a definite health reason."[61]

Robert Dickinson, one-time president of the American Gynecological Society, particularly disparaged the CRB data. In January of 1924, Dickinson conducted a surprise inspection of the clinic, which led him to criticize the Bureau's data publicly as insufficiently scientific because of its association with lay propaganda.[62] The agitators and laypersons, whose activities made the subject impossible to "handl[e] as clean science, with dignity, decency and directness," could never produce acceptable data.[63] Yet he realized that "in the face of this tremendous

[59] Robert Dickinson, "Brief Outline of Report of Committee of New York Obstetrical Society," March 1923, NCMH-CL. See also letter of Robert Dickinson to Margaret Sanger, 20 November 1925, MSP-LC.

[60] Letters of Gertrude Sturges to Robert Dickinson, 16–30 December 1925 and 22 July 1926; and of George Kosmak to Robert Dickinson, 16 February 1925, NCMH-CL.

[61] Stone, "Therapeutic Contraception," p. 4. The article did not enumerate those reasons. Throughout 1927 Hannah Stone, with Robert Dickinson's help, tried unsuccessfully to get her case studies published. Letter of Louise Bryant to Margaret Sanger, 16 February 1928, MSP-LC; and Reed, "Doctors," p. 119.

[62] On women professionals' dual commitment to research and advocacy, and on their male colleagues' disdain for such publicity, see Muncy, *Creating a Female Dominion*, pp. 21, 44–45, 62, 140–41.

[63] Dickinson was accompanied by George Kosmak, editor of the *American Journal of Gynecology*, who thought the CRB was wildly illegal and wanted it closed. See Robert L. Dickinson, "Contraception: A Medical Review of the Situation: First Report of the Committee on Maternal Health of New York," pp. 584, 600–601. Sanger contested this

public demand, to stand pat on doing nothing or to refuse to investigate or give counsel, is to leave the whole matter in the hands of the agitator," and he urged his colleagues to take up the issue themselves.[64] With a long-standing interest in female sexuality, Dickinson had supported contraceptive prescription since 1916. He attributed the rising divorce rate to sexual maladjustment. Birth control was, for him, a means to increase sexual adjustment and thereby stabilize family life. "In all marriages . . . birth control and the mechanism of love loom large as techniques of happiness."[65] However, he believed scientific studies, conducted by recognized gynecologists in full accordance with the law, were needed to make contraception respectable before the profession.[66] Dickinson set out to produce them himself.

In March 1923, after hearing rumors that Sanger was planning to open a second clinic, Dickinson established the Committee on Maternal Health (CMH) to conduct professionally endorsed, scientific investigations of contraception, sterility, abortion, and related issues.[67] Although on paper it had over fifty members, the CMH served primarily as the organization backing Dickinson's own agenda. By conducting a survey, Dickinson convinced the New York Obstetrical Society that its membership supported proper research on therapeutic contraception and obtained the Society's sponsorship of such research in hospital outpatient clinics.[68] The CMH's rigid rules for the study frustrated its

report, calling Dickinson's impartiality into question. See Margaret Sanger, "Contraception: A Medical Review of the Situation," pp. 20–21. See also letter of George Kosmak to Robert Dickinson, 9 March 1925, NCMH-CL.

[64] Robert Dickinson, "Statement at the Hearing on Application for License of Clinic for Birth Control before the Committee of the State Board of Charities," 15 January 1926, p. 2, MSP-LC. See also Dickinson, "Suggestions for a Program for American Gynecology," pp. 1–13; and the New York Obstetrics Society Committee on Contraception, minutes, 29 March 1923, NCMH-CL.

[65] As quoted in Reed, *The Birth Control Movement*, p. 186. For a complete biography of Dickinson, see also pp. 147–66.

[66] Dickinson, "Contraception," p. 584; and CMH, "Outline of Procedure for the Study Relating to Contraception," c. March 1923, NCMH-CL.

[67] Initially, the CMH received primary financial backing from a disaffected Sanger supporter, Gertrude Minturn Pinchot. To ensure its impartiality, the CMH decided to forbid persons with connections to the birth control movement from becoming members. Opponents of contraception were not excluded, however. Perhaps in a strategy of keeping one's enemies close, Dickinson worked hard to keep Kosmak as a member of the CMH, although he stymied Dickinson's plans on many occasions. CMH organization meeting, minutes, 9 March 1923; treasurer's report, CMH, 9 July 1923; and secretary's report, CMH, 10 January 1924, NCMH-CL.

[68] New York Obstetrical Society Committee on Contraception, minutes, 29 March 1923, NCMH-CL.

efforts to collect reliable data. Only patients with clear and significant medical conditions qualified to receive contraception, and physicians of recognized standing were required to refer these patients in writing to the CMH's hospital-based clinics. Many doctors who privately advised patients to go to Sanger's clinic refused to sign for referrals to the CMH's clinic.[69] Three years into the study the CMH had produced only 124 incomplete case histories. Gertrude Sturges, the executive secretary of the CMH in 1925, reported that the main causes for the poor results were that "we refuse patients who present only economic indications. . . . There is great inconvenience in securing admission [to CMH clinics] whereas admission to an independent clinic (e.g., American Birth Control League) is convenient and simple." By this time the CRB was gathering twelve to fifteen hundred case records a year.[70]

Unsuccessful in his attempt to surpass the research of this lay clinic, Dickinson was increasingly drawn to the CRB. The birth control movement was, in his eyes, the primary cause of his profession's continued avoidance of contraception. If the matter were properly handled, he believed, his colleagues would be convinced to incorporate contraception into their specialty; the League's methods were not proper. Still, this lay organization was the only group successfully conducting an "open-minded clinical study of the subject," and he "personally and unofficially" thought it should be supported.[71] The problem for Dickinson was to dissociate open-minded research from the ABCL propaganda that he and his colleagues despised. For this dissociation the CRB had to be under the control of recognized medicine.[72] Dickinson got a chance to orchestrate the separation of research and propaganda in 1925.

Dickinson's published criticism of the Bureau discredited the two-year demonstration to which Sanger had committed the ABCL. Rather than abandon the project, Sanger sent James Cooper, the ABCL's new medical director, to consult with Dickinson on how to improve the quality and ethicality of the Bureau's data. Dickinson advised Cooper that the medical aspects of the Bureau had to be supervised by recognized

[69] CMH, outline. Because so few patients were referred, this rule was eventually changed.
[70] Letter of Gertrude Sturges to Robert Dickinson, 9 March 1926, NCMH-CL.
[71] Robert Dickinson, "Relation of Committee on Maternal Health to Sanger Birth Control Clinic," 17 March 1924, NCMH-CL. As late as 1930–31 Dickinson still blamed the birth control movement for medical opposition to contraception. See NCMH, annual report, 1930–31, NCMH-CL.
[72] Secretary's report, CMH, 11 December 1924 and 19 March 1925, NCMH-CL.

medical organizations for its data to be accepted. Such supervision would be difficult to obtain for a lay clinic, but Dickinson suggested that the New York Academy of Medicine might be willing to provide it if the ABCL formally requested it. In March, at Dickinson's request, a special meeting of the Public Health Committee of the New York Academy of Medicine was held to receive Cooper's formal offer "to place the medical work of the League under a Committee of leading members of the profession." In a motion brought by Dickinson, the Academy authorized a subcommittee, chaired by Dickinson, to investigate the matter.[73] This subcommittee concluded that New York City needed an extramural clinic in which to conduct contraceptive research for the next two to three years. After that time area hospitals could be persuaded to carry on this work. The subcommittee report, written by Dickinson, also indicated that Sanger was willing "to accept regular counsel and inspection from gynecologists and obstetricians of recognized standing" and recommended that the Academy accept Sanger's offer, if the clinic was properly licensed.[74] At the same time, Dickinson paid a visit to the State Board of Charities to discuss the "means for control of the birth control clinic," and ascertained that the Board might "issue a license, not to the ABCL but to a group of physicians who would supervise it."[75]

Between March, when the favorable Academy report was issued, and June the ABCL and Dickinson negotiated the terms for proper supervision of the medical end of the CRB. Because the ABCL could not get the necessary license, it was suggested that a separate group be incorporated to secure one. That group, named the Maternity Research Council (MRC), would consist of five members each from the CMH and ABCL with one additional member jointly elected.[76] In June the Sangerists and the CMH met to draw up a certificate of incorporation, the first step in obtaining a license. The incorporation papers stated that the purpose of the MRC was to "provide clinical facilities, licensed, when necessary, by the State Board of Charities, for such patients as may be entitled to contraceptive advice under the laws of the

[73] Ibid., 19 March 1925, NCMH-CL.

[74] Report of the subcommittee, Public Health Committee, Academy of Medicine, 16 March 1925, NCMH-CL. The subcommittee visited the clinic on 7 March 1925.

[75] Secretary's report, CMH, 19 March 1925; and Robert Dickinson to Executive Committee, CMH, c. March 1925, NCMH-CL.

[76] See letter of Robert Dickinson to George Worthington, legal counsel of CMH, 11 May 1925, NCMH-CL. Dickinson does not record who suggested this organizational structure.

State of New York and to undertake a scientific investigation of contraceptive methods."[77] As a condition of CMH participation in the MRC, Dickinson insisted that Sanger publicly affirm that propaganda and research should be separated. To this end he insisted that the CRB be detached physically and legally from the ABCL and that "no Birth Control literature or propaganda be displayed, given away or sold at the clinic." Sanger complied. In September the CRB moved to new quarters, and in November movement posters and literature were removed from the clinic offices.[78]

Sangerists accepted the MRC proposal for several related reasons. The big foundations had been unwilling to fund the clinic without the supervision of a recognized medical organization. With the new quarters and the incorporation under way, Dickinson secured a $10,000 grant from the Bureau of Social Hygiene to fund the Bureau.[79] Thus even without a dispensary license, coalition with physicians opened the doors for the clinic to receive stable funding from the big philanthropies. However, Sanger's main reason for agreeing to the incorporation of the MRC was to get a license. As Sanger told her Advisory Board, "In case you should be fearful of getting too many boards, may I say that the object of the Maternity Research Council is to get a license from the State Board of Charities to establish birth control clinics throughout the city and the state."[80] Endorsement from the State Board of Charities and the New York Academy of Medicine would also advance efforts to open clinics throughout the nation.

For Dickinson, gaining control of Sanger's clinic meant the opportunity to wrest birth control research from the hands of agitators. In the

[77] "Historical News," p. 2. The phrase "licensed, when necessary," was included to prevent the possibility of the CRB being declared illegal if the dispensary license was denied.
[78] Conference of the Clinical Research Committee of the ABCL and the CMH, minutes, 29 November 1925, NCMH-CL. Secretary's report, CMH, 28 November 1925; letter of Betram Ireland to Robert Dickinson, 12 September 1925, MRC; minutes, 21 November 1925, NCMH-CL; and Dickinson, "Hearing Statement," 15 January 1926.
[79] This money went directly to the CRB, so even if the MRC plan fell through, it had already helped to fund the clinic for one year. Dickinson was also receiving pressure from the big philanthropies to include sociological aspects in CMH research. Unable to persuade the CMH to change its research rules, access to the CRB offered Dickinson the best hope of foundation support as well. See letters of Katherine B. Davis to Margaret Sanger, 7 October 1925; and of Margaret Sanger to Katherine B. Davis, 14 and 19 October 1925, MSP-LC; CMH, minutes, 23 June 1924; and the report of the subcommittee, NCMH-CL. See also Borell, "Biologists," pp. 65, 77; and Chesler, *Woman of Valor*, pp. 279–82.
[80] Letter of Margaret Sanger to Adolph Meyer, 28 May 1925, MSP-LC. This announcement was sent to each member of the CRB Advisory Board.

incorporation papers for the MRC he included the recommendation that "scientific investigation of contraceptive methods [be] under the supervision and inspection of a board of gynecologists and obstetricians and other physicians of recognized authority who shall guide and inspect the work."[81] The ABCL initially agreed to this arrangement. But in October Dickinson proposed an "interim working plan," devised in consultation with the CMH and the Bureau of Social Hygiene director, Katherine B. Davis, in which the CMH physicians would "take over the control of the new clinic until such time as incorporation was completed and a license from the State Board of Charities procured." Dickinson proposed the immediate takeover of the CRB by the CMH because he hoped that if faced with a fait accompli the State Board of Charities would be more likely to grant a license.[82] Or, if the license was denied, the CMH might be willing to continue supervising the clinic if it were already doing so.

Thinking that Dickinson seemed "anxious (wildly anxious) to get in control," Sanger and her existing advisors became suspicious of his intentions. After consulting with her Advisory Board, Sanger rejected Dickinson's interim plan. The CRB Advisory Board, organized in response to Dickinson's public criticism, consisted of several biologists who were already supervising the Bureau's research.[83] One member of the Board, Clarence C. Little, a noted geneticist and eugenicist and the president of the University of Michigan, became particularly concerned about Dickinson's intentions. Although he saw strategic value in medical endorsement for the clinic, he felt Dickinson desired complete control of the clinic and would squeeze out scientists and laypersons. He wrote to both Sanger and Dickinson of his objections, saying, "The medical profession has not lived up to its obligations or opportunities in this particular matter." In Little's estimation, medical men "had not

---

[81] "Historical News," pp. 1–2. This changed the agreed-upon language for the incorporation papers. See CMH and ABCL meeting, minutes, 15 May 1925; letter of Robert Dickinson to Anne Kennedy, 19 May 1925, MSP-LC. See also CMH, "Proposed Standards for Medical Direction of the Clinical Research Bureau with the American Birth Control League," 17 April 1925, NCMH-CL.

[82] Letters of Robert Dickinson to Gertrude Sturges, 30 December 1925; and of Anne Kennedy to Robert Dickinson, 14 October 1925, NCMH-CL. Dickinson's usual style was to present potential opponents with a fait accompli.

[83] Letters of Margaret Sanger to James Cooper, 13 November 1925; of James Cooper to Margaret Sanger, 2 and 26 November 1925; and of C. C. Little to Margaret Sanger, 28 October 1925, MSP-LC. Kennedy, *Birth Control in America*, p. 198. Among the members were C. C. Little, Raymond Pearl, and E. M. East, each of whom had unofficially advised Sanger in the past.

earned the right to take over the work in a field which others have tilled for them." In an attitude of professional rivalry, Little rejected Dickinson's claim that physicians alone could adequately supervise contraceptive research. He and the other biologists on the Board were primarily interested in the nonmedical aspects of contraception. They supported Sanger's efforts to legitimate social and economic indications for birth control by guiding the clinic's research on these issues. Little did not think that physicians had the inclination, training, or prudence to oversee such important research. He proposed that the MRC Board consist, at the minimum, of two medical persons, two sociologists, and two biologists.[84]

Dickinson immediately and wholeheartedly rejected Little's plan. He promised that the scientists and birth control activists would not be pushed out, but he refused to formalize this promise in the MRC structure, saying it would delay incorporation.[85] Sanger agreed with Little "from the broad point of view" and suspected that "it will be Dr. D.'s aim to keep all of us off the Research Council." Yet she advised Little to go along until after the license was granted. The ABCL lawyers assured her that they could change the MRC structure to suit them better after it was incorporated. What she feared more was, as Dickinson warned, that Catholic opposition would organize and suppress the dispensary license if too much time were wasted haggling over the details. Obtaining the license remained her primary goal.[86] Little agreed, for the time being, but "advise[d] strongly that [Sanger] obtain from Dr. Dickinson in writing the confirmation of the promises mentioned." Little did not trust Dickinson to make good on his assurances and told Sanger to "watch" him.[87]

Little's objections led Sanger, in late November, to call a conference

[84] Letters of C. C. Little to Margaret Sanger, 26 October 1925; and of C. C. Little to Robert Dickinson, 26 October 1925, MSP-LC. Little was specifically concerned that physicians were reckless in attempting X-ray induced infertility, a project Dickinson supported. See also letter of C. C. Little to Margaret Sanger, 12 November 1925, MSP-LC, in which Little castigates the medical profession's ability to do sociological research.

[85] Letters of Robert Dickinson to Margaret Sanger, 23 October 1925; and of Robert Dickinson to C. C. Little, 28 October 1925, MSP-LC; and "Historical News," p. 2. A letter of Robert Dickinson to Michael Davis, 19 September 1925, NCMH-CL, indicates that Dickinson sought complete control of the CRB by his Medical Board.

[86] Letters of Margaret Sanger to Raymond Pearl, 10 November 1925; of Margaret Sanger to James Cooper, 13 November 1925; and of Margaret Sanger to C. C. Little, 26 October and 7 November 1925, MSP-LC.

[87] Letters of C. C. Little to Margaret Sanger, 28 October 1925; and of Frank Robbins, assistant to C. C. Little, to Margaret Sanger, 17 December 1925, MSP-LC.

between the clinic Board and the CMH to reexamine the details of the MRC. The CRB Board sought to establish a clear understanding of how authority would be structured when the MRC was incorporated. They wanted data collection to be in the hands of scientific members according to Little's plan. Dickinson and the CMH were unanimously opposed to Little's plan.[88] A compromise was reached whereby the clinic would continue under its existing management until the license was obtained; the policy against distributing literature and propaganda would continue; and the case-record forms would be "revised and extended to meet both the research and medical requirements." Once the license was obtained, then "the purely medical side of the clinic involving the actual giving of contraceptive advice, and the selection of patients to receive it would be entirely in the hands of physicians." If, on the other hand, the license was denied, "the medical members of the [MRC would] be obliged to withdraw their active participation in the clinic." Dickinson was not satisfied with this arrangement and continued to press Sanger to agree to medical dominance on the MRC Board.[89]

Sanger and the CRB Board, however, were willing to submit the clinic to proper medical supervision *only* if the dispensary license was obtained. Giving up control of the clinic's practices to 'proper medical supervision' might have narrowed the circumstances under which birth control would be prescribed.[90] Sanger was willing to risk the breadth of the clinic's practices only if the Bureau gained something substantial in return. A dispensary license would be a substantial ideological and practical victory because it would give state legitimacy to the clinic. In fact, the license was denied in February 1926 because "the Board is too much afraid that such [a] license will be widely exploited as a victory for Mrs. Sanger." The official reason given was that the State Board of Charities resolved that it was "inexpedient from the point of view of public policy that the Board approve the incorporation or grant the dispensary license."[91]

Dickinson continued to press the State Board for a dispensary license through 1926 and 1927, but the MRC never amounted to more

---

[88] Letter of Margaret Sanger to Robert Dickinson, 6 November 1925, MSP-LC; and CMH, minutes, 2 November 1925, NCMH-CL.

[89] Conference, 29 November 1925. See also letter of Robert Dickinson to Margaret Sanger, 7 December 1925, NCMH-CL.

[90] CMH, "Proposed Standards for Medical Direction of the Maternity Research Council," 17 April 1925, MSP-LC.

[91] "Historical News," p. 4.

than a paper organization. In 1927 the Board of Charities suggested that Dickinson should affiliate the clinic with a hospital. Dickinson pursued this avenue for a brief time, but Sanger rejected the idea, fearing the clinic would be buried in administrative red tape.[92] Thereafter, the MRC plan languished for some time. However, when Sanger, taking the Bureau with her, resigned from the ABCL in late 1928 the Bureau lost its medical director because James Cooper remained behind. Sanger requested Dickinson's assistance in securing a new medical director, and he took this request as an opportunity to pursue the MRC plan once again. Then, the Bureau was raided by city police in April 1929. The New York Academy of Medicine protested the raid because patient files had been seized, which was an affront to doctor-patient confidentiality. Sanger took the opportunity of the positive publicity to request an investigation by the Academy, once again, with an eye to endorsement. Once again, Dickinson headed the investigation and used the opportunity to obtain the Academy's endorsement of the MRC. When everything was set according to his understanding of Sanger's request for assistance, he outlined his proposal to Sanger. She, however, was reluctant to "turn over the clinic completely."[93]

In part, her reluctance was motivated by the fact that the plans of the MRC were sketchy and contained none of the things for which she had initially sought his help. Dickinson had not secured a license, nor had he located a new medical director. Most important, he had not secured new funding for the clinic. Sanger, who was about to expand her clinic into Harlem, was particularly interested in any funding the MRC might attract. The Bureau of Social Hygiene had renewed its $10,000 donation in 1926 but had given the CRB no money thereafter. By 1929, the Bureau's annual deficit was approaching $25,000, and Sanger was competing with the independent ABCL and the CMH for the few funds that the movement could attract. A license and the financing it might generate were the chief assets in which Sanger was

---

[92] Ibid., p. 6.
[93] Letter of Margaret Sanger to Robert Dickinson, 19 October 1929, p. 2; CMH, minutes, 11 June 1929; letters of Louise Bryant and Robert Dickinson to Margaret Sanger, 17 July 1929; of Louise Bryant to Margaret Sanger, 21 September 1929, NCMH-CL; and of Robert Dickinson to Margaret Sanger, 22 October 1929, MSP-LC. Kennedy, *Birth Control in America*, pp. 202–8, asserts that Sanger's need to be in control motivated her to reject the MRC. He concludes that if she had accepted Dickinson's proposal the entire course of the movement would have been changed for the better. I agree with Reed, *The Birth Control Movement*, p. 373, that this conclusion has no basis in fact.

interested.[94] Although reluctant, Sanger told Dickinson that if he had a concrete proposal she would submit it to her Board. In October, he offered a plan for the MRC in which the Board would have only one nonmedical member, and the Bureau would be reorganized as a hospital-affiliated, fee-for-service clinic. On 20 November 1929, the CRB Advisory Board voted unanimously to reject Dickinson's offer because it would curtail the scope of the clinic's research, practice, and governance. They decided instead to organize an independent Medical Board.[95]

Trying to orchestrate this takeover put Dickinson in a difficult position. He was caught between a medical profession hostile to lay intrusions and a social movement threatening to usurp the profession's responsibility for contraception. Yet his mode of address when dealing with his reluctant colleagues always deferred to their professional defensiveness. He repeatedly reiterated that the profession rightfully had the sole legal authority for contraceptive prescription and research. Likewise, he acquiesced to the profession's claim that contraception would remain unproven until it was validated by 'gynecologists of recognized authority.' Throughout his dealings with the CRB, he jealously defended his profession's domain by dismissing the Bureau's activities as propaganda.[96]

Dickinson's mode of action when dealing with the ABCL was to try both to contain them and to position himself as the arbiter of their respectability.[97] Before the State Board of Charities Dickinson testified that "the State Board and the medical profession have two choices, and

[94] The Bureau of Social Hygiene gave $10,000 in 1929 to a joint committee of CMH and CRB for publication of Marie Kopp's analysis of the clinic's first ten thousand cases. See letter of Ruth Topping, Bureau of Social Hygiene, to Margaret Sanger, 20 January 1930, MSP-SSC. Louise Bryant, notes, 3 January 1929; and letters of Louise Bryant to Margaret Sanger, 25 February, 21 September, and 10 October 1929; and of Margaret Sanger to Louise Bryant, 30 September 1929, NCMH-CL. On the clinic's finances, see also Reed, *The Birth Control Movement*, pp. 116–17.

[95] Sanger was to hold the one nonmedical position. Letters of Margaret Sanger to Louise Bryant, 17 October and 30 September 1929; and of Robert Dickinson to Margaret Sanger, 22 October 1929, and of Margaret Sanger to Robert Dickinson, 17 October 1929, NCMH-CL. Once again, C. C. Little was instrumental in convincing the Board to reject Dickinson's plan. See Advisory Board meeting, minutes, CRB, 20 November 1929; and letter of Ira Wile to Margaret Sanger, 18 November 1929, MSP-LC.

[96] See CMH, minutes, 11 June 1929; and NCMH, annual report, 1930–31, p. 3, NCMH-CL. On Dickinson's deferential posture toward his medical colleagues see also Borell, "Biologists," pp. 69–70; and Reed, "Doctors," p. 115.

[97] See Dickinson's review of the CMH accomplishments in CMH, annual report, 1940, NCMH-CL.

only two. One is to let the clinic go on in its present fashion with scant professional guidance and control. The other is to help secure for it the best available guidance. Nothing can stop it."[98] While he was reassuring the ABCL that his interim plan was not an effort to squeeze them out of the MRC, he announced to his Committee "the beginning, next week, of the birth control clinic formerly conducted by the American Birth Control League but now under responsible medical management." In January 1926, he reported the progress of the MRC to the CMH under the heading "Removal of the Sanger Clinic."[99] When the CRB staff produced adequate data, he tried to disconnect it from the movement by appropriating it to the respectable CMH.[100] Dickinson avoided public entanglement in the movement's political activities and castigated Sanger whenever he heard a rumor that the clinic might not be operating with proper regard to the law.[101]

His harshest criticism came in 1929. Angered by the CRB's rejection of his plans, Dickinson circulated a letter to Academy members and prospective funding sources criticizing Sanger's administration of the clinic. Representing the Board's decision as Sanger's alone, he complained that her sudden and irresponsible action left "one of the country's largest gynecological services" without proper medical supervision.[102] He characterized the clinic's administration by a lay-

[98] Dickinson, "Hearing Statement," 15 January 1926, p. 2.

[99] Secretary's report, CMH, 2 November 1925; and summary report of the chairman, CMH, 12 January 1926, NCMH-CL.

[100] Dickinson attempted to appropriate the research of both Hannah Stone and Marie Kopp. In exchange for aid in finding a publisher, Dickinson edited Stone's 1928 article and wrote a foreword to it. Sanger was annoyed that the CRB received little credit for both publications. See Louise Bryant, notes, 25 March 1927, NCMH-CL; Kopp, *Birth Control in Practice*, title page; letters of Penelope Huse to Margaret Sanger, 14 January 1928; of Margaret Sanger to Penelope Huse, 30 January 1928, MSP-LC; and of Margaret Sanger to Robert Dickinson, 5 October 1933, MSP-SSC.

[101] Dickinson was most concerned with rumors that the clinic gave birth control to unmarried and/or healthy women and that the clinic sent practical advice to women through the mail. His concerns were justified: the clinic did not operate in a manner Dickinson would regard as proper. See, for example, letters of Robert Dickinson to Margaret Sanger, 20 October 1925, and 10 and 17 October 1929, MSP-LC.

[102] Letters of Robert Dickinson to "Dear Doctor," 4 December 1929, p. 2; and of Margaret Sanger to C. C. Little, 6 December 1929, MSP-LC; and Louise Bryant, notes, 11 November–3 December 1929, NCMH-CL. He also complained that Sanger had reneged on her previous pledge to accept the plan. But if Sanger had in fact ever agreed to his proposal, there is no record of it in her words. As early as March the scientists on the Board opposed renewing the MRC plan. See letters of E. M. East to Margaret Sanger, 14 March 1929; of Ira Wile to Margaret Sanger, 15 March 1929; and of C. C. Little to Margaret Sanger, 20 March 1929, MSP-LC.

woman as "anomalous" and claimed that it had never had a director or attending physician with "experience above the grade of the lowest dispensary position."[103] In part his evaluation was based upon the gender of the clinic's all-female staff. In Dickinson's eyes, Stone and the other women physicians at the clinic were not sufficiently qualified to handle the great diversity of gynecological ailments they might encounter or to conduct the research he so ardently advocated. In listing candidates for the MRC's board of gynecologists of "recognized standing and authority" who would oversee the clinic's operation, Dickinson included only male physicians.[104]

Dickinson's perspective on the lay organization and women doctors who supervised the CRB was not atypical. Part of the AMA's opposition to the renewal of the Sheppard-Towner Act was that the Children's Bureau, which administered it, was directed by a woman who was not a physician. Women physicians, who composed about 6 percent of all physicians, were themselves rarely regarded as true professionals by their male colleagues. Women doctors were often represented by their male colleagues as temperamentally unsuited for dispassionate and objective research. The male-dominated medical profession tended to characterize women doctors more as social workers than doctors, because they were concentrated in maternal and infant welfare agencies. Moreover, although women were admitted to the AMA in 1915, they had little influence or "recognized standing" in the organization. Thus, Dickinson's attitude to Sanger and the CRB reflected the wider gender politics of his profession, which particularly contested the authority that women reformers and physicians had established over maternal health.[105]

Dickinson's "high-handed" tactic of publicly circulating his criticisms of the CRB outraged Sanger and the CRB Board. They immediately

---

[103] Letter of Robert Dickinson to "Dear Doctor." Hannah Stone was not affiliated with any hospital; she had been forced to resign in 1924 because of her involvement with the CRB. Dickinson discounted her nearly five years of practical experience running the clinic. On the clinic's staff, see John Price Jones, "Survey on Plans for Fund-Raising for the Birth Control Clinical Research Bureau and National Committee on Federal Legislation for Birth Control," 1930, p. 77, MSP-LC.

[104] Secretary's report, CMH, 28 November and 19 March 1925; and letter of Louise Bryant and Robert Dickinson to Margaret Sanger, 17 July 1929, NCMH-CL.

[105] On male physicians' attitudes toward their female colleagues see Muncy, *Creating a Female Dominion,* pp. 135–40; Leavitt, *Brought to Bed,* p. 113; Penina Migal Glazer and Miriam Slater, *Unequal Colleagues,* pp. 69–79; and Regina Morantz-Sanchez, *Sympathy and Science,* pp. 312–60.

sought to repair any damage his criticisms might cause.[106] Bypassing Dickinson, they tried to convince other members of the New York Academy of Medicine that they wanted "official medical endorsement" of the clinic. This, Sanger argued, did not mean "maternal health committee dictation," however. The Academy was not convinced. Sangerists' efforts to secure the Academy's endorsement and organize an independent Medical Board were thwarted by the continuing accusations that the CRB engaged in propaganda.[107] Sanger was told that "a private and independent clinic" could never "function in a scientific manner."[108]

In part the Academy's response expressed the profession's preference for hospital clinics organized on a fee-for-service basis.[109] But behind the Academy's ongoing concern about birth control propaganda was the profession's continued refusal to countenance any lay authority for medical matters. The medical profession's intensifying resistance to the intrusion of social reform into its domain culminated in the 1929 defeat of the Children's Bureau's efforts to renew Federal funding for maternal and infant health services. As the medical profession extended its authority over birth even physicians who supported the Sheppard-Towner Act questioned the involvement of laypersons in that maternal health program.[110] The profession's rejection of Sangerist birth control clinics was part of its overall resistance to infringements on the profession's independent authority over health matters. Because promoting contraception was less socially acceptable than reducing maternal and infant mortality, it was easy for physicians to char-

---

[106] Letters of Margaret Sanger to C. C. Little, 22 January 1930, and to Ira Wile, 14 January 1930, MSP-SSC; of C. C. Little to Margaret Sanger, 13 January 1930; and of Ira Wile to Margaret Sanger, 2 January 1930, MSP-LC. The Bureau of Social Hygiene, aware of this conflict with Dickinson, did reject Sanger's 1930 applications for CRB funding.

[107] Letters of Margaret Sanger to Ira Wile, 14 January 1930, MSP-SSC; of John Hartwell to Margaret Sanger, 20 December 1929; of Margaret Sanger to John Hartwell, 31 December 1929; of C. C. Little to Margaret Sanger, 11 April 1930; and of Margaret Sanger to Leon Cole, 17 October 1930, MSP-LC.

[108] Letters of Linsly Williams to Margaret Sanger, 23 May 1932, 31 December 1931, and 25 February 1932; of Margaret Sanger to Linsly Williams, 2 March 1932; and of Margaret Sanger to the CRB Board of Trustees, 28 September 1936, MSP-LC.

[109] In the 1929–32 spermicide study conducted under CMH auspices, the CMH chose a British researcher, in part because he had access to hospital-based clinical facilities for the project. See Borell, "Biologists," p. 71.

[110] Underlying AMA opposition was the profession's concern for its economic independence. See Muncy, *Creating a Female Dominion*, pp. 124–25, 136–42; and Meckel, *Save The Babies*, pp. 207–8, 215–22.

acterize the birth control movement's demands for wide access to contraception as irresponsible propaganda.

Throughout the 1920s the medical profession refused to endorse the practices of extramural birth control clinics and rejected the birth control movement's economic and social reasoning for contraception. However, when this same reasoning was expressed by recognized physicians it became more acceptable to the profession. When the CMH represented such factors as "age, numbers of living children, physical and mental condition of the husband, housing, [and] occupation" as part of a patient's general health profile it framed contraception in a manner that would become acceptable medical practice by 1940.[111]

In 1927 the CMH Medical Indications Committee denounced contraceptive prescriptions made solely for economic reasons and reaffirmed its position that contraceptives should be prescribed only in cases of "active disease" necessitating "therapeutic abortion." However, the Committee called for careful analysis of maternal and infant mortality rates to evaluate whether child spacing might be medically legitimate, asserting that the potential pathology of pregnancy was "inextricably associated" with "economic considerations."[112] By the early thirties "scientific" fertility studies began to show that child spacing reduced maternal and infant mortality by allowing women to regain their health between pregnancies. This reduction was most likely an artifact of the connection between mortality, fertility, and poverty. That is, poorer women, who generally had little access to obstetrical care or contraception, had higher fertility rates, higher mortality rates, and shorter intervals between births. Nonetheless, child spacing was the primary therapeutic category by which doctors incorporated the economic considerations of birth control advocates into their professional domain.

In framing the medical aspects of child spacing, Dickinson harked back to the symbol of the traditional family physician who treated pa-

[111] Caroline Hadley Robinson, *Seventy Birth Control Clinics*, pp. 157, 152–56. This study was issued by the CMH, and Dickinson wrote this chapter himself (pp. 127–64). See also Robert Dickinson, foreword to Eric Matsner, *The Technique of Contraception*, pp. 3–4. Likewise, maternal and infant health programs framed by male physicians were also more acceptable to the profession. See Meckel, *Save The Babies*, pp. 222–23; and Muncy, *Creating a Female Dominion*, pp. 146–50, on Herbert Hoover's attempts to revive these programs under the auspices of the Public Health Service in 1930.

[112] Medical Indications Committee, report, CMH, 15 January 1927, NCMH-CL. The Committee ignored existing studies by the Children's Bureau that showed as early as 1919 that with a two-year interval between pregnancies, infant mortality was reduced by 50 percent. See Meckel, *Save The Babies*, pp. 178–82.

tients with regard to their total family situation. In the interests of public health, he argued, modern scientific physicians likewise had to be mindful of their patients' economic and social situation. Child spacing with contraception reconciled economic and sexual strains on marital happiness while reaffirming the imperative of couples to reproduce.[113]

With this rhetoric, Dickinson constituted contraception as one more tool within the increasingly medicalized domain of maternal and infant health. Thus, for Dickinson, women were to rely on the expertise of obstetricians and gynecologists before, during, and after pregnancy. His articulation of the economic ethic of fertility within a medical frame defined the physician, not the woman, as the arbitrator of fertility decisions. Deferential to the physician's authority, this rhetoric defined the medical profession's eventual support for contraception.[114]

After a decade of effort by Dickinson and the CMH, the AMA gave hesitant assent to its articulation of social and economic indicators for contraception. By 1935 the booming "feminine hygiene" business compelled the AMA to form a committee to investigate. The 1936 report of the Committee on Contraception, noting the general use of contraception, indicted all contraception and the lay organizations that sponsored it; it said little about the practices of commercial feminine hygiene producers. The Committee specifically disputed the social and economic reasoning of Sangerists and delineated a restrictive list of severe illnesses warranting contraceptive prescription. In fact, listing the relevant diseases that contraindicated pregnancy, the Committee recommended that persons with serious ailments should not even marry, thus precluding their need for contraception. Disregarding all the research produced by the movement and its biologist allies, the report asserted that no contraceptive was reasonably adequate and effective for the large portion of the population, and "no contraceptive technic [*sic*] other than actual continence is intrinsically 100 per cent safe." In contradiction to Sangerist claims that legal access to contraception would reduce the depression-era epidemic of illegal abortion, the report suggested that contraception actually contributed to the increase in illegal abortion because women sought abortion when it failed. The Committee's final recommendations included a strongly worded condemnation of the "propaganda" of lay birth control orga-

[113] Dickinson, foreword to Eric Matsner, *The Technique of Contraception*, p. 3.
[114] On the increasing medicalization of maternal and infant health in the 1930s see Meckel, *Save The Babies*, pp. 220–25; and Leavitt, *Brought to Bed*, pp. 180–88.

nizations and all physicians who supported them, stating that "an entirely false sense of values with respect to the important function of childbearing and of parenthood had been created by the activities of such organizations."[115]

Both Dickinson's CMH and birth control activists were disappointed with this report, although Sangerists were not surprised by its indictment of the movement. The AMA voted to continue investigation of contraception and, over the next year, Dickinson's CMH inundated the Committee with data. The 1937 Committee report effectively reversed the position of the 1936 Committee and gave tentative endorsement for contraception. But the report was very carefully worded to avoid any explicit approval of extramural clinics. It reaffirmed the narrow list of specific diseases warranting contraception that had been listed in the previous year's report. It recognized that child spacing might improve maternal and infant health, although the Committee concluded that more research was needed before optimal intervals could be specified. Foreshadowing the concept of privacy articulated in *Roe v. Wade*, the report concluded that in evaluating the child-spacing indications for contraception, "Each case must be determined by the individual judgments of parents and physician, based on the conditions present."[116] By not listing any specific conditions that would make child spacing necessary, the report reaffirmed the individual physician's authority to determine appropriate conditions. This tepid endorsement left room for the profession's ongoing commitment to encouraging every healthy married woman to have more children. The privacy of contraceptive decision making articulated by the report deferred to the physician's right to independent practice rather than to the woman's right to contraception.

With the 1937 Committee report Sangerists received at least a partial endorsement for the latitude in contraceptive prescription that they had long sought, without sacrificing their clinical practices to the

[115] Sanger's old foe, George Kosmak, chaired the Committee. See "Report of Reference Committee on Executive Session" (1936), p. 1911. See also Regine Stix, "A Study of Pregnancy Wastage," p. 357. This study showed that women whose accidental pregnancies resulted from a contraceptive failure were more likely to induce abortion than those who used no contraception.

[116] "Report of Reference Committee on Executive Session" (1937), p. 2218. Dickinson personally lobbied each member of the 1937 committee. See Reed, *The Birth Control Movement*, p. 187; and Kennedy, *Birth Control in America*, pp. 215–16.

profession's dominion.[117] In the decade after the AMA endorsed contraception, the medical profession continued to criticize extramural clinics. As late as 1946 the New York Academy of Medicine recommended that Planned Parenthood clinics be taken over by hospitals, calling its female and foreign staff inadequate. By 1947 a national survey indicated that in their private practices more than half of America's physicians prescribed contraception to any married woman who wanted it, yet the profession remained critical of clinics that did the same thing.[118] Criticism of the prescription practices in extramural clinics exemplified the ongoing struggle between lay organizations and the medical profession for control of contraceptive practices. As long as medical indications were needed for legitimate prescriptions of birth control, medical authority legitimately dominated clinical procedures.

While Sangerist clinics continued to pay lip service to proper medical indications, they practiced open access. The lay organizations continued to promote social and economic reasoning for contraception, but their clinical publications deferred to the medical profession's criticisms by reaffirming the requirement of medical indications. Even so, lists of medical indications published by all the lay organizations included child spacing, marital adjustment, recent abortion or parturition, and nervous anxiety, as well as the more life-threatening diseases.[119] It is difficult to determine what practical consequences the debate about medical indications had for women's access to contraception. Sangerists deferred rhetorically to medical indications, but, by concurring with the individuality of each case and the privacy of the prescription process, they maintained the space in their clinics to give women contraception for any reason.[120] Social and economic concerns brought women to extramural clinics, and in most clinics they received contraception under the euphemism of child spacing. In accommodating the medical profession's criticisms ideologically, however, Sanger-

[117] In fact, even in 1956 the CRB operated without a license. See Reed, "Doctors," p. 132, n. 32.
[118] "Summary and Recommendations of Report on Planned Parenthood Clinics" (1946), pp. 553–56. Joyce Ray and F. G. Gosling, "American Physicians and Birth Control, 1936–1947," pp. 402–3.
[119] Matsner, *The Technique of Contraception*, pp. 7–8; CRB, "Suggestions for the Establishment of a Birth Control Clinic," a pamphlet, c. 1932, pp. 3–4, MSP-LC; "Medical Indications for Contraceptive Advice," Birth Control Federation of America, October 1939, PPFA-SSC; and PPFA, "Medical Indications for Giving Contraceptive Advice in Affiliated Clinics" c. 1942, CJG-CL.
[120] CRB, "Suggestions," p. 4.

ists also condoned, in their rhetoric, the authority of physicians over women's contraceptive decision making. The rhetoric of child spacing, and later that of family planning, reaffirmed the ideological imperative to have children, tempered by economic restraint. In it, contraception as a tool of women's sexual and reproductive self-determination was recast as a tool of family health and stability. In the decision about contraception, physicians were positioned with the authority to weigh the factors affecting individual, marital, and familial health. Women's individual concerns were relevant only to the extent that they influenced marital, and thus familial, stability.

Through the forties, Sanger continued to resist attempts to narrow access to contraception that medical hegemony brought with it. She objected strenuously to all efforts by PPFA physicians to tighten indications for contraception and insisted that they should not be allowed to "dominate" clinic administration.[121] Sanger, absolutely opposed to their control of the movement and its education campaigns, maintained that "the movement will die a slow death from stagnation if we let too many of our activities be conducted under medical auspices."[122] But the medical hegemony over contraception successfully set the terms of women's access to contraception both ideologically and economically. Women's access to contraception depended upon their access to privately funded clinics and fee-for-service physicians, both of which were increasingly structured by physicians' ideological commitments and exclusive authority over pregnancy and childbirth. In the context of declining population growth in the thirties, white, middle-class women were encouraged to have children, and poor women and women of color were discouraged. In the fifties, women were encouraged to have more children to fulfill their renewed domestic roles. Even today, women's access to contraceptive services is effected by their ability to pay.

But even in its success the medical hegemony was not uncompromised. By the time the AMA endorsed contraception in 1937, the evidence from demographic and biological studies had demonstrated contraceptive effectiveness in preventing unwanted pregnancies and improving maternal and infant health. Also, by 1937, American sexual ideology had shifted so that marital abstinence was an unjustifiable way to reconcile fertility and income. Thus, the profession was unable to

[121] Letter of Margaret Sanger to D. Kenneth Rose, 4 January 1945, MSP-LC; and Reed, *The Birth Control Movement*, pp. 136–37.
[122] Letter of Margaret Sanger to Clarence Gamble, 4 February 1940, MSP-SSC.

limit contraception to cases of active disease. Child spacing effectively usurped the disease requirement for contraception and instituted the economic ethic of fertility as medically appropriate. Nor was the profession's hospital system able to reclaim extramural clinics. Although birth moved to the hospital in the 1940s, birth control did not. Throughout the 1940s, extramural clinics continued to see more than 80 percent of all clinic patients in more than eight hundred clinics nationwide.[123]

[123] Ray and Gosling, "American Physicians," pp. 404–7.

CHAPTER FOUR

Birth Control
and Racial Betterment

Only upon a free, self-determining motherhood can rest any
unshakable structure of racial betterment.
—Margaret Sanger, "Birth Control and Racial Betterment"

Woman's power can only be expressed . . . when we declare to the
nation; "Show us that the best possible chance in life is given to
every child now brought into the world, before you cry for more!"
—Margaret Sanger, *Pivot of Civilization*

Throughout the 1920s Sangerists endeavored to maintain a delicate
balance between currying the support of the medical profession and
resisting medical hegemony. At the same time, they tried unsuccessfully to persuade welfare feminist organizations to endorse contraceptive legalization. In the course of its struggles with medicine and
feminism, the birth control movement depended on the language of
eugenics to legitimate contraception. By articulating the goal of contraceptive legalization in a eugenic frameworks, the movement defined
birth control as a necessary component of national efforts to promote
racial betterment. If, as eugenics represented it, the American race was
deteriorating because of inefficient breeding, birth control's application of "reason and intelligence" to reproduction could regenerate the
race and ensure public health and the national welfare.[1]
    Despite the Sangerists' efforts, eugenicists were not immediate or
automatic allies of the birth control movement. The American eugenics movement was concerned primarily with differential birth rates between old-stock Americans and new immigrants and the "colored

---

[1] Sanger, *Pivot*, p. 172. On similar uses of eugenics in the infant welfare movement see
Meckel, *Save the Babies*, pp. 101–3, 116–17, 130–31, 153.

races."[2] To eugenicists, differential fertility rates represented compelling evidence that Nordic-Teutonic America, in danger of committing race suicide, was being swamped by a "rising tide of color." The major fertility measures espoused by eugenicists were negative eugenics, the permanent sterilization or enforced celibacy of the unfit, and positive eugenics, the increase of birth rates among the "better stocks." The use of contraception by the "better stocks" represented part of the problem; it contributed to Nordic-Teutonic race suicide by artificially lowering their birth rates even further. General access to contraception would not, eugenicists feared, alleviate the problem, because the less fit were too irresponsible to use it.[3] At the very least, however, eugenicists realized that birth control could "not now be stopped" and had to be "reckoned with."[4] Because many of its members feared the consequences of contraceptive legalization, the American Eugenics Society (AES), the organizational center of the American eugenics movement, kept its distance from birth control until the late 1920s. But eugenics was not a uniform ideology narrowly articulated by social reactionaries; individual eugenicists supported the birth control movement throughout its history.[5]

As a reputable science, eugenics provided the birth control movement with an authoritative language through which to legitimate women's rights to contraception. By situating birth control within the eugenic terrain of racial betterment, Sanger appropriated the authority and prestige of eugenics to birth control as a tool of racial health. Both advocates of birth control and eugenicists were "seeking to assist the race toward the elimination of the unfit." However, as she also pointed out, eugenicists and birth control advocates put "emphasis upon different methods."[6]

In the first half of this chapter I discuss the contours of eugenics ideology and practice and examine the points of contention and agreement between the eugenics movement and the Sangerist position on

[2] Edward M. East, *Mankind at the Crossroads*, pp. 111, 126. East defined only three races as primary: "the white, the yellow, and the black." The brown races resulted from intermixture of these three primary groups.

[3] Paul Popenoe, *Conservation of the Family*, p. 152.

[4] Paul Popenoe, "Birth Control and Eugenics," p. 6.

[5] William Robinson elaborated the eugenic benefits of the proper means of preventing conception as one of several arguments in his 1916 pro–birth control book, *Birth Control or The Limitation of Offspring*. See pp. 124–30.

[6] Sanger, "Racial Betterment," p. 11.

racial betterment. Sanger's articulation of eugenics was a contradictory mix of adherence to the dominant American version of this ideology and resistance to it. She accepted as fact eugenicists' descriptions of the extent of racial deterioration, but she contested their interpretations of its cause. Drawing primarily from radical British eugenicists, Sanger's articulations were not biologically determinist. She located the causes of racial decay in economic environmentalism and conventional sexual morality.

The second half of the chapter assesses the benefits and costs of eugenical alliance to the birth control movement. The scientific authority of eugenics lent weight to Sangerist challenges to the conventional religious condemnation of contraception as unnatural. Eugenic expertise for population studies lent weight to Sangerists' data against the medical profession's charges of amateurism. The sexually neutral, scientifically legitimate language of eugenics helped Sangerists frame contraception as a proper issue for women's rights advocates. Using eugenic logic and nomenclature, Sanger constituted women who used contraception as the authors of racial betterment, thereby linking birth control to the racial maternalism of welfare feminists.

But the costs of this alliance with eugenics for the feminist basis of the birth control movement must be assessed as well. Paternalistic assumptions about people of color, resulting from the conflation of economic dependency and ethnicity, were firmly encoded in eugenics and articulated in eugenical criteria for fertility choices. Sangerists resisted the eugenicists' equation of poverty with ethnic inferiority and the extreme proposals of white supremacists who wished to increase fertility rates of white, middle-class women. But the white, middle-class perspective of Sangerists' racial maternalism limited their effective resistance to eugenic distortions of birth control and thereby undercut their goal of reproductive self-determination for all women.

Sanger and Eugenicists: Contentions and Agreements

The term *eugenics* was first used in 1883 by Sir Francis Galton, the founder of modern statistics and distant cousin of Charles Darwin. Deeply influenced by Darwin's work, Galton spent much of his life studying the social agencies "which may improve or impair the racial qualities of future generations." His purpose was to improve humanity by giving "the more suitable races and strains of blood a better chance of prevailing speedily over the less suitable."[7] Most of the statistical techniques that he is credited with inventing were developed in his studies of heredity.

The close connection between statistics and eugenics continued in the twentieth century with Karl Pearson, who developed, in eugenical studies of human heredity, many of the basic statistical measures of significance currently used in the social sciences.[8] Apart from the Census Bureau and Children's Bureau, the collection and analysis of demographic statistics received its greatest impetus from eugenicists. Likewise, the study of human genetics was dominated by biologists who were active in the eugenics movement.[9] Although the most widely read eugenicist texts had been published before 1920, the popularity and influence of eugenics continued to grow through the twenties.[10] These eugenic analyses of vital statistics not only constructed scientific knowledge about the extent of human biological diversity but also gave scientific authority to preexisting racial taxonomies.

In the early 1910s eugenics was not rigidly hereditarian, because biologists were still uncertain about how heredity actually worked. Many Progressives worked simultaneously for environmental and eugenic reforms. There was no contradiction between these two strategies because most lay people still held some version of belief in the inheritance of acquired characteristics. Thus within Progressive ideology, the relationship between environment and heredity was quite elastic. What we would today distinguish as genetic diseases, apparent at

[7] Galton, as quoted in Henry Fairchild Osborn, "Birth Selection versus Birth Control," p. 175; Francis Galton, *Inquiries into Human Faculty*, pp. 24–25, as quoted in Kevles, *In the Name of Eugenics*, p. ix.

[8] Galton is credited with discovery of regression correlation and with developing applications of the normal curve to frequency distributions of discrete events. Pearson developed the techniques of standard deviation, chi-squares, and regression and correlation coefficients. See Ruth Schwartz Cowan, "Francis Galton's Statistical Ideas," p. 511; and Lyndsay Farrall, "Controversy and Conflict in Science," p. 287.

[9] In the midtwenties, geneticists began tentatively to criticize the blatantly racist propaganda of eugenics, but the criticisms were mild. Geneticists did not work actively to dissociate their discipline and strongly criticize eugenics until the rise of Nazism. See Ludmerer, *Genetics and American Society*, pp. 48–62, 121–34; Kevles, *In the Name of Eugenics*, pp. 69, 172–76, 193; and Garland Allen, "Genetics, Eugenics and Class Struggle," pp. 36–41.

[10] Madison Grant's book, *The Passing of the Great Race*, which was referred to by Tom Buchanan in *The Great Gatsby* (1925), was first published in 1916. Henry Goddard's study of the Kallikaks, originally published in 1912, was reprinted in 1923. In addition, eugenical articles appeared frequently in newspapers, magazines, and other popular literature. By 1928 courses in eugenics were taught in 75 percent of the nation's colleges. Allen, "Genetics," p. 33.

birth, and congenital diseases, which, though not genetic, are acquired in utero, were often conflated in the early twentieth century. Perhaps the best example of this confusion can be seen in the discourse on venereal diseases, in which syphilis in newborns was often understood to be hereditary.[11] With an elastic relationship between biology and destiny, the dangers of ethnic differences could be ameliorated. With the acceptance of Mendelian genetics after 1910, the inheritance of acquired characteristics became a more difficult principle to sustain, and the extreme hereditarianism of eugenic ideology became more pronounced.[12]

Mendelian genetics posited that germ plasm, the substance of heredity, consisted of discrete and nonblendable factors that were passed unaltered from parent to offspring in sexual reproduction. In the first decade of the century, biologists in Europe and America replicated Mendel's now-famous experiment with peas, testing a wide variety of physical characteristics.[13] Based upon these data, eugenicists concluded that improvement of the human stock could best be accomplished by sorting out undesired traits from each generation. Following the implications of this logic, they formulated a range of social policies to regenerate the race by containing the reproduction of "the unfit." Despite developments in biological theory, which by the late 1920s discredited most of the specific hereditarian principles underlying eugenic theory, the American eugenics movement increasingly ignored any influence that the environment might have on human traits, taking all socially important characteristics to be biologically determined.[14]

In Britain the eugenics movement was torn asunder by disagreements over Mendelian genetics. In the United States, however, Mendelian genetics was not as controversial. Charles Davenport, a noted

[11] Robinson, *Birth Control or the Limitation of Offspring*, pp. 127–28. See also Brandt, *No Magic Bullet*, pp. 14–15.

[12] Ludmerer, *Genetics and American Society*, pp. 7–20, 38–39; Haller, *Eugenics*, pp. 60–63; and Garland Allen, *Life Sciences in the Twentieth Century*, pp. 52–57.

[13] Allen, *Life*, pp. 52–57. *Germ plasm* was Charles Davenport's term. I use it instead of our term, *gene*, because the language of genes and chromosomes had not yet acquired popular currency in the twenties. Mendel's work was not immediately accepted. Before 1910 the staunchest critics argued that there was no concrete evidence of his theorized factors. Thomas Morgan's famous fruit fly experiments demonstrating the function of chromosomes as Mendelian factors silenced critics beginning in 1910.

[14] Both Allen, "Genetics," p. 32, and Ludmerer, *Genetics and American Society*, pp. 76–77, point out that in particular the principle of single-gene causation of human traits was discredited early in the twenties. See also Haller, *Eugenics*, p. 159.

biologist who converted to Mendelianism early in the century, led the American eugenics movement through the twenties.[15] Between 1904 and 1907 he undertook various breeding experiments with domestic animals at a laboratory in Cold Spring Harbor, Long Island, which he had persuaded the Carnegie Institution to establish. Increasingly interested in tracing simple Mendelian ratios in humans, in 1907 he published his first eugenics text on the inheritance of human eye, skin, and hair color. A year earlier he had become secretary of the American Breeders' Association Committee on Eugenics. As the first official eugenics organization in America, it promoted the application of stock-breeders' principles to humanity. By 1910 Davenport's activities expanded to include directing the Eugenics Record Office at Cold Spring Harbor, the center of both research and propaganda for the American eugenics movement. There Davenport supervised the collection of the primary data on which eugenicists relied—human pedigrees collected in family genealogies.[16]

Unable to do experiments in human breeding, eugenicists constructed genealogies as the text through which to trace human heredity. Mendel's experiments had shown that if one mated two known pure breeds, the frequency with which each breed's traits would appear in succeeding crossbreeding could be accurately predicted. Reversing this process, genealogies of human characteristics were analyzed to determine if any characteristics were repeated in the same proportions one would expect using Mendel's laws. If a particular trait showed up frequently within a genealogy, eugenicists took this as evidence of the hereditary basis of the trait. By their logic, traits repeated across several generations could not have an environmental basis, since acquired characteristics could not be inherited. These genealogies were collected without rigorous definitions of the very traits they purported to record.[17] Eugenic analyses ignored the possibility that observed traits were actually a complex interaction of genes and environment; instead, complex human behaviors were represented as simple genetic effects. In his 1911 book *Heredity in Relation to Eugenics*, Davenport

[15] See Farrall, "Controversy and Conflict in Science," pp. 279–87; and Kevles, *In the Name of Eugenics*, pp. 45–54.

[16] Haller, *Eugenics*, pp. 63–68; and Kevles, *In the Name of Eugenics*, pp. 45–49.

[17] Kevles, ibid. According to Stephen J. Gould, *The Mismeasure of Man*, p. 168, Goddard preferred to employ women, who constituted the majority of eugenic field workers, because they could intuitively spot feeblemindedness on sight.

claimed that mechanical skill, artistic and musical ability, and shift-lessness were simple recessive traits.[18]

In 1912, Henry Goddard published the most famous eugenics gene-alogy of the twentieth century, *The Kallikak Family.*[19] The study traced the two families of a Revolutionary War soldier, Martin Kallikak. One family was a fine upstanding bunch resulting from Martin's marriage to a Quaker woman of good family, the other a horde of misfits, pau-pers, and morons resulting from his union with a feebleminded bar-maid. The persuasiveness of the Kallikak genealogy lay in its juxtaposing two branches of a family tree: one fit, the other unfit. It purportedly proved that regardless of the underlying cause of feeble-mindedness, it followed Mendelian rules of inheritance; feeblemind-edness was "transmitted as regularly and as surely as color of hair or eyes."[20] The criticism that it was impossible to determine if a long-dead woman, whose name was not even known, was feebleminded did not affect the weight the genealogy carried in popular consciousness. Her willingness to bear a child without the benefit of marriage was suffi-cient evidence of her feeblemindedness, of which moral laxity was commonly held to be an irrefutable sign. Tracing the degeneracy of individual families to a single defective ancestor, this genealogy re-vealed the social cost of unrestrained breeding among individual unfit white persons.[21] It stood as a lesson to white America of the dangers involved in allowing the lower classes to reproduce the bulk of the race. In the absence of public criticism by geneticists, this "lesson" carried great weight in popular discourse. For more than a decade the Kallikak

[18] Charles Davenport, *Heredity in Relation to Eugenics*, pp. 48–51, 58, 80–82. Before the 1911 experiments of Wilhelm Johannson there was no distinction in biological theory between genotype, an individual's genetic makeup, and phenotype, the visible character-istics of an individual that result from the interaction of his or her genotype and environ-ment. Yet even by the standards of the day Davenport's theories were speculative. See Allen, *Life Sciences*, p. 55; Haller, *Eugencies*, pp. 106–11; and Kevles, *In the Name of Eugen-ics*, pp. 44–54.

[19] Henry Herbert Goddard, *The Kallikak Family*. The family name is a pseudonym of the Greek words for good and bad, *kalos* and *kakos*. The other prominent genealogy, *The Jukes*, was originally published by Richard Dugdale in 1877 and argued for environmen-tal as well as hereditary causes of degeneracy. A 1915 update, *The Jukes in 1915*, pro-duced by the Eugenics Record Office, confirmed Dugdale's results but dismissed his environmental interpretations. See Kevles, *In the Name of Eugenics*, p. 71; Elof Axel Carl-son, "R. L. Dugdale and the Jukes Family," pp. 535–39; and Arthur Estabrook, *The Jukes in 1915*.

[20] Goddard, as quoted in Kevles, *In the Name of Eugenics*, p. 79.

[21] Both the Kallikaks and the Jukes were old-stock Caucasians.

family stood as the popular emblem of the "menace of the feeble-minded."[22]

Sanger utilized the eugenically demonstrated danger of unrestrained breeding as scientific proof that legalized contraception was essential to national well-being. But her writings, which did not display any profound grasp of biological theory, construed the source of danger differently from mainline American eugenicists. Sanger derived her eugenical ideas from the radical wing of the British eugenics movement, in particular from Havelock Ellis, who represented racial deterioration as the consequence of the repressive Victorian class and sexual order. According to Ellis, whereas nature had once provided the mechanism for the selection of human traits, social institutions provided the mechanism now. Under capitalism the effects of social selection had been disastrous. The "'best stocks' were not 'necessarily the stocks of high social class,' but were spread through all social classes." Class distinctions that "cut humanity into small cliques" kept people from "choosing genetically optimal partners." A system that defined potential marriage partners by their class rather than by their genetic traits amounted to "indiscriminate breeding," which in turn produced poverty. Eugenics provided a rational, scientific basis for guiding human reproduction and regenerating the race. Abolition of class distinctions was the first step, but Ellis also believed "eugenic improvement required women's sexual liberation from the shroud of repressive Victorian attitudes."[23]

In her articulation of racial betterment, Sanger concurred with Ellis, her lifelong friend and mentor. Besides economic pressure, the social factor most relevant to the process of racial decay was the sexual enslavement of women: "Abused soil brings forth stunted growth. An abused motherhood has brought forth a low order of humanity." Based upon eugenical data, Sanger constructed a scientific rationale

[22] This was Goddard's term. Kevles, *In the Name of Eugenics*, pp. 78–79; Ludmerer, *Genetics and American Society*, pp. 77–78; Haller, *Eugencies*, pp. 110–11; and Gould, *The Mismeasure of Man*, pp. 168–71. Gould includes copies of photographs originally published with the study. The negatives were altered in pen to accentuate physical characteristics associated with feeblemindedness.

[23] Ellis, as quoted in Kevles, *In the Name of Eugenics*, pp. 87, 65. Kevles included Ellis among the social-radical British eugenicists, whom he distinguishes from the mainstream of the British movement because of their connections to Socialism, the Labor Party, and the women's movement. In the United States he identified no radical faction. Perhaps if he had considered eugenicist involvement with the birth control movement he would have argued that the Sangerist birth control movement constituted the radical wing of the American movement. See pp. 85–89.

for women's natural right to birth control that opposed the traditional morality, "founded upon ignorance and submission" of women. According to her interpretation, it was during the centuries in which women had, by law, no means to control their reproduction that the human race had degenerated terribly. Thus birth control was not a "violation of natural law" but the first tool toward achieving racial betterment:

> Birth control . . . is nothing more or less than the facilitation of the process of weeding out the unfit [and] of preventing the birth of defectives. . . . If we are to make racial progress, this development of womanhood must precede motherhood in every individual woman. Then and then only can the mother cease to be an incubator and be a mother indeed. Then only can she transmit to her sons and daughters the qualities which make strong individuals and, collectively, a strong race.[24]

Sanger's attempt to position birth control as a eugenic technology met resistance from many eugenicists. In the second decade of the twentieth century, warnings expressed by Karl Pearson about differential fertility rates renewed the prospect of race suicide. Generalizing from limited statistical studies, Pearson claimed that one-half of each generation was the product of about one-quarter of its married predecessors. That prolific quarter was represented disproportionately by the unfit. From the premises of evolutionary theory, eugenicists reasoned that the higher fertility among the inferior class of humanity, purportedly revealed by Pearson, was biologically determined. As among animals, eugenicists held that intelligence and prolificacy were inversely related; the lower a life form was on the evolutionary scale the greater was its production of progeny. Thus, fecundity, the biological capacity for reproduction, was greater among the feebleminded, dependent, and delinquent humans than among the better stocks.[25] To counteract this natural phenomenon and increase their proportion of the next generation eugenicists proposed that the "better stocks" needed to have more babies. Intoning the rhetoric of race suicide, eu-

[24] Sanger, *Woman*, pp. 234, 167, 229. Borell, "Biologists," pp. 54–57, and Chesler, *Woman of Valor*, pp. 122–23, 195–96, make a similar argument regarding Sanger's eugenic perspective.

[25] Kevles, *In the Name of Eugenics*, p. 33. Darwin's observation that lower life forms were more prolific than higher ones was applied to humans by Herbert Spencer.

genicists criticized the birth control movement's efforts to curtail natural fertility rates by artificial means.

Paul Popenoe, an active member of the American eugenics movement, elaborated this criticism in a 1917 article published in the *Birth Control Review*.[26] He defined as eugenic a "measure" that favored "the reproductivity of the happier and more efficient parts of the population and discourage[d] the increase of the less capable parts." In his assessment, birth control propagandists were carrying on a one-sided, dysgenic campaign because they made "unfounded claims of the merit of small families and delayed parenthood." Birth control advocates were partially accurate; "some people need[ed] fewer children," but "some need[ed] more." Small families, per se, were not necessarily a desirable thing racially. As it was currently practiced in the United States, Popenoe claimed, birth control tended toward "racial deterioration" because it contributed to a differential birth rate. Birth control was practiced only by the "superior parts of the population, . . . while the increase of inferior families [was] checked only by the death-rate." For "racial betterment" to be achieved, "the differential nature of the birth-rate must be changed." This would not likely result from the spread of contraceptive knowledge. Such a dispersal of knowledge would cut "down the racial contribution of inferior stocks." However, "the gain" would be minimal because it seemed probable that those who would "practice birth control most effectively are the prudent, far-sighted, conscientious parents, whose children the race needs; while even possession of a knowledge of contraceptive methods will not affect the reckless and improvident, . . . whose children the race would be better off without."[27]

In a gesture common to mainstream eugenic ideology, Popenoe interpreted "the superior and inferior parts of the population" in terms of economic standing. For eugenicists, inferiority was demonstrated by poverty and economic dependency. Under Davenport's leadership, mainstream eugenic ideology represented the poor as poor because they did not have the biological wherewithal to prosper; their circumstances of poverty were unaffected by their environment. To Daven-

---

[26] Popenoe helped set up and evaluate eugenical sterilization practices in California state institutions for the insane and the retarded. By 1931, the practices he and his fellows initiated accounted for California's performance of over seventy-five hundred of the twelve thousand state sterilizations done nationwide. Haller, *Eugenics*, pp. 136–38. See also Judith Grether, "Sterilization and Eugenics," p. 90.

[27] Popenoe, "Birth Control."

port, pauperism reflected "relative inefficiency [which] in turn usually means mental inferiority."[28] By extension, many social problems purportedly associated with poverty were held to demonstrate genetic incompetence. The AES declared that "unfit human traits such as feeblemindedness, epilepsy, criminality, insanity, alcoholism, pauperism, and many others run in families and are inherited in exactly the same way as color in guinea pigs."[29] The conventions of white racism implicitly reinforced this association of poverty and biological inferiority. As did most whites, eugenicists assumed that peoples of color were mentally inferior to Caucasians, and their greater poverty rates stood as evidence that economic status was a clear indicator of mental efficiency.[30] In this circular logic the association of poverty, ethnicity, and biological merit was reinforced.

Popenoe concluded that "the universal practice of birth control . . . [would] . . . increase the task of eugenics, since it [would] require vigorous measures to augment the birth-rate of eugenically superior families." He predicted that only if the birth control movement would support eugenic encouragement of larger families among the fit could they "count on the active support of most eugenicists in endeavoring to reduce the size of families among the inefficient and destitute." While birth control advocates could not be expected "to carry on a simultaneous campaign on these two sides of the question," they at least should not "throw unnecessary obstacles in the way of eugenics." He insisted that "if it is admitted that parents should have no more children than they can afford to bring up decently, it ought perhaps to be equally admitted that they should have as many as they *can* afford to bring up decently."[31]

Sanger responded to eugenicists' demands for a balanced program by contesting their framing of the issue, advancing the customary response that women's rights advocates made to race suicide charges. As far back as 1870 there had been predictions in the United States of racial deterioration owing to differential birth rates. Francis Walker, using evidence from census returns that the birth rates of native-born

---

[28] Davenport as quoted in Kevles, *In the Name of Eugenics*, p. 46.

[29] American Eugenics Society exhibit at the 1929 Kansas Free Fair, as quoted by Kevles, ibid., p. 62.

[30] Allen, "Genetics," p. 34. Birth rates among African-Americans were lower than the eugenics theory of natural fecundity predicted. Popenoe explained this discrepancy as the consequence of their purportedly high rates of venereal diseases. See Popenoe, *Conservation*, p. 99.

[31] Popenoe, "Birth Control" (emphasis in original).

whites were declining, suggested that "old stocks" were committing race suicide. Such declining birth rates were frequently attributed to the vicious selfishness of suffragists, who, in demanding the masculine privilege of voting, were abandoning their natural maternal duty to the state. The charge that feminine selfishness was contributing to race suicide was renewed in the twentieth century by President Theodore Roosevelt.[32] In response to charges of "race suicide" suffragists argued that only voluntary motherhood could be virtuous motherhood. Motherhood continued to be women's chief duty, but virtuous motherhood involved delaying childbearing until financial resources were ensured: "A woman may be the best of wives and mothers, but unless she can bear healthy children and be sure that they will be properly fed, clothed and educated, and unless she can give them an excellent father, the worst thing she can do for the world is to become a mother."[33] In this 1903 statement, Ida Harper, like other women's rights advocates, countered the charge of race suicide by asserting an economic ethic of fertility. They refused to accept the premise that control of fertility led to race suicide. Instead, they argued that by limiting their fertility to the level of their economic resources women would indeed fulfill their racial duty.

Like this earlier generation, Sanger intoned both the rhetoric of voluntary motherhood and an economic ethic of fertility by which American women would fulfill their racial duty. To the eugenicists' claim that race suicide was the consequence of women's selfishness, Sanger responded that women were not "avoiding motherhood" because they were "afraid to die." Rather, women feared a "life of poverty and drudgery, weighed down by the horror of unwanted pregnancy and tortured by the inability to rear decently the children" already born.[34] In their diatribes against women's abandonment of cradle, hearth, and home for economic and political independence, it seemed to Sanger that eugenicists believed "that a woman should bear as many healthy children as possible as a duty to the state." While eugenicists "insist[ed] that a woman's first duty [was] to the state," the birth control movement

[32] Roosevelt, "Race Decadence," pp. 765–66.

[33] Quoted in Kraditor, *The Ideas*, p. 118. See Kraditor on race suicide arguments of anti-suffragists, pp. 117–19, 14–42; and Kevles, *In The Name of Eugenics*, on eugenicists' attitudes toward feminism, pp. 65–66, 87–89, and 107. See Petchesky, *Abortion and Woman's Choice*, on nineteenth-century debates about women's duty to the race, pp. 41–42.

[34] Margaret Sanger, "An Answer to Mr. Roosevelt," p. 14. This was a response to Theodore Roosevelt's article published in the October 1917 issue of *Metropolitan Magazine*, entitled "Birth Control—From the Positive Side."

contended that "her duty to herself is her first duty to the state."[35] To fulfill her duty to herself, woman must "know her own body, its cares and its needs," including "knowledge of her sexual nature."[36] Sanger maintained

> that a woman possessing an adequate knowledge of her reproductive functions is the best judge of the time and conditions under which her child should be brought into this world. We further maintain that it is her right, regardless of other considerations, to determine whether she shall bear children or not, and how many children she shall bear if she chooses to become a mother.[37]

For Sanger, birth control, made accessible to all, was the first and greatest step toward racial betterment.

Social factors, primarily economic pressure, rather than biological endowment, were at the heart of Sanger's version of racial betterment. The differential birth rate, which she accepted as a fact, did not result from the greater fecundity of the "lesser stocks," nor did the higher birth rates among the poor serve as evidence of their mental inferiority. The differential birth rate was to Sanger the direct consequence of differential access to birth control. "Even in the most unenlightened sections of the community, among mothers crushed by poverty and economic enslavement, there is the realization of the evils of the too-large family, of the rapid succession of pregnancy after pregnancy." And, she noted, women were "dying by the thousands" because contraception was "withheld from them."[38] Eugenicists erred, she argued, in failing to recognize, as the birth control movement did, "the vast amount of native and latent intelligence among the mothers and fathers of the poor." The intelligence of the poor was demonstrated by their demand for access to birth control.[39] Feeblemindedness and poverty were the consequence, not the cause, of high fertility. Feeblemindedness, defined by Sanger as retardation of normal development, was environmentally caused. "The fruits of the most perfect eugenic marriage" were "likely to be bad health" for women and children without birth control. Having too many children at too frequent inter-

[35] Sanger, "Racial Betterment," p. 11.
[36] Sanger, *Woman*, p. 183. See also Sanger, *Pivot*, pp. 243–59.
[37] Sanger, "Racial Betterment," p. 11.
[38] Sanger, *Pivot*, pp. 251–52.
[39] Sanger, "The Need for Birth Control," pp. 227–28. See also Sanger, "The Eugenic Value of Birth Control Propaganda," p. 5.

vals "wreck[ed] women's health, ... demoralize[d] the father [and] stunt[ed] ... children through bad living conditions and early toil," leading "in that generation or the next" to feeblemindedness, insanity, and criminality: "Children who are underfed, undernourished, crowded into badly ventilated and unsanitary homes and chronically hungry cannot be expected to attain the mental development of children upon whom every advantage of intelligent and scientific care is bestowed."[40] Moreover, as she pointed out, the significance of differential birth rates was overblown because although the "upper classes" gave birth to fewer children, their lower infant mortality rates meant that they brought "to maturity almost as many as the poor succeed[ed] in doing."[41]

Framing the issue of racial decay as socially caused, Sanger did not endorse the positive eugenics program as part of the birth control movement.[42] Eugenics, Sanger concluded, was "futile and impractical" unless "allied and strengthened by birth control." Racial decay, she charged, could "never be rectified by the inauguration of a cradle competition."[43] To assume that in an overcrowded world comfortably situated families could remain so regardless of the numbers of children they had was an "absurdity." Eugenicists were acting irresponsibly when they implored the eugenically healthy to produce as many children as possible. Such demands ignored the "furious winds of economic pressure which [had] buffeted into partial or total helplessness a tremendous proportion of the human race." If the positive program of eugenics were to be followed, it would only produce a "cradle competition between the 'fit' and the 'unfit'" that would lead society down "the road to universal imbecility," where "the fit would very soon become the unfit."[44] For Sanger, the "all-conquering power of machinery

[40] Sanger, "Racial Betterment," p. 12, and *Pivot*, p. 241. In some limited instances of gross abnormality, such as cretinism, Sanger recognized that feeblemindedness was genetic. But overall she emphasized environmental causes of "artificial retardation," such as child labor. See Sanger, *Pivot*, p. 64.

[41] Sanger, "An Answer," p. 13.

[42] Reed, *The Birth Control Movement*, pp. 135–36. Gordon, *Woman's Body*, p. 281; and Kennedy, *Birth Control in America*, p. 115, incorrectly attribute to Sanger a 1919 quotation endorsing more children from the fit. She did not make that statement and, in fact, criticized it when it appeared in an *American Medicine* editorial, reprinted in the *BCR*. See Valenza, "Was Margaret Sanger a Racist?" p. 45.

[43] Sanger, "Politicians," p. 4, and *Pivot*, p. 25.

[44] Sanger, *Woman*, p. 67, "Racial Betterment," p. 12, and "Politicians," p. 4. Although infant welfare advocates tended to ignore neonatal mortality as obviously caused by biological unfitness, Meckel indicates that, like Sanger, they objected to eugenical characterizations of poverty as racially and ethnically based. See Meckel, *Save the Babies*, pp. 158, 119.

and capitalistic control" brought with it the "complex problem of sustaining human life in surroundings and under conditions flagrantly dysgenic." The existing effects of economic pressures were registered by the increase in feeblemindedness, dependency, and delinquency and most especially in the high rates of infant and maternal mortality among the poor. Instead, opposing large families even among the middle class, Sangerists endorsed the use of contraception whenever there was "not economic means of providing proper care for those who [were] born in health."[45]

Sanger was convinced that eugenicists' exhortations to "enter again into competitive child-bearing . . . [would] fall on deaf ears." Women were aware that they could not continue to produce high-quality babies if they had a large family. That was why middle-class women used contraception and poor women demanded it. With birth control, pregnancies could be spaced at intervals to allow women to maintain their health and enable a family to keep its size within the limit of its resources. Thus, each child could be better born, better cared for, and better educated. To meet women's demands, Sangerists "insist[ed] that information in regard to scientific contraception be made open to all." For the birth control movement to "extend" its program to include positive eugenics would "lamentably" weaken the effort to educate "those vast sections of the human family to which . . . contraception has been denied."[46]

The voluntarism by which Sanger represented all women's rights to contraceptive knowledge and devices was a fundamental point of contention between the birth control and the eugenics movements. The positive programs eugenicists articulated to improve the race rested on voluntarism. However, when it came to the "inferior portions of the population" there was always an edge of anxiety within eugenic discourse about individual choice. Representing social hierarchies as the reflections of biologically based incompetence, eugenicists thought the best hope for racial betterment was to intervene and contain individual fertility choice. Only if "human mating" was put on "the same high plane as that of horse breeding" could the social problems resulting from poverty be solved. Eugenicists suggested that the conven-

[45] Sanger, *Pivot*, p. 105, and "Racial Betterment," p. 11. Sanger did not repudiate Marxism in the 1920s. Rather, she criticized it for being too limited. Orthodox Marxism's solitary focus on the economic aspect of life ignored the issue of sex and thus limited its usefulness: "You cannot solve the problem of hunger and ignore the problem of sex" (p. 126). For Sanger's critique of Marx, see *Pivot*, pp. 138–69.

[46] Sanger, ibid., p. 180, "Racial Betterment," p. 11, and "Editorial," p. 164.

tional bases of spousal selection—family tradition, religion, and love—should be replaced with eugenic criteria, and the Eugenics Record Office upon request provided eugenic evaluation of proposed marriages.[47] Eugenicists also proposed to weed out the unfit through restrictive marriage laws, sex-segregated custodial care, and compulsory sterilization.

Marriage licensing laws, which mandated a waiting period between obtaining a license and the actual marriage ceremony, would reduce the numbers of dysgenic marriages made in haste. Eugenics also championed marriage restrictions to prevent the coupling of fit and unfit persons, which, by Mendelian logic, would spread hereditary taints.[48] But marriage restrictions were inadequate by themselves to stop racial decay. Those people whose marriage should be restricted, eugenicists reasoned, lacked the moral fiber to be dissuaded from procreating by the taint of illegitimacy. Thus, compulsory sterilization and sex-segregated institutionalization of the feebleminded, insane, and syphilitic were also required.[49] By 1931, twenty-seven states had enacted laws requiring sterilization of the feebleminded and insane. Some laws included criminals as well. The eugenic logic supporting compulsory sterilization laws received judicial endorsement in the 1927 Supreme Court decision *Buck v. Bell*. With this decision, the Court affirmed that "in order to prevent our being *swamped with incompetence*, . . . the principle that sustains compulsory vaccination is broad enough to cover the cutting of the Fallopian tubes."[50] Thus bodily integrity could be breached to ensure the quality of citizens. Compelling vaccination was a legitimate use of police power, because the state obligation to protect the public health from the spread of contagious disease outweighed the individual's right to bodily integrity. In ruling that sterilization came under the same principle, the Court extended the state obliga-

[47] Davenport as quoted by Kevles, *In the Name of Eugenics*, p. 48. Eugenicists also advocated that the government give financial incentives to fit women for procreation and bonuses to married veterans; see also pp. 56, 68–69, 91–92.

[48] Ibid., pp. 92–94, 99–100. Such restrictions were directed at preventing the marriage of diseased persons to healthy persons. The restrictions included, for instance, persons with venereal diseases, the deaf, the blind, and the epileptic. Eugenics rhetoric also played a role in the passage of antimiscegenation laws; eugenicists opposed the "mongrelization" of the "old stocks" that racial intermarriage caused.

[49] Haller, *Eugenics*, pp. 95–96, 109–10, argues that institutionalization was the most widely supported eugenics reform.

[50] *Buck v. Bell*, 274 U.S. 205–7, 1927 (emphasis added). See Kevles, *In the Name of Eugenics*, pp. 110–12. Carrie Buck, a caucasian woman who was the appellant in the case, was certified to suffer from hereditary feeblemindedness.

tion to protect the public health to include protection from the spread of hereditary taints.

At the same time, with respect to racial diversity, the facet of eugenics that sought to explain race differences in biological terms came to the fore after the First World War. This edge of racial thinking, which dated back to Galton's work in the 1880s, was sharpened particularly in debates surrounding immigration restriction. Eugenicists disparaged the prospects for cultural assimilation. As Davenport argued, "The idea of the 'melting pot' belong[ed] to a pre-Mendelian age." "Now we recognize that characteristics are inherited in units and do not readily break up."[51] Equating national origin with racial identity and assuming a person's behavior was shaped by his or her race, eugenicists concluded that unrestricted immigration posed a grave danger.[52] The 1920 census revealed that there had been a sizable influx of immigrants from cultures originating outside the Germanic forests and English countryside where, according to eugenicists, the instinct for democracy was born.[53] This increased immigrant population threatened to upset the balance of national political power. Defining government as "the visible expression of the ideals . . . of the people," restrictionists argued that "a change in the character or composition of population must inevitably" lead to a change in the form of its government: "If, therefore, the principle of individual liberty, guarded by constitutional government . . . is to endure, the basic strain of our population must be maintained."[54] Across the nation, fear of such a change was palpable in the aftermath of the Bolshevik revolution. For the first time in its history the U.S. Congress refused to reapportion Congressional representation.[55] In 1921, with the resumption of the high prewar rates of immigration, Congress passed emergency legisla-

[51] Davenport did not support racial quotas as the basis for restrictive immigration. Believing that "no race per se" was "dangerous and none undesirable," he supported restrictions to exclude individuals with poor heredity. But by the passage of the 1924 Immigration Restriction Act his perspective no longer represented the mainstream of eugenic ideology. See Kevles, ibid., p. 47.

[52] See Margo Anderson, *The American Census*, pp. 144–49, about the uncertainty involved in determining national origin.

[53] Gossett, *Race*, pp. 88–118, 303; Mink, *Old Labor*, pp. 124–28.

[54] John B. Trevor's testimony before Congress as to why the national-origins basis of immigration restriction was needed. Quoted in Anderson, *The American Census*, p. 146.

[55] In 1920, Congressional reapportionment, required by the Constitution after each decennial census, would have shifted power from native-born, old-stock rural communities to immigrant cities. Reapportionment was not approved until 1930. See Andersen, ibid., pp. 131–58.

tion restricting immigration to 3 percent of the foreign-born population from each European country as it was recorded in the 1910 census.

In 1921 racial thinking was outweighed by economic concerns and the fear of radicalism; but through eugenicists' extensive lobbying, by 1924 racial reasoning dominated legislative debate on the permanent Immigration Act.[56] Eugenicists sponsored publication of the Army I.Q. test results that revealed low scores of ethnic immigrants. These data lent credence to representations of southern and eastern Europeans as biologically inferior. Based on a huge sample and touted as testing only innate ability, the Army I.Q. tests apparently demonstrated Nordic supremacy as a "fact." By representing the performance of each ethnic group in terms of an average mental age, eugenicists constructed a racial hierarchy of intelligence, which, by ignoring the range of scores for each group, represented Nordic Americans as the supremely intelligent, self-governing race.[57]

The Army I.Q. data reinvigorated eugenical taxonomies that ranked all ethnic groups by intelligence and political nature. With such taxonomies of racial merit, the mainstream of the American eugenics movement became increasingly articulated to America's racial order. Through the twenties eugenics provided scientific legitimacy to white supremacy, justifying racial segregation at home and imperialism abroad. Through offensive characterizations of the political nature of each race, eugenicists defined the threat each posed to American democracy. "Orientals" tended naturally to despotism, justifying their continued exclusion from the United States and a guarded stance toward the "yellow peril." The restlessness of the various brown races for independence resulted from the white components of their makeup.[58]

[56] Eugenicists focused on southern and eastern European immigrants, paying little attention to peoples of color, most of whose immigration was already restricted. However, the Immigration Restriction Act of 1921 and 1924 did put an absolute limit of one hundred per annum on the number of immigrants from Asian and African countries.

[57] Kevles, *In the Name of Eugenics*, pp. 80–82; East, *Mankind at the Crossroads*, pp. 116–17, 121, 145. Gould, *The Mismeasure of Man*, pp. 192–234, provides an excellent critique of the Army I.Q. tests from World War I. Going beyond the standard critique, Gould discusses the conditions under which the tests were given, the errors in administering written tests to illiterate men, and the jerry-built data analysis.

[58] See East, *Mankind at the Crossroads*, pp. 110–33, esp. 117–18, on his assessment of the purported statistical basis for the "yellow peril" and threat of revolution within colonies of the brown races (India, Philippines). East, ibid., pp. 120, 142, likewise characterized intelligence and political restlessness among African-Americans as attributes of their white components.

Eugenicists declared that the "Negro race," having "failed miserably and utterly by the white man's standards," was incapable of self-government. Representing the genetic differences between the primary races as vast, eugenicists justified complete social segregation of blacks and whites to prevent any racecrossing because it would disturb "the balanced whole of each [Mendelian] component."[59]

Sanger distinguished her position from that of immigration restrictionists who, seeing racial difference as immutable, would secure American institutions by excluding those who were different. Although Sanger articulated birth control in terms of racial betterment and, like most old-stock Americans, supported restricted immigration, she always defined fitness in individual rather than racial terms. In her most ardently eugenical book, *Pivot of Civilization*, Sanger makes no references to racial taxonomies. Throughout the book the only mention of race is to show that, in fact, the new immigrants, "so despised by our respectable press," and old-stock Americans faced the same disasters of uncontrolled fertility. When Sanger did specify the race that she sought to improve, it was the hybrid race developing in America's melting pot: "We have been told times without number that out of the mixture of stocks, the intermingling of ideas and aspirations, there is to come a race greater than any which has contributed to the population of the U.S." Sanger did not explicitly exclude any racial group from this new American race, nor did she explicitly oppose racecrossing. She represented each ethnic group within the United States at the time as part of the new race.[60]

Sanger endorsed sterilization, as did most of the nation.[61] Her endorsements, however, were strategically coupled with arguments about the limited value of sterilization. If sterilization were widely imple-

[59] Ibid., 138, 132. East argues that the balance of components within the Negro race were on the whole so undesirable that complete social segregation was eugenically justified to prevent racecrossing with whites. Despite this statement, East rejects the belief in the general superiority of all of one race over all of another race as indefensible. See also pp. 140–44.

[60] Sanger, *Pivot*, p. 64, and *Woman*, p. 30. She discusses all major U.S. ethnic groups except Native Americans. On the concept of the melting pot, see Mink, *Old Labor*, pp. 221–23.

[61] Sanger was, however, very specific in supporting sterilization to a limited number of well-defined conditions. See Sanger, "The Need," p. 228, and "Editorial," p. 164. Kevles, *In the Name of Eugenics*, pp. 90, 93–94, argues that there was a near-consensus nationwide on sterilization of the institutionalized insane and feebleminded. Sanger shared support for this measure with Theodore Roosevelt, William Robinson, and even Emma Goldman. On pro-sterilization perspectives among infant welfare advocates see Meckel, *Save the Babies*, p. 118.

mented, then legal access to contraception might appear to be unnecessary to racial betterment. Supporting sterilization of only the most obvious, the undeniably feebleminded, insane, and syphilitic, Sanger's endorsements were always situated within arguments that sterilization would have only limited effectiveness in achieving racial betterment. And Sanger, finding the eugenicists' reasoning to be unsound and paternalistic, contested their wider criteria for compulsory sterilization. She likewise objected to the sterilization of habitual criminals: "More certainty of the justice of our laws and the honesty of their administration" was necessary before making "rulings of fitness or unfitness merely upon . . . a respect for the law."[62]

The great hopes eugenicists pinned on compulsory sterilization reflected what was, in her view, their gravest error: pitting nature against nurture. Eugenicists were wrong to "elevate" heredity "to the position of an absolute," because heredity and environment, Sanger noted, could not be "disentangle[d]." Which socially important human traits were genetically determined and which were environmentally produced could not be accurately determined. As she observed, "To the child in the womb . . . the mother is 'environment.' She is, of course, likewise 'heredity.'"[63] If biology could not yet even assess adequately what was and was not genetically caused, then eugenicists certainly could not distinguish who was and was not fit to reproduce. Sanger repeatedly criticized eugenicists' impertinence in presuming "to predetermine" whose children would "give promise of being of value to the community." In "the writings of the representative Eugenists," she noted, one could not "ignore the distinct middle-class bias that prevails."[64] Until there was a definite dividing line between the fit and the unfit that did not reflect class and prejudice, no "just, constructive policy" to prevent the reproduction of the unfit could be enacted.[65] Sanger held this perspective for many years. In her 1939 speech at the first annual meeting of the Birth Control Federation of America, she said, "We have got to change the inference that the quality of our population depends upon the birth rate of college graduates. To me this is tinsel thinking. There are just as sound qualities to be found in the Arizona cowboys, in the artisans, the mechanics, and the artists."[66]

[62] Sanger, *Pivot*, p. 184.
[63] Ibid., p. 188. See also p. 174.
[64] Sanger, "Editorial," p. 164, and *Pivot*, p. 181.
[65] Sanger, "The Need," p. 228.
[66] Annual meeting minutes, 1939, BCFA, PPFA-SSC.

The biases in eugenic definitions of fitness for both reproduction and immigration exemplified for Sanger "the dangers of external standards." She disdained the audacity with which eugenicists told people how many children to have. The birth control movement did not support "placing in the hands of external authority the power over behavior. Birth control, on the contrary implie[d] voluntary action."[67] Sangerists were convinced "that racial regeneration, like individual regeneration, must come 'from within.' . . . it must be autonomous, self directive and not imposed from without."[68] They did not aim "to interfere in the private lives of poor people, to tell them how many children they should have, nor to sit in judgment upon their fitness to become parents." Rather, their aim was "to awaken responsibility, to answer the demand for a scientific means by which and through which each human life may be self-directed and self-controlled."[69] Any other position was foolhardy and bound to fail because

> an idealistic code of sexual ethics, imposed from above, a set of rules . . . [that] . . . fail to take into account the living conditions and desires of the masses, can never be of the slightest value in effecting change in the customs of the people. Systems so imposed in the past have revealed their woeful inability to prevent the sexual and racial chaos into which the world has drifted.[70]

The proposals of eugenicists, based upon the "conventional and traditional morality and middle-class respectability," and "handed down to the populace with benign condescension," were a "waste of time and effort."[71]

The leaders of American eugenics, rigid in their adherence to hereditarianism, opposed Sangerist birth control. Popenoe was right in his 1917 prediction that without Sangerist support for an increased birth rate among the Nordic middle classes, mainstream eugenicists would not support birth control.[72] Sanger's arguments that economic

---

[67] Sanger, *Pivot*, pp. 183, 254. See also "Editorial," p. 163. This editorial repudiated the "eugenic" resolution passed at the final session of the Sixth International Neo-Malthusian and Birth Control Conference, which the ABCL sponsored. That resolution endorsed the positive eugenic program of encouraging the fit to have more children. Sanger denounced the resolution and dissociated the ABCL from any such position.

[68] Sanger "The Eugenic Value," p. 5.

[69] Sanger, *Pivot*, p. 23.

[70] Ibid., p. 24.

[71] Ibid., p. 249.

[72] Rabid racists, such as Madison Grant, did not support Sanger's efforts at all. Charles Davenport refused a 1925 invitation to preside at the ABCL Conference. Lathrop Stod-

pressures in large families contributed to the numbers of unfit were unpersuasive to eugenicists, who saw the class divisions of American society as evidence of racial hierarchy. Harry Laughlin, the chief eugenic witness for immigration restriction, wrote in 1926 that although contraception could be eugenic, "Birth Control . . . work[ed] too strongly from the economic . . . view." Eugenics, on the other hand, had "the sounder foundation because it [was] primarily biological."[73]

The eugenicists who did support the ABCL and CRB in the 1920s, such as Raymond Pearl, Edward M. East, and Clarence C. Little, were more moderate both in their predictions of doom and in their prescriptions for regeneration. Shifting their concern from the race to the population, they were among the few American biologists who publicly criticized the racial dogmatism of the mainstream eugenics movement. Some of that criticism was articulated in support of birth control.[74]

Raymond Pearl, director of the Institute of Biological Research at Johns Hopkins, unlike most American eugenicists, was a biometrician who conducted extensive research on the biological aspects of population dynamics. Although he lamented differential birth rates as biological fact, he also recognized environmental causes of birth rates. He strongly disputed the mainstream eugenic doctrine that high fertility indicated racial unfitness. Their claim that there was a "gene or combination of genes for poverty" was untenable to him, and so was the assumption that the poor could not and would not use contraception. Rather, he inquired whether or not high birth rates among the poor really reflected their legally denied access to contraception.[75] Edward M. East, a botanist, was a Mendelian, but after his own research discredited the one-gene–one-trait principle he shifted to rely more on population dynamics to ground his eugenics. Although the expression of racism in his writings was often palpable, East was critical of the racial

dard's association with Sanger is cited by Gordon as evidence of her commitment to racist eugenics. Although his name appeared on the masthead of the *BCR* as a director of the ABCL, he was not actively associated with the ABCL at any time after the clinic opened in 1923. Popenoe himself reiterated his objection to birth control in 1925. See *The Conservation*, pp. 142–53. Sangerists criticized Popenoe's book reiterating their commitment to self-determination. See Annie Porritt, "An Opponent of Birth Control," pp. 375–77.

[73] H. H. Laughlin, "Eugenists on the Place of Birth Control: The Two Aspects of Control," p. 7.

[74] See also Borell, "Biologists," pp. 58–71; and Chesler, *Woman of Valor*, pp. 215–17, on the relationship of biologists to the birth control movement.

[75] Kevles, *In the Name of Eugenics*, pp. 122–23; and Raymond Pearl, "The Differential Birth Rate," p. 300.

dogmatism of the mainstream eugenicists. He dismissed their arguments as being "moved" by "race pride" alone. East's reasoning in support of white supremacy relied on what he considered to be sound principles of population. Those principles dictated legalized contraception to decrease the menace of overpopulation.[76]

Like Sanger, C. C. Little was critical of the arrogance with which mainstream eugenicists presumed to decide who was and was not fit. "It was an erroneous and dangerous assumption" that such distinctions could be made scientifically. Likening compulsory sterilization to prohibition, Little opposed in principle attempts by one social group to dictate the behavior of another. Birth control, which he likened to temperance, left it "up to the individual if he is intelligent, to exercise what his intelligence tells him to be the best use of such methods for his or her particular purpose in life."[77] As a biologist he knew that fitness was not an abstract quality; it was definable only in relation to particular environmental conditions. If those conditions changed, then the traits best fitted to the new conditions would likely be different from those best fitted to the old conditions. Eugenic definitions of fitness were shortsighted. The value of variety was that it enabled a species to adapt and progress in a changing environment. Still, the immense racial diversity in the United States gave him pause; because "no other country had ever tried such a biological experiment," there was no way of knowing how those diverse racial elements might mix.[78] Birth control, by "placing in the hands of women the right to determine their own reproductive activity," provided the necessary brake on America's biological experiment—a brake that would "magnif[y] the chance of survival of this civilization."[79]

These close allies of birth control held more rigidly deterministic views than Sanger did. As Kevles notes, what distinguished these men from other social reformers was their firm belief that biology mattered.[80] In disparaging the racial prejudice of mainstream eugenics, they did not dispute its goals, only its methods. They shifted their focus from the fitness of the various races to that of the entire population. But underlying their new focus on population, the older eugenic as-

[76] East, *Mankind at the Crossroads*, pp. 130–32.
[77] C. C. Little, "Unnatural Selection and Its Resulting Obligations," p. 243.
[78] Ibid., p. 244. See also C. C. Little, "Another View," p. 34.
[79] C. C. Little, "Will Birth Control Promote Race Improvement?" p. 344; and "Unnatural Selection," p. 257.
[80] Kevles, *In the Name of Eugenics*, p. 173.

sumptions about racial differences in the capacity for reason and re-production remained intact. Thus they saw birth control as a way to adjust for the natural biological differences in birth rates between the better and lesser stocks and supported Sanger's clinics as a way to reach those segments of the population whose greater fecundity threatened to swamp the old stock. Sanger, whose own perspective was closer to Britain's radical eugenicists, relied on these allies but did not want birth control to be subsumed by them. When she discovered in 1928 that the leadership of the ABCL in her absence was considering a merger of the *Birth Control Review* with an AES publication, she turned quickly to the ABCL membership to disapprove of the plan. The June 1928 *Review* published an excerpt from Sanger's letter to members of the ABCL National Council requesting their opinion of merging the *Review* with an AES magazine. Letters written in response to Sanger's artfully slanted request, most of which opposed the merger, were re-printed in the *Review* throughout 1928.[81] Nonetheless, the "critical and diagnostic aspects" of eugenics were valuable for the birth control movement, and Sanger used them to strengthen her demand for legal contraception.[82]

Scientific Respectability: The Benefits and Costs of Eugenics

In a variety of ways eugenics gave scientific credence to the move-ment's insistence that contraception should be included within the ter-rain of public health. Eugenics supplied the tools by which the movement could potentially overcome public resistance to birth con-trol. It provided the ideological ground upon which to contest the principle that the rate of reproduction was "God's will." Eugenic au-thority for statistical research on human reproduction countered the medical hegemony over birth control. Its doctrine of racial betterment through selective breeding grounded the movement's effort to insinu-ate birth control into the welfare feminist agenda. Most important, eugenics, focused on breeding populations rather than sexual individ-uals, offered a discreet language through which the movement could

[81] Sanger's letter was quick to point out that in such a merger the name *birth control* would be lost. By December the issue was moot. The AES brought out its own magazine, and Sanger, having resigned from the ABCL, was embroiled in a conflict with the ABCL over editorial control of the *BCR*, which she lost. See *BCR* 12 (June 1928): 188; 12 (August 1928): 238; 12 (October 1928): 290–91; and 12 (November 1928): 306, 323, 329.

[82] Sanger, *Pivot*, p. 104.

articulate its goals without sexual controversy.[83] By using this language Sangerists diminished the sexual connotations in birth control rhetoric that welfare feminists took exception to.

Science, particularly evolutionary theory, stood as a strong counter-hegemony to the Christian discourse of God's will. Science in general justified the secular-humanist projects of mastering nature through revealing its laws. Evolutionary social thought was a powerful resource against the representation of the natural order as expressed by birth control's major opponent, the Roman Catholic Church. Through eugenics and psychoanalysis, Sanger was able to represent the control of reproduction as adherence to, rather than a violation of, natural law. Psychoanalysis, Sanger argued, had shown that sexuality was a natural force that, rationally controlled, leads to progress but is perilous when repressed. Abstinence was unnatural; sexual expression was healthy, even necessary, apart from procreative concerns.[84] At the same time, eugenics demonstrated that uncontrolled fertility was a disaster. If heterosexual expression was essential to individual psychological health and uncontrolled fertility was a social disaster, then birth control was necessary. The traditional restriction of sexuality to procreation was both unnatural and unscientific. To Sanger, American eugenicists had an unfortunate tendency to reiterate the traditional injunction to be fruitful and multiply: "It [was] the limited, inhibited conception of sex that vitiate[d] so much of the thought and ideation of the Eugenists." However, eugenics carried greater legitimacy than psychoanalysis, which was not widely accepted or understood in the United States in the 1920s; and while Sanger never abandoned psychoanalytic sexual theory, she relied more heavily on the language of eugenics to legitimate contraception.[85]

Her articulation of evolutionary theory was eccentric within the American eugenic discourse because she explicitly linked women's sexual subjectivity to evolutionary progress. As opposed to the evolutionary theory underlying the mainstream of the American eugenics movement, in which women figured primarily as the incubators of the evolutionary progress of "man," Sanger's version of evolutionary bi-

[83] Kevles, *In the Name of Eugenics*, pp. 65–66. See also letters of Marguerite Benson to George J. Ryan, president of the Board of Education, New York City, 19 March 1935, MSP-SSC; and to Sidney Cohen, 19 March 1935, MSP-LC. These letters refer to the controversy generated when a Sangerist lecturer displayed contraceptive devices and explicit diagrams explaining their use.

[84] Sanger, *Pivot*, pp. 214, 228–29, 230, 271–76.

[85] Ibid., pp. 140, 228–42, 249–59.

ology, articulated in *Woman and the New Race,* positioned women as the subject-agents of racial progress and efficiency. Evidence from the animal kingdom demonstrated that it was "through the female alone" that "those modifications of form, capacity and ability which constitute evolutionary progress" were developed: "It was the mothers who first developed cunning in chase, ingenuity in escaping enemies, skill in obtaining food, and adaptability. It was they also who attained unfailing discretion in leadership [and] adaptation to environment. . . . In a word, natural law makes the females the expression and conveyor of racial efficiency."[86] Such evidence also revealed that the female role was not limited to motherhood. Rather, development of every faculty of an individual woman was a prerequisite to racial progress. To comply with "nature's working plan," society had to "permit womanhood its full development" before it expected "efficient motherhood." Full development of womanhood for Sanger included a satisfying sex life.[87] Thus by Sanger's rendition, human evolution was forestalled by the oppression of women in maternity; racial regeneration was possible only through the power of womanhood liberated by access to contraception. In this way Sanger's rhetoric used eugenic language to define women with self-determined maternity as the autonomous agents of racial betterment.

The data of eugenics were also valuable. As we saw in Chapter 3, eugenicists gave their greatest practical support to Sangerists in their struggle against the medical hegemony. It was to eugenicists that the nation was "most indebted for the proof that reckless spawning carries with it the seeds of destruction."[88] Sanger, and the nation, accepted eugenicists' statistical studies that purportedly demonstrated the differential birth rate and the rise of feeblemindedness. Thus the presence of eugenicists on the Board of Directors of the CRB as technical advisors helped improve the credibility of its data against the medical profession's criticism. By making clinic records available to several researchers, Sangerists were able to turn the CRB data on contraceptive efficacy into powerful weapons against the medical profession's con-

[86] Sanger, *Woman,* pp. 228–29.
[87] Ibid., p. 229.
[88] Sanger, *Pivot,* p. 178. This book was an attempt to persuade the American scientific community to engage in research on birth control.

demnation of birth control as unproven.[89] Eugenic concern with racial health and betterment lent ideological credence to social and economic indicators for birth control against the medical profession's strict interpretation of "the cure and prevention of disease." The practical research eugenicists directed was instrumental in showing that birth control improved maternal and infant health even when prescribed in the absence of disease.[90]

From Sanger's perspective, the salient point of eugenical data was that they demonstrated that "uncontrolled fertility is universally correlated with disease, poverty, overcrowding, *and* the transmission of hereditable traits."[91] Thus, whether one considered heredity or environment to be at the root, uncontrolled fertility was the problem, and "birth control [was] really the greatest and most truly eugenic method." It was the "pivot of civilization," because it offered "the means whereby the individual may adapt himself [*sic*] to and even control the forces of environment and heredity." Her claim was substantiated in 1934 by eugenicist Raymond Pearl's research, which showed that the single greatest factor in the differential birth rate was knowledge of and access to birth control.[92]

Eugenic logic by endorsing social and economic indications for the prescription of contraception indirectly supported the Sangerist contention that women's desire for birth control was reasonable and responsible given the conditions of their lives. But, the most important contribution made by eugenics to the Sangerist effort to legitimate birth control was its antiseptic language. The terminology of eugenics (genetic capacity, reproductivity, pregnancy wastage, expressed fertility, and birth rates) desensitized the public discussion of birth control by obscuring the sexual activity that occasioned contraceptive use. It provided Sangerists with a language with which to discuss contracep-

[89] Raymond Pearl, Regine Stix, Frank Notestein, and Marie Kopp all used CRB records in their studies. See "Preliminary Survey of Data from Case Histories," c. 1931; letters of Raymond Pearl to Margaret Sanger, 16 and 24 July 1926; and of Margaret Sanger to E. M. East, to Leon Cole, to C. C. Little, and to Adolph Meyer, 13 October 1926; MSP-LC.

[90] See the following articles on the effect of contraception on pregnancy wastage (i.e., stillbirth and abortion): Regine Stix and Frank Notestein, "Effectiveness of Birth Control" and "Effectiveness of Birth Control: A Second Study."

[91] Sanger, *Pivot*, p. 174 (emphasis added). She cites Karl Pearson's work for this assertion.

[92] Ibid., p. 189. Pearl, "Second Progress Report," p. 268; Raymond Pearl, "Contraception and Fertility in 4,945 Married Women," p. 400. See also C. C. Little's speech as president of the ABCL; ABCL annual meeting, 1936, PPFA-SSC.

tion without vulgarity, and Sangerists used this sexually neutral language to legitimate birth control as just one more public health and welfare issue. In its neutrality, however, eugenical language desexualized birth control altogether.[93]

Raymond Pearl's terminology in particular effectively disconnected sex and contraception. In pursuing his goal of producing "sound data," Pearl argued that the *"potential"* effectiveness of contraception, measured by successful use among intelligent, educated women who were obsessed with preventing unwanted pregnancies, had to be carefully distinguished from the *"actual"* effectiveness of contraception among the "general population." To distinguish actual from potential effectiveness, Pearl constructed an "objective" measure of "exposure to risk of pregnancy" as a base of comparison. He defined exposure to the risk of pregnancy not as heterosexual intercourse but as the total of ovulation events while married.[94] By this definition sexual intercourse disappears as the event that exposes women to the risk of pregnancy. Rather, marriage is the condition of all women studied, and it was the rhythms of their reproductive biology that put women at risk for pregnancy. Without sexual intercourse as the event that necessitated birth control there was no place from which to contest the sex rights of women. The sense of birth control as a tool by which women could experience (hetero)sexual pleasure without the fear of pregnancy was obscured by a language that divorced sexuality itself from the possibility of pregnancy. Thus, in the same moment that it muted the sexual controversy of birth control, eugenical language also displaced women's sexual subjectivity from debates about contraceptive practice.

Devoid of sexual controversy, eugenically framed birth control rhetoric was more morally respectable to both welfare feminists and a wider culture that feared the implications of women's sexual independence. Sangerists never intoned the jargon of ovulation events. However, the female sexual subject of earlier Sangerist rhetoric, who demanded sexual freedom, was replaced in their eugenically framed rhetoric by the responsible maternal subject, who practiced rational

---

[93] Petchesky, focusing on class, makes this point with regard to Malthusianism and demography. See *Abortion and Woman's Choice*, pp. 9–10, 35–40, 92–93.

[94] Raymond Pearl, "Contraception and Fertility in 2,000 Women," pp. 365, 367, 399–401 (emphasis in original). See also Pearl, "Contraception and Fertility in 4,945 Married Women," pp. 356–58, 366–77; and "Second Progress Report," pp. 254–55.

control of her reproductive biology.[95] Through the logic of her version of evolutionary biology, using the language and data of eugenics, Sanger endeavored to prove that birth control was a necessary component of the welfare feminist project of racial uplift. Fashioning her rhetoric to resonate with the racial maternalism of welfare feminists, Sanger argued that if supporting motherhood was the means by which to achieve cultural assimilation and thus protection of American democracy, then mothers needed to have control over their fertility. Without birth control the best intentions of good motherhood would be overwhelmed by the size of its task.[96] By defining birth control as one more tool of good mothering, the birth control movement, like welfare feminists, repositioned itself with respect to the women it sought to support.

Birth Control and Racial Maternalism

In the twenties, the centerpiece of welfare feminism, maternal support programs, offered instruction in the old-stock American precepts of infant care, child care, and housekeeping. Through these programs, welfare feminists recast their gender solidarity with poor, ethnic women into a patron-client relationship in which the welfare feminists served as the models of successful womanhood. In this way, the programs' focus on the individual mother's behavior obscured the social basis of poverty. If a poor, ethnic mother strove hard enough to duplicate middle-class, old-stock standards of domestic and maternal excellence, then poverty would not thwart her efforts to raise "good children." Yet, although training was given to poor mothers, the means to enact the demonstrated practices were not furnished. The Sheppard-Towner Act provided instruction in infant care but dispensed no funds with which to fulfill its prescribed standards.[97]

[95] In *Woman's Body,* pp. 284–88, Linda Gordon condemns Sanger's reliance on eugenics, describing it as a "desertion of feminism." I contend that Sanger did not desert feminism. Rather, in her articulation of eugenics, she divested birth control of a candid feminine sexuality, thus making it morally respectable to welfare feminists within an increasingly antifeminist political terrain. If this constitutes abandonment of feminism, then there were no feminists in the period, because no women's reform groups candidly supported women's sex rights.

[96] Sanger, "The Need," p. 228.

[97] I am indebted to Mink, *Wages,* chapter 1–5, for this analysis of maternal support programs. See also Mink, "Lady," pp. 97, 101, 103–6; Meckel, *Save the Babies,* pp. 100–101, 119–20, 157, 169–70, 220–21; and Muncy, *Creating a Female Dominion,* pp. 108–11.

Likewise, training in proper contraceptive technique was the focus of the birth control movement in the 1920s. Its practices differed, however, from maternal support programs to the extent that the movement clinics did provide the means of contraception about which its pamphlets gave instruction. Yet over the course of the twenties, birth control rhetoric, like welfare feminist rhetoric, came to obscure the societal basis of poverty and disease by focusing on the individual mother's private fertility decisions. And simultaneously, the movement's educational practices recast the relationship between poor and middle-class women to one of client and patron.

The 1915 first edition of *Family Limitation* was directed at a working-class audience at war with the ruling class. It denounced the societal restraints on working-class self-determination.[98] By 1920 the revised pamphlet spoke of uplifting the poor to the standards of reproductive hygiene employed by the middle class. It claimed that "only the workers" were "ignorant of the knowledge of how to prevent bringing children into the world." The opening disclaimer against presuming to tell working-class men and women why they needed birth control was gone. Instead, working-class women were told that they should have no more than two children, because they could not support more in a "decent fashion."[99] Implicit here were old-stock, middle-class standards of a decent upbringing. The injustice cited in the 1920 version of the pamphlet was not economic exploitation as it had been in 1915. Rather, it concerned the individual woman whom the state wronged when it prohibited her access to birth control:

> Every mother feels the wrong that the State imposes upon her when
> it deprives her of information to prevent the bringing into the world
> of children she cannot feed or clothe or care for. She resents this
> with all the bitterness of her strength and will rejoice to find some in-
> formation contained herein, to help the mothers of America free
> themselves from the burden of too-frequent pregnancies.[100]

Only the "indolent" woman and the "selfish" man would refuse the knowledge offered in the pamphlet. The 1920 version closes with a brief discussion of the public need for birth control to conserve the

---

[98] Sanger, *Family Limitation* (1915), p. 3.
[99] Ibid. (10th ed., 1920), p. 4, MSP-LC.
[100] Ibid., p. 3.

lives of physically unfit women and "to prevent the birth of diseased and defective children."[101]

By the time the 1928 version appeared, *Family Limitation* was directed at an audience of middle-class women who, it said, had a duty to agitate for the right of their working-class sisters to methods they already possessed:

> These women resent the fact that the educated women are able to obtain safe, scientific, harmless information of birth control, while Society condemns its use among the working women who need it most. Present day Society is generous in doling out pittances for the unfit and diseased, thus encouraging their multiplication and perpetuation, while it prevents and discourages the use of scientific knowledge which would enable mothers to avoid bringing into the world children they cannot feed, clothe or care for.[102]

Gender solidarity, in terms of women's right to contraception, continued to be the movement's rallying cry, but the middle-class women's duty to educate and uplift their poor and ignorant sisters was preeminent in 1928. As with welfare feminists, gender solidarity within the birth control movement was recast into a patron-client relationship. What middle-class white women had to offer to their poor sisters was training in "conscious responsibility to the race," which was embodied in the principles that "children should be conceived in love, born of the mother's conscious desire, and only begotten under conditions which render possible the heritage of health."[103]

The first two principles uphold women's sexual subjectivity in referring to consensual sexuality and voluntary motherhood, but underlying the last principle—a heritage of health—was the assumption that health was a commodity to be purchased privately with the individual family's income. A heritage of health was possible only if a woman's fertility was kept within the limits of her husband's income to provide food, clothing, shelter, and medical care to the resulting children. In what amounted to an economic calculus of fertility control, Sanger reasoned that a family should not have more children "than the mother

---

[101] Ibid., pp. 3, 23.

[102] Ibid. (17th ed., c. 1928), p. 5, MSP-LC. This pamphlet begins with a discussion of preventing births among the unfit and includes sterilization as a birth control method. The "unfit" are defined as the insane, syphilitic, idiotic, and feebleminded.

[103] Ibid., p. 4.

could look after and the father could make a living for."[104] In 1915 the economic ethic of fertility was cast in terms of an argument for working-class self-determination based upon a critique of capitalism. By 1920 the ethic was detached from any such argument or critique of inequality, obscuring the socially constructed limits on family income. Through this abstract economic ethic, the movement helped to reconfirm the dominant culture's standards of the "decent fashion" in which to raise children. Without considering the social basis of making a living, the movement judged harshly those women who had children despite their poverty. Increasingly over the course of the twenties, in the movement's rhetoric, the inability to raise socially worthwhile children became less a question of deprivations of the market and more the failure of individuals to act responsibly. Those who did not calculate their desired family size in terms of the old-stock, middle-class definition of the necessary financial means to rear children decently were implicitly irresponsible and thus were likely to be unfit citizens.[105]

The gendering of this economic calculus, by which a decent upbringing required a stay-at-home mother, is another pitfall of racial maternalism shared by the birth control movement. Like welfare feminists, Sangerists reified the woman citizen's contribution as housebound maternity. Although for Sanger birth control enabled woman's self-expression, this expression was fulfilled in motherly protection of children: "When motherhood becomes the fruit of a deep yearning, not the result of ignorance or accident, its children will become the foundation of a new race. . . . children [will not] die by inches in mills and factories. No man will dare to break a child's life upon the wheel of toil." By locating women's political agency in their maternity, Sanger supplanted her own articulation of women's sexual rights in favor of racially responsible motherhood. To Sanger, "the miracle of free womanhood [was] that in its freedom it becomes the race mother."[106] In this way, Sanger's use of eugenics to insert birth control politically into the agenda of welfare feminists was flawed in much the same way as were their maternal support programs: both faltered under the weight of the dominant culture's gender conventions.

Also like welfare feminists, by confirming an economic calculus of fertility control, the birth control movement linked the politics of fertility to the future of America's race order. Sanger's economic ethic of

[104] Sanger, *Woman*, p. 64.
[105] See Sanger, "The Need," p. 228, and "Editorial," pp. 67–68.
[106] Sanger, *Woman*, pp. 231–32.

fertility was one means by which she distanced herself from the bio-determinism of hereditarian eugenicists. But because ethnicity and poverty were indelibly associated in this period, her framing of this economic ethic within the terms of racial maternalism did not fully challenge the conventions of American racism. Those among the ethnic and racial poor who did not restrain their fertility as a means to ensure the racial uplift of their children acted irresponsibly. And irresponsibility slipped easily into social incompetence, the catch-all of eugenic standards of unfitness. Sanger never abandoned her commitment to individual control of fertility; this commitment was repeated by Sanger throughout the 1920s, especially against eugenic proposals to increase birth rates among the middle class. Yet the movement's articulation of racial maternalism, if not premised on the biological superiority of the Nordic race, was premised on its cultural superiority. Responsible action, the key indicator of social competence, required adherence to dominant culture standards.[107]

While articulating her goal of reproductive self-determination for women in general, Sanger's language used singular nouns that obscured racial (and class) differences entirely. She appealed for the right of *woman* to decide when and whether *she* would become a mother. Likewise, her language tended to obscure racial differences in appeals for the betterment of *the race* through free womanhood. Sanger's language articulated women's basic need for freedom from unwanted pregnancies, but its singularity obscured the different conditions under which women of diverse ethnic communities might or might not want a pregnancy. This singularity obscures too the white racial perspective of who was fit and unfit; who should and should not reproduce; and how many children a family should have. Sangerist rhetoric continually confused women's rights to reproductive self-determination with women's role in bettering the race. It confused individual women's interests in controlling their fertility and white America's interests in maintaining numerical and cultural supremacy.[108] In articulating the model of good mothering solely in terms of their own racially situated ambition to raise good children, Sangerists unself-consciously generalized the white perspectivity of that maternal ambition.

[107] See, for example, Sanger, "The Need," pp. 227–28, and "Editorial," pp. 163–64.

[108] This was not unprecedented; the nineteenth-century voluntary motherhood movement did the same thing. See Petchesky, *Abortion and Woman's Choice*, pp. 41–44; and Gordon, *Woman's Body,* pp. 126–30. Also, Sanger was not alone in her acceptance of eugenics. Both Charlotte Perkins Gilman and Emma Goldman also utilized eugenical ideas.

The right of all women to reproductive self-determination was compromised by the premise that all women should conform to the dominant ideology of proper family size. Racial maternalists, in recasting the relationship between themselves and poor, ethnic mothers, defined these minority-culture women as the objects of social programs for racial homogenization. Although racial maternalists simultaneously positioned themselves as the subject-agents who guided "other" mothers' actions, the objectification of some kinds of women undercut the assertion of all women's agency. In the case of birth control, Sanger's re-encoding of eugenic evolutionary theory to cast women as the agents of racial progress could not be sustained against the objectification of "other" women in her rhetoric. Training ethnic women in middle-class white techniques and values of contraception eventually recast the social right to contraception into a social prescription. As among welfare feminists whose programs required adherence to dominant cultural standards as a prerequisite to equal opportunity, Sangerists likewise required adherence to their definition of reproductive responsibility as a prerequisite to self-determination.[109]

However, it is important not to overstate the racism constituted within Sangerist rhetoric. Simply labeling Sangerists as racist tells us little about how they were situated within the expanse of white racism. Sanger's rhetoric did not fully challenge eugenics' rigid racial hierarchies. Yet, while her discussion of the American race tended to whitewash people of color, she did not concur with the disparaging opinions of people of color expressed by most eugenicists. Although Sanger's representation of women as the agents of human evolution may have been unique among women's rights advocates, her racial thinking was not. Like welfare feminists, Sangerists posited the possibility of racial pluralism. Subscribing to the ideal of the melting pot, they positioned birth control to serve racial uplift but not to limit overall diversity. They sought to assimilate all cultural groups, including the "old stock," to the values of the birth control movement. Although their rhetoric required assimilation of an old-stock perspective, they, like welfare feminists, opposed immigration restrictionists and eugenicists who discounted the possibility of assimilation. Instead, Sangerists tried to position themselves with the welfare feminists for whom assimilation

---

See Petchesky, *Abortion and Woman's Choice*, p. 93; and Kevles, *In the Name of Eugenics*, pp. 64, 106.

[109] On welfare feminists see Mink, *Wages*, chapters 1–2, and "Lady," pp. 97, 104; and Chapter 2 herein.

of ethnic diversity through maternalism dissipated its danger.[110] In a decade of race consciousness in which fear of diversity reigned within public discourse and state policy, the suggestion of racial pluralism was a liberal position on racial difference.[111]

Sangerists tried to reencode eugenics to support women's reproductive self-determination, but their own racial maternalism undercut their resistance to the white racial paternalism inherent in eugenics. Sangerist reliance on eugenical allies prejudiced contraceptive clinical practices, displacing women from the position of subjects of their own fertility. Eugenicists were concerned with the social control of human reproduction; they had no concern that this control would be enacted on the bodies of women. In the language of population dynamics, the individual disappears entirely. The population is the unit of measurement, and the ratios of fit to unfit are the primary focus. These eugenicists hoped family planning would encourage the "better stocks" to have more children and the "lesser stocks" fewer, thereby shifting the ratios of population composition. They were less concerned with individual women's rights, needs, or desires to prevent pregnancy. The eugenicists' paternalistic goal was to become the expert guides for women's reproductive choices. Enlightened mothers would necessarily remain dependent upon eugenical experts to guide their fertility decisions. This kind of control is not friendly to women's individual self-determination, because eugenical guidance would be predicated on racially imbued evaluations of fitness.

Sanger followed eugenicist recommendations on how to improve the data collection at the clinic, including the suggestion that information on race and national origin be recorded on the patient history cards. Through this practice, the clinic could become a source of data on the differential in fertility rates between the races.[112] With this revamping of the clinic's record-keeping system, eugenically framed racial think-

[110] In the twenties, however, her main focus was upon the recent white immigrants from southern and eastern Europe, who carried in their bodies and souls all the glorious elements of "Old World" civilization, which, when given expression, would make a valuable contribution to America. She made no statements about the value of Asian, African, Chicano, or Native-American heritages to the future American race. See Sanger, *Woman*, pp. 30–46. On welfare feminists see Mink, "Lady," pp. 97–104.

[111] Sangerists' perspective, like that of welfare feminists, is not simply one of social control. See Muncy, *Creating a Female Dominion*, pp. 109–11.

[112] Kennedy, *Birth Control in America*, p. 200; Gordon, *Woman's Body*, pp. 286–87; and letter of E. M. East to Margaret Sanger, 9 February 1925, MSP-LC. "Report of Conference of Maternal Health Committee and Clinical Research Committee of the American Birth Control League, 29 November 1925, NCMH-CL. See also n. 89 above.

ing was brought into the center of America's contraceptive delivery system. Although a number of studies published in the thirties demonstrated that access to contraception was the key factor in both class and race birth-rate differentials, they reiterated stereotypes of African-Americans, in particular, as less capable of precision and forethought.[113] This eugenically framed racial thought set the stage for the eventual incorporation of differential treatment of patients based on race. The prescriptive edge of population control took on greater significance during the depression. The national collapse of the economy and the extension of welfare in the New Deal heightened concerns about whether the poor and ethnic were reproducing responsibly. By 1939 the Birth Control Federation of America, formed a year earlier by the remerger of the CRB and ABCL, incorporated positive eugenics into its official objectives when it endorsed more babies for the fit. Sanger was livid about this policy but could not sway the Federation Board to change it. Thus, while eugenics was useful in legitimating contraception, ultimately the cultural baggage eugenics carried with it undercut Sanger's rhetorical encoding of women as the subjects of fertility control. And although Sanger supported racial pluralism in principle, in practice the tension between racial prescription of family size and reproductive self-determination continued to shape the course of the movement as it won legalization and began to develop a national network of clinics. As detailed in the next chapter, this tension is clearest in the CRB coalition with African-American professionals during the 1930s.

[113] Pearl, "Contraception and Fertility in 2,000 Women," pp. 395, 403; and "Contraception and Fertility in 4,945 Married Women," pp. 381, 384, 391, 398.

CHAPTER FIVE

Better Health for Thirteen Million:
The Interracial Coalition for Birth Control

Again and again white people, competent in every other particular,
get confused in the face of interracial endeavor. Lack of deep seated
interest generally accounts for this.
                                                    —M. O. Bousfield

Why should the Negroes who are conducting a desperate struggle
against the social and economic forces aimed at their destruction
continue to enrich the morticians and choke the jails with unwanted
children? It were far better to have less children and improve the
social and physical well-being of those they have.
                                    —George Schuyler, "Quantity or Quality"

In 1943 Planned Parenthood's Division of Negro Service (DNS) promised that the use of contraception would bring "better health" for the
nation's "thirteen million" African-Americans.[1] Established in 1938 to
coordinate efforts to provide contraceptive information and services
to the African-American community, the DNS was the central locus of
a national interracial coalition for birth control before 1945. Along
with the Harlem clinic opened by the CRB in 1930, the DNS represents the birth control movement's specific efforts to address the contraceptive needs of African-American women. As such, these projects
were crucial sites where the racially imbued tension between birth control as a social right or a social prescription was played out.

Previous histories of birth control have treated the Harlem clinic and
the Division of Negro Service as minor episodes, tending to focus
solely on whether these projects were manifestations of Sanger's and

[1] PPFA, *Better Health for Thirteen Million*, FRP-SSC.

the movement's racist intentions. But based on the questionable premise that African-Americans had no intrinsic interest in contraceptive legalization, these interpretations assume that the Harlem clinic and DNS imposed white values on the unreceptive African-American community.[2] The debate has been about whether or not these projects were intended for ill—social control—or for good—social uplift. Such accounts have been one-sided; they have ignored both the demographic evidence of African-American contraceptive use and the record of rhetorical and practical support by African-Americans for birth control.

Between 1880 and 1940, African-American fertility rates fell so dramatically that the differential fertility between the races was nearly eliminated during the record low-birth years of the depression.[3] Demographers have attributed this decline in fertility to the consequences of poor health among African-Americans rather than to conscious fertility control. The health hypothesis, as it has been called, attributes the low completed fertility and high childlessness rates among African-American women in the 1930s to their higher rates of venereal disease, puerperal infections, tuberculosis, and rickets.[4] Recent studies, however, have disputed the health hypothesis, arguing that it rests on the dubious assumptions that African-Americans rarely used contraception and that when they did, they used ineffective methods ineffectively.[5] These assumptions rely on ironic twists of white ra-

[2] Gordon, *Woman's Body,* pp. 332–34, concludes that the DNS had no "socially progressive meaning." See also Kennedy, *Birth Control in America,* pp. 259–60; and Rodrique, "The Black Community," pp. 333, 340. Reed does not discuss either project explicitly. Chesler, *Woman of Valor,* p. 388, argues that the projects were experiments in social engineering but the intentions were not racist. Angela Davis, *Women, Race, and Class,* pp. 202–21, likewise rejects the premise that African-Americans had no interest in birth control. However, she underestimates these interracial efforts to organize clinics.

[3] The gap increased again after 1940 as the fertility rates of both African-Americans and whites increased during the baby boom.

[4] Phillips Cutright and Edward Shorter, "The Effects of Health," pp. 191–97. They also argue that the health hypothesis rests only on indirect data that high disease rates compromised African-American reproductive capacity. Particularly pernicious is the assertion referred to on pp. 194–95, that high rates of venereal disease produced high rates of sterility. Although African-Americans were popularly represented as the syphilis-soaked race, few studies at the time showed that the purported high rates existed, and no studies showed that high levels of sterility resulted. Cutright and Shorter dispute this cause and favor both the demonstrated high rates of puerperal fever and rickets as the primary health causes of involuntary fertility control.

[5] See Joseph McFalls and George Masnick, "Birth Control," pp. 89–106. This article contains an excellent review of the health-hypothesis literature. They also argue that the

cial thinking. The only direct evidence on which the health hypothesis is based is taken from the 1930s demographic studies of contraceptive use cited in Chapter 4. The lower rates of contraceptive use among African-Americans reported in those studies ground demographers' retrospective conclusion that birth control was primarily a white cultural practice before 1940. But those early studies also demonstrated that access to effective contraception, and not race, was the primary factor in rates of successful contraceptive use. Differential access to effective contraception, and not differences in interest, motivation, or ability, accounted for the differential fertility rates in the studies. Even though it is not biologically deterministic, the health hypothesis is consistent with traditional white racial thinking. In concluding that African-Americans did not want effective contraception, it obscures the racism that caused African-Americans rarely to get effective contraception. Moreover, the health hypothesis is fundamentally inconsistent with its own data. In fact, middle-class, urban African-Americans had, within their communities, the lowest fertility rates, and they also had the lowest rates of the diseases thought to cause low fertility. They were the group with the greatest access to contraception both from private physicians and from movement clinics, and they gave the greatest public support to the birth control movement. Certainly poor health influenced the decline in fertility, especially in the early years, but the proponents of the health hypothesis err in concluding that fertility control played only a minimal role.

Yet even those who dispute the health hypothesis are unable to account for the birth control knowledge that they insist existed in the African-American community.[6] Apparently they are unaware of the interracial coalition for birth control, out of which came virtually every study of African-American contraceptive use in the 1930s and 1940s cited to dispute the health hypothesis.[7] Moreover, like the proponents

---

health hypothesis rests only on indirect data that high disease rates compromised African-American reproductive capacity. See also Stanley Engerman, "Changes in Black Fertility, 1880–1940," pp. 126–53.

[6] McFalls and Masnick, "Birth Control," pp. 92, 99–102, conclude, based on a retrospective study, that 50 percent of African-American women used contraception in the 1930s. This compares to a white contraceptive-use rate of 71 percent. Moreover, the top three methods of contraception—condoms, douching, and withdrawal—were the same for both groups. See Deborah A. Dawson, Denise J. Meny, and Jeanne Clare Ridley, "Fertility Control," p. 76.

[7] McFalls and Masnick, "Birth Control," pp. 89, 94–96, cite the Regine Stix and Raymond Pearl studies discussed in Chapter 4 and the Seibels studies discussed in notes 98,

of the health hypothesis, they are unaware of the public support given the birth control movement by African-Americans, thus diminishing their own assertion that African-Americans knew about and used contraception. Closer examination of the Harlem clinic and the DNS provides a window on the range of African-American support for birth control and its ideological underpinnings. Instead of focusing only on the intentions of white advocates in the racial politics of birth control, I examine in this chapter the process by which those politics were articulated in the interactions between white and African-American birth control advocates.

Proceeding chronologically, the first section describes the Harlem clinic, considering in detail both the location of African-Americans within U.S. population politics and the racial dynamics in that particular clinic. The second section describes the Division of Negro Service and considers the racial dynamics that shaped it. In both sections the analysis focuses on ideological common ground between white and African-American birth control supporters as well as their conflicts. Because these projects arose at a moment when population politics were increasingly focused on birth rates among the poor, these projects also illustrate the continuing conflation in America of poverty and race. The indelible connection of race and poverty undergirded both the agreements and the disagreements between African-American and white birth control advocates. In particular, the middle-class paternalism of African-American birth control advocates toward poor blacks undercut their effective resistance to the racial maternalism of Sangerists. Examining these interactions of white and African-American birth control supporters further illuminates the textures of racial maternalism among white birth control advocates and reveals how African-Americans' responses to white racial maternalism shaped each group's perspective on birth control. Finally, the struggle between Sangerists and the new Planned Parenthood Federation leadership about how to organize the DNS also sheds light on the wider struggle in the movement between laywomen and professional men. In the final section of the chapter I return to consider what these projects reveal about the racism articulated in the American birth control movement

---

111, and 112 below. See also Clyde Kiser, "Fertility and Harlem Negroes," pp. 273–85; not connected with the birth control movement, this article is one of the earliest to posit high venereal disease rates to account for the low fertility rates found, p. 282.

and how those politics interacted with the gender politics undergirding the movement.

Birth Control in Harlem

The Harlem Branch of the Birth Control Clinical Research Bureau, or the Harlem clinic as it was commonly called, was operated by Margaret Sanger from 1930 to 1935 in coalition with members of the Harlem community, including James Hubert, executive secretary of the New York Chapter of the National Urban League and president of the Harlem Social Workers' Club; Mabel Staupers, executive director of the National Association of Colored Graduate Nurses; Louis T. Wright, medical secretary of the Harlem Hospital; May Chinn, the only African-American woman practicing medicine in Harlem; and William Lloyd Imes, the assistant pastor of the Abyssinian Baptist Church.[8] Although the Harlem clinic was the first sustained effort, concern about the contraceptive needs of African-Americans was not new for either Sangerists or African-Americans. In 1919 the *Birth Control Review* published a "special number" about "the Negroes' need for birth control, as seen by themselves."[9] As early as 1922 W. E. B. Du Bois publicly endorsed birth control in *The Crisis*, saying, "Birth control is science and sense applied to the bringing of children into the world, and of all who need it we Negroes are first."[10] Shortly after Du Bois's article appeared, the ABCL Board voted that Sanger should accept all invitations to speak before African-American audiences.[11] Eighteen months after the CRB opened its doors, James Hubert approached Sanger about the possibility of opening a clinic in a black neighborhood. For several months in 1924 a clinic was operated in conjunction with the National Urban League in the Columbus Hill neighborhood, but there were so few patients that the clinic was closed and the patients were transferred to the CRB. This clinic's failure may well reflect the fact

[8] Advisory Council meeting, minutes, 23 September 1931; HBBCCRB, announcement, 25 March 1932; and 1932 list of Advisory Council members, MSP-LC.

[9] *BCR* 3 (September 1919), front cover. The special issue included short stories by Mary Burrill and Angelina Grimke, an interview with Chandler Owen who co-edited the *Messenger* with A. Philip Randolph, and an editorial by Isaac Fisher of Fisk University that called for interracial cooperation on birth control.

[10] W. E. B. Du Bois, "Opinion," p. 248.

[11] ABCL, minutes, 13 December 1922, PPFA-SSC.

that in the 1920s Harlem was becoming the primary center of the African-American community and its institutions.[12]

During the twenties, Harlem became the largest and most densely populated black community in the nation. Home of the literati and intellectuals of the New Negro Renaissance, Harlem was popularly represented as the "Mecca of the New Negro." It was a mecca, as well, to white "slumming parties" who "discovered black magic" in its speakeasies and nightclubs.[13] But on the eve of the depression, beneath the veneer of exotic and sensuous nightlife described by whites, living conditions in Harlem were horrendous. Its tremendous growth resulted in part from increasing residential segregation. Barred from living in other sections of the city, African-Americans were forced to pay exorbitant rents for deteriorating and congested living space. Racial discrimination in employment left Harlem's residents with few options besides low-paying service jobs. The combination of high rents and low wages produced the congested and unsanitary conditions evidenced by high rates of illness and death. The overall death rate was 42 percent higher in Harlem than in other sections of New York City. Although death rates from heart disease, cancer, tuberculosis, and pneumonia were also higher than whites' rates, two statistics stood out: both maternal and infant mortality rates were twice those of whites, and increasing.[14] The recognition of higher rates of maternal and infant mortality may well have been the immediate catalyst leading the Urban League to pursue the establishment of a birth control clinic in Harlem. Both the Columbus Hill and Harlem clinics were initiated shortly after studies revealed the excessive maternal mortality of African-Americans in New York City. At the organizing meeting of the Harlem clinic's Advisory Council, Louis Wright noted that his interest in the clinic resulted from the "appalling number of deaths that come to his attention . . . following abortions."[15]

[12] Dorothy Bocker, "Monthly Report," June 1924, MSP-LC; Anne Kennedy, memo, 21 October 1924; and ABCL, "Report of the Clinical Research Department for 1925," p. 5, MSP-LC. Columbus Hill referred to the area from Sixtieth to Sixty-fourth Streets and from Tenth to Eleventh Avenues. On the shift of the black population from Columbus Hill to Harlem see Gilbert Osofsky, *Harlem*, pp. 112–13.

[13] Claude McKay, as quoted in Osofsky, *Harlem*, pp. 181, 184–85.

[14] Ibid., pp. 141–44, 150–51, 179–87.

[15] Advisory Council meeting, minutes, 20 May 1931, MSP-SSC. James Hubert's reasons for contacting Sanger are not recorded. It may be inferred from the timing of his contacts shortly after publication of the following studies, however, that the maternal health conditions of African-American women were among his reasons. See New York

In the midst of Robert Dickinson's last effort to take over the CRB, in 1929, Sanger met with members of the New York National Urban League and the Social Workers' Club of Harlem on several occasions to discuss the feasibility of opening a clinic in the community.[16] In October the Social Workers' Club publicly endorsed the work of the CRB and resolved to urge the CRB "to establish a birth control clinic somewhere in Harlem accessible to Negro women," pledging "to cooperate in every way possible."[17] By 1 February 1930, Sanger had secured $10,000 to fund the clinic.[18] The clinic opened three days later. Located in the second-floor rooms of a storefront on Seventh Avenue, off 138th Street, the clinic was announced as the Clinical Research Bureau by a small, hand-lettered sign at its entrance.[19]

In its day-to-day operations, the clinic was run as a branch office of the CRB—hence the name, Harlem branch. It was staffed by a medical director who supervised patient services and by a varying number of consulting physicians, two registered nurses, and a receptionist. In the beginning, the clinic was open to patients one afternoon a week, but its hours were gradually expanded; and by December 1930 it was open six afternoons and two evenings a week. The clinic, like the CRB, offered women a gynecological examination by a physician; provided contraceptive instruction by a nurse; and dispensed pessaries. The stated fee for the service, as with the CRB, was five dollars—three dollars for the exam and two dollars for a pessary and a six-month supply of spermicidal jelly. And no woman was refused service because of an inability to pay. Records show that less than 10 percent of the patients paid the full fee, and more than half of the African-American patients paid no fee at all. So, in effect, the clinic operated on a sliding-scale

---

Association for Improving the Condition of the Poor, *Health Work for Mothers and Children in a Colored Community*; and Louis Dublin, "The Health of the Negro," pp. 77–85.

[16] Edwin Embree, president of the Rosenwald Fund, had expressed interest in supporting the "clinic you have been asked to open in . . . Harlem" as early as April. See letters of Edwin Embree to Margaret Sanger, 1 April 1929; and of Margaret Sanger to Edwin Embree, 17 October 1929, and to the New York Foundation, 20 November 1929; of Morris Waldman to Margaret Sanger, 10 July 1929; and of Margaret Sanger to Morris Waldman, 7 October 1929, MSP-LC.

[17] Social Workers' Club of Harlem, resolution, 10 October 1929, MSP-LC.

[18] Sanger secured a $5,000 donation from her longtime benefactor, Carrie Fuld, and a $5,000 matching-fund grant from the Rosenwald Fund. See letters of Margaret Sanger to Edwin Embree, 27 December 1929; of Edwin Embree to Margaret Sanger, 29 April 1930; and of Michael Davis to Margaret Sanger, 21 March 1931, MSP-LC.

[19] Letter of Margaret Sanger to W. E. B. Du Bois, c. 21 November 1929; HBBCCRB, *Annual Report*, 1930, MSP-LC.

basis. There were over nineteen hundred patient visits recorded in 1930 and several thousand each year thereafter. Until 1933 about half its patients were white women referred from downtown.[20]

Education programs and fundraising were directed by Sanger in consultation with an Advisory Council of community leaders. Initially, the Advisory Council of the main clinic served the Harlem clinic as well, but by the end of 1930, Sanger organized a separate Council for the Harlem clinic.[21] The Harlem Advisory Council, which included the people mentioned above along with several additional African-American physicians, nurses, and clergy, was set up to "help direct" the clinic's "activities and policies" so that "birth control [would] be a constructive force in the community." Sanger hoped the Council would provide "advice and help in operating" the clinic—"to determine the best way of reaching the women who most need help; to decide the best methods to use for educating the public concerning the aims and purposes of Birth Control"; and to help maintain the "confidence and co-operation" of African-American public health professionals.[22] She also hoped the Council would be able to help raise funds for the clinic. As with the CRB, the Harlem clinic's costs were covered by a combination of private donations, patient fees, and Sanger's personal resources. The core of fee-paying white patients helped offset the deficit at the Harlem clinic caused by Harlem's higher rate of nonpaying patients. Most of the clinic's annual costs still had to be met by other means, however, so the need for outside funding remained great.

The members of the Advisory Council came to the project with an understanding of birth control that both shared common ground with white Sangerists and was racially specific. Certainly an ideal of racial betterment was an important principle within the African-American

[20] Advisory Council meeting, minutes, 20 May 1931, MSP-SSC. HBBCCRB, *Annual Report*, 1930, 1931, 1932, 1933, and 1934; letters of Marie Levinson to Margaret Sanger, 11 July 1933; and of Margaret Sanger to Marjorie Prevost, 8 May 1932, MSP-LC. The fee for African-American patients was reduced to $1.00 at the end of 1932, Advisory Council meeting, minutes, 25 January 1933, MSP-LC.

[21] Letter of Antoinette Field to Margaret Sanger, 5 November 1930; list of prospective Advisory Council members, n.d.; letter of Antoinette Field to Margaret Sanger with additional list of names for Harlem Advisory Council, n.d.; letters of Margaret Sanger to Michael Davis, 13 November 1930 and 20 June 1931, and to Antoinette Field, 26 November 1930, MSP-LC.

[22] Letter soliciting members for the Council, dated 2 December 1930 and signed by Margaret Sanger; and letter to prospective Harlem Advisory Council members announcing the organizing meeting, 20 May 1931, signed by Margaret Sanger, MSP-LC. See also Harlem Advisory Council Organization meeting, minutes, 20 May 1931, MSP-SSC; and letter of Margaret Sanger to James Hubert, 3 December 1930, MSP-LC.

community, and birth control served as a tool by which to achieve that goal. Blacks needed birth control, Du Bois had argued in 1922, because they were "becoming sharply divided into the mass who have endless children and the class who through long postponement of marriage have few or none." This pattern robbed the community of the stable childbearing families that would ensure racial progress, because "children" were "the only real Progress, the sole Hope, the sure Victory over Evil." Because "parents owe their children, first of all, health and strength," which birth control facilitated, it enhanced racial progress and integrity. However, Du Bois's ideal of racial progress, unlike Sanger's, was imbued with the vision of securing racial justice. He identifies birth control, along with stable marriage and education, as a tool in African-Americans' ongoing struggle for racial progress within a racist society: "With children brought with thought and foresight into intelligent family circles and trained by parents, teachers, friends, and society, we have Eternal Progress and Eternal Life. Against these, no barriers stand; to them no Problem is insoluble."[23] Like Du Bois, the Advisory Council saw racism as posing the primary obstacles to racial progress. The high infant and maternal mortality rates resulted directly from racial discrimination in housing, education, and employment.[24]

As with the white Sangerists, the ideal of racial progress articulated by African-American birth control advocates dovetailed with an economic ethic of fertility: "Children should come into the world at intervals which will allow for the physical, economic and spiritual recovery of the parents."[25] This mild expression of the economic ethic of fertility by Du Bois in 1922 was more clearly articulated in the 1930s. For example, in his presidential speech of 1932 before the National Medical Association, W. G. Alexander stated, "Mass production of Negro babies has become an anachronism—an economic fallacy with a correlated living problem, that is both a racial and a community liability."[26] Burdened with numerous children born in rapid succession, the family's and community's resources to raise those children were depleted. However, here again the difference between the white economic ethic of

[23] Du Bois, "Opinion," pp. 248, 247, 250, 253.
[24] Advisory Council meeting, minutes, 20 May 1931, MSP-SSC; letter of Alonzo Smith to Margaret Sanger, 28 March 1933; and Advisory Council meeting, minutes, 31 March 1933, MSP-LC for Harold Ellis's reasons for working in the Harlem clinic.
[25] Du Bois, "Opinion," p. 250.
[26] W. G. Alexander, "Birth Control for the Negro," p. 37.

fertility and that articulated by African-Americans is that the latter was connected to a wider culture of opposition. The anachronism to which Alexander refers was produced by racial population politics in which generations of "high pressure methods in the slave business meant the encouragement of prolific reproduction." Fewer children, well reared, would do more to ensure the future of the race.[27] With these statements, Alexander, like other African-Americans, specifically represented their race's high fertility as a legacy of slavery rather than an inherent biological trait. In so doing he opposed the myth of racial degeneracy that dominated white racial thinking in the early twentieth century.[28]

Since the 1870 census inaccurately estimated that the African-American population was declining, white supremacists had been predicting that the "Negro problem" would solve itself. The race's "failure in the struggle for existence" would lead to its extinction. This solution, however, was refuted by early twentieth-century censuses that showed the African-American population was indeed growing. When nature proved unreliable in quickly achieving the white supremacist fantasy of racial homogeneity, government was harnessed to achieve that goal. Political disenfranchisement and rigorous Jim Crow segregation that ensured white supremacy throughout the South was justified by this potent myth of racial degeneracy.[29] Inherent degeneracy also rationalized the abandonment of African-American health care and education by southern states. If the race was dying out anyway, which the death and despair behind the color line seemed to indicate, then its disease and low intelligence were irremediable. The best course of action was simply to ensure the integrity of the white race by segregation. As African-Americans moved north before and after World War I to escape renewed oppression in the South, the myth of degeneracy followed them, justifying Jim Crow laws and willful blindness to horrendous living conditions in the North.[30]

[27] Ibid., p. 36. See also Du Bois, "Opinion"; Peter Marshall Murray, letter to the editor, *BCR* 16 (July–August 1932): 216; E. Franklin Frazier, "Birth Control for *More* Negro Babies"; and Charles H. Garvin, "The Negro Doctor's Task," pp. 269–70.

[28] See also Charles S. Johnson, "A Question of Negro Health," pp. 167–69; Elmer Carter, "Eugenics for the Negro," pp. 169–70; and Newell Sims, "Hostages to the White Man," pp. 214–15, who specifically discuss the degeneracy myth and birth control.

[29] George Fredrickson, *The Black Image in the White Mind*, pp. 256, 257–71, 298–304, 325.

[30] George Fredrickson, *White Supremacy*, pp. 189–91, 274; Edward Beardsley, *A History of Neglect*, pp. 12–27, 130; and Osofsky, *Harlem*, pp. 21–24, 35–37, 42–43.

Yet by the late twenties, intensive research had failed to prove the inherent biological differences between the races that undergirded the myth of degeneracy and the practice of segregation. In fact, science increasingly demonstrated that there were no races; "no measurements of human beings, of bodily development, of head form, of color or hair, of psychological reaction, have succeeded in dividing mankind into different recognizable groups."[31] Such African-American intellectuals as Du Bois, Charles S. Johnson, and E. Franklin Frazier argued that science had instead proved that observed differences between the races were actually the consequence of social and economic circumstances, not of biology. If "the Negro" was less efficient, less moral, and less intelligent than whites—and most of these middle-class intellectuals accepted that some poor, southern Negroes were—then it was because of "his" [*sic*] differences in circumstances. They insisted that the unfavorable traits that white America attributed to blacks were caused by centuries of oppressive exclusion from the mainstream economy and society.[32] If, as they argued, observed differences were not the inherent consequences of race or color, then racial hierarchies were a temporary consequence of prejudicial social organization that could and should be changed. Racial bigotry, they argued, was an irrational attitude sustained by perceptions of blacks as poor, lazy, inferior, and immoral—perceptions reinforced by the low socioeconomic status of the mass of African-Americans. Reflecting the middle-class status of its authors, the logic within this oppositional perspective posited economic improvement as the key route to racial betterment for the entire community. Raise the economic standards of African-Americans, they believed, and prejudice, along with the inequality it supported, could be overcome. The goal of black activism in the thirties was to integrate America racially.[33] Eliminating poverty and assimilating all African-Americans into middle-class culture was their principal strategy for

---

[31] W. E. B. Du Bois, "Race Relations in the United States," in *The American Negro*, p. 6.

[32] Ibid. See also E. Franklin Frazier, "The Negro Family," pp. 44–51; and Charles S. Johnson, "The Changing Economic Status of the Negro," pp. 128–38. I use the generic masculine, which was the custom of the time, to emphasize the tendency in using the concept "the Negro" to represent the African-American community as monolithic and male. See nn. 70 and 119 below.

[33] Kirby, *Black Americans*, pp. 191–202; see also pp. 97–102. Only Du Bois believed that racial prejudice and bigotry were so deeply ingrained in American culture that rational changes in black living standards would not effectively counter racial bigotry. On Du Bois's changing attitudes during the depression see also Raymond Wolters, *Negroes and the Great Depression*, pp. 231–65.

ending racial prejudice.[34] Segregation had not produced two distinct racial cultures; it had only set the terms of an unequal relationship between two classes of the same culture.[35] Since a common culture was assumed, integration and assimilation would be unproblematic; racial integrity was not threatened.[36] Conscious restriction of fertility based on an economic calculus of family resources was one such value that they thought the black community should assimilate.

It was a call to community responsibility for racial betterment that African-American birth control advocates heeded, and there was little mention of individual sexual freedom among their rationales. This may have been partly a result of the times. Sexuality was not generally a topic for public discussion in either racial community.[37] However, the long-standing racist tradition of manipulating images of African-American sexuality to justify repression, as in the discourse on lynching, made sexual respectability a highly charged topic in the African-American culture of opposition. In particular, representations of "Negro promiscuity," as evidenced by the purportedly higher rates of illegitimacy and marital instability, supported the wider myth of racial degeneracy. The connotations of immorality associated with birth control may have made African-American professionals reluctant to broach the subject of sexual freedom explicitly. Their rhetoric invariably situated support for birth control in terms of stabilizing family life, without which there could "be few future workers and torch bearers."[38] Du Bois's early opinion presumes the necessity of a nuclear family in which the mother at home provides the basis of proper rearing. He condemned the trend of illegitimacy as producing "poor, little, in-

[34] Kirby, *Black Americans*. The other main axis of African-American opposition to racism, the separatist black nationalism of Marcus Garvey, was on the wane after 1925 because of government repression. The economic collapse of the thirties further devastated this working-class movement. Garveyism, which many African-American intellectuals disparaged, did not support the birth control movement. On Garvey, see Giddings, *When and Where I Enter*, pp. 180, 193–95; Kirby, *Black Americans*, p. 98; and Omi and Winant, *Racial Formation*, pp. 40–42.

[35] Kirby, *Black Americans*, pp. 196–98; and S. P. Fullinwider, *The Mind and Mood of Black America*, pp. 105–7.

[36] Frazier's opinions changed in the later years of his life, but in the 1930s he was a prominent spokesperson for the "economic" school. See Kirby, *Black Americans*, pp. 153–55, 176–77, 196–98.

[37] Du Bois, "Opinion," p. 247, and "Black Folk and Birth Control," p. 167. In both articles, Du Bois comments on this taboo against public discussion of sexual matters.

[38] Du Bois, "Opinion," p. 253.

nocent waifs, homeless and half–cared for."[39] Women's sexual subjectivity was submerged beneath the rhetoric of family health. Certainly women's right to health always justified birth control, and the notion of a husband's exclusive rights to his wife's childbearing capacities was labeled archaic, but women's sexual rights were not mentioned directly.[40] Perhaps, as one author suggested, because African-American women were not subject to the sexual "hypocrisy and illusions" of white culture, they did not have to fight for the right to pleasure in the same way that white women did.[41] In any case, African-American endorsements represented birth control as a tool by which women could fulfill their duty to help uplift the race through good mothering in stable families.

Sanger's representations of birth control as a tool of family health and economy that promoted racial betterment resonated within the culture of opposition to racism in which the Advisory Council resided. But despite their ideological common ground, conflicts based in racial politics are apparent in the records of the Advisory Council's meetings.

Throughout its history, the Harlem clinic grew slowly and was plagued by financial instability. Obviously a major portion of the clinic's financial problems resulted from its untimely opening at the beginning of the depression. The amount of the Rosenwald grant that had enabled the clinic to be opened was contingent upon the amount of money that Sanger raised independently. Following the standard practice of public health philanthropy, the Rosenwald Fund generally gave short-term seed money to fund demonstration clinics, expecting that worthy projects would become self-sufficient in a short period of time.[42] Although Sanger realized that it would be difficult to make a

[39] Ibid., Frazier, "The Negro Family," p. 45, also discusses the issue of family instability and illegitimacy, and attributes these problems, along with high fertility, to slavery's legacy.

[40] DuBois, "Opinion," p. 250. See also Carl Roberts, "The Birthright of the Unborn," p. 87.

[41] George Schuyler, "Quantity or Quality," p. 165. Or perhaps Schuyler, an author in the New Negro Renaissance that celebrated the natural sensuality of the Negro, overstated the case. Some African-Americans did fear that women's greater independence from hearth and home would lead to race suicide. See Rodrique, "The Black Community," p. 336. See also Sharon Harley, "For the Good of Family and Race," pp. 336–49, who discusses the related topic of wage-earning mothers and the tension in the African-American community about women's roles.

[42] Letters of Margaret Sanger to Edwin Embree, 27 December 1929, and to Antoinette Field, 12 January 1932; and of Margaret Woodbury to Stella Hanau, 28 June 1934, MSP-LC. The Fund, which had reorganized in 1928 to focus on African-American health,

clinic in Harlem self-supporting, she wanted to provide "the opportunity anyway."[43] But what little money was available in the white community to support a birth control clinic vastly exceeded funds available in the African-American community, where the unemployment rate was nearly double that of whites and the cost of relief services nearly bankrupted the community's charitable agencies.[44] The depression also caused a precipitous decline in charitable contributions nationwide, making philanthropic support undependable. The Rosenwald Fund failed to renew its support after 1932, and Carrie Fuld, the primary remaining contributor, made further support contingent on matching funds.[45] But Sangerists discounted the constraints on funding in assessing the clinic's problems. In the October 1932 Council meeting, when Sanger raised the possibility of having to close the clinic, she attributed its slow growth and financial instability to a lack of publicity and to low interest in birth control within the community. In contrast, the Advisory Council repeatedly insisted that the clinic's slow growth and financial problems resulted from racially specific implications of the clinic's location, name, and staff.

The Advisory Council pointed out that the clinic's location on a side street, its identification by a placard containing the word *research,* and its white staff raised suspicions among many potential patients that the clinic intended to encourage race suicide.[46] Birth control "could not find a quick response in a group which has been led to believe that its racial status was dependent on its ability to increase and multiply." In a context in which "social and economic forces" are "aimed at their

---

usually required recipients to bear part of the costs. See Beardsley, *A History of Neglect,* pp. 115–16; and James H. Jones, *Bad Blood,* p. 54.

[43] Letters of Margaret Sanger to Edwin Embree, 27 December 1929, and to Rosenwald Fund, 29 December 1930 and 28 August 1931, MSP-LC.

[44] In fact, the Urban League was forced, because of financial problems of its own, to insist that the clinic pay rent for the space it utilized. Advisory Council meeting, minutes, 21 February, MSP-LC, and 13 November 1934, MSP-SSC; and letters of Margaret Sanger to Julius Rosenwald, 29 December 1930, to Michael Davis, 31 January 1931, and of William Lloyd Imes to the HBBCCRB staff, 14 March 1934, MSP-LC.

[45] Letters of Rosenwald Fund to Margaret Sanger, 29 January 1932; of Margaret Sanger to Michael Davis, 23 March and 30 December 1932; and of Michael Davis to Margaret Sanger, 12 November 1932, MSP-LC. The Rosenwald Fund was suffering from its own financial crisis and suspended funding of many of its projects in early 1932. See Beardsley, *A History of Neglect,* pp. 117–18. See also Kenneth Manning, *Black Apollo of Science,* pp. 121–23, 157, 182, 206, 242–43.

[46] Advisory Council meeting, minutes, 20 May 1931 and 25 October 1932, MSP-SSC; and 17 June, 23 September, and 28 October 1931, 25 January 1933, and 21 February 1934, MSP-LC.

destruction," conscious restriction of birth seemed to aid the effort to extinguish the race.[47] Although African-American supporters disputed the logic that restricting fertility would lead to race suicide, they certainly understood that birth control promoted by whites could easily be perceived as the newest plan to promote the race's extinction.[48] The Council argued throughout 1931–32 that, at the very least, African-Americans had to be included on the staff before the community's trust could be won. The presence of blacks on the clinic staff would help to demonstrate that there was no intent to promote race suicide.[49] Staff changes would also alleviate the community's related suspicion that the clinic was a segregationist establishment designed to conduct bizarre experiments on Harlem's women.[50] Fear that white doctors would use them for experiments made many blacks reluctant to use health services provided by whites.[51] The Council members argued that given greater authority they would prevent such community relations problems in the future. After all, as residents of the community, they were well acquainted with its reservations about birth control and were best able to address them.

Sanger readily agreed to give the Council greater say in the clinic's educational work.[52] But less easily convinced that the clinic's name, staff, and location were problems, she initially insisted that greater publicity alone would overcome the community's suspicions.[53] The ra-

---

[47] Carter, "Eugenics for the Negro," p. 169; Schuyler, "Quantity or Quality," p. 165.

[48] For explicit arguments against the notion that prolific reproduction would prevent race suicide see Carter, "Eugenics for the Negro"; Schuyler, "Quantity or Quality"; Sims, "Hostages to the White Man"; Garvin, "The Negro Doctor's Task"; Johnson, "A Question"; Du Bois, "Black Folk"; and Lemuel Sewell, "The Negro Wants Birth Control," p. 131. The fact that nearly all African-American authors address this issue indicates that they perceived it to be a very important and widespread concern.

[49] Advisory Council meeting, minutes, 23 March and 25 October 1932, MSP-SSC.

[50] "The Feminist Viewpoint," *New York Amsterdam News*, 5 September 1932, contains a statement that the Harlem clinic was not opened as a segregation measure. Letters indicate, however, that white patients at the downtown clinic had complained about having to share the waiting room with black women. Although the CRB staff never turned black women away, they were aware that the presence of African-American women in the clinic caused tension. Letters of Margaret Sanger to Morris Waldman, 2 July 1929, to Julius Rosenwald, 9 October 1929, and to the New York Foundation, 20 November 1929, MSP-LC.

[51] Beardsley, *A History of Neglect*, pp. 35–39.

[52] Advisory Council meeting, minutes, 20 May 1931, and 23 March and 25 October 1932, MSP-SSC; and 25 January 1933, MSP-LC.

[53] Advisory Council meeting, minutes, 25 October 1932, MSP-SSC; and letter of Margaret Sanger to Marjorie Prevost 11 April 1932, MSP-LC. Records support the Council's view. Of those women attending the clinic in 1930 and 1931, 56 percent were referred by other patients and friends; only 11 percent were referred by publicity.

cial implications of the name, in comparison to the legal constraints on the clinic's operation, did not constitute sufficient grounds for removing the word *research*.[54] The suspicion provoked by the name was discounted by Sangerists as superstitious misunderstanding of science, not a reasonable assessment of racial politics. But by October 1932 she agreed to add the words *birth control* to the clinic placard. At the end of 1932, under severe financial strain, the clinic was moved to a more central location in the Urban League building. By January 1933, an African-American physician, Harold Ellis, two African-American nurses, Lou Thompson and Dorothy Ruddick, and a social worker, Emmy Jenkins, had been hired to work in the clinic. From that point on, the clinic staff was predominantly African-American. The accuracy of the Advisory Council's argument became clear when, after these changes, more African-American women used the clinic.[55]

Although the Council's advice was accurate and Sanger did finally agree to their recommended changes, the issues at stake in the Council meetings went beyond questions of the clinic's staff, location, and name. The report of M. O. Bousfield, the African-American physician sent by the Rosenwald Fund to inspect the clinic, aptly described— although referring specifically to Hannah Stone—the racial dynamics in the clinic's operation. He noted that "trying to work out one social problem (Birth Control) . . . [she] suddenly found herself enmeshed in another (color or race.) She did not have the patience to see it through."[56] Part of Sanger's resistance to the Council's advice resulted from her reluctance to let any group of supporters have authority

[54] Although it was a deterrent to African-Americans, the clinic's name was an attempt to comply with the law restricting the word *clinic* to licensed agencies. See Chapter 3. Sangerist clinics were determined not to contribute to the dangerous conditions under which women attempted to control their fertility but rather to end them, and therefore they refused to experiment with untried methods.

[55] HBBCCRB, annual report, 1933–34, MSP-SSC. Letter of Marie Levinson to Margaret Sanger, 11 July 1933, MSP-LC. Advisory Council meeting, minutes, 25 October 1932, MSP-SSC; and 25 January and 31 March 1933, MSP-LC. Having difficulties with the clinic landlord, Sanger wanted to move as well. Harold Ellis participated in the clinic and Council beginning in 1932. He was hired to work in the clinic on a regular basis in 1933 and was the first and only man to work in Sanger's clinics until the 1940s, when Grant Sanger and Abraham Stone worked in the CRB. See letter of Margaret Sanger to Harold Ellis, 4 May 1933, MSP-LC.

[56] Letter of M. O. Bousfield to Michael Davis, 9 April 1932, MSP-LC. Bousfield was hired by the Rosenwald Fund a year later to oversee its Negro health programs. See Beardsley, *A History of Neglect*, pp. 88–93. Michael Davis, Medical Director of the Rosenwald Fund and one of the nation's leading authorities on alternatives to fee-for-service medicine, was a long-term advisor to Sanger. On Davis's career see Jones, *Bad Blood*, pp. 53–55, 83–89, 93–94; and Beardsley, *A History of Neglect*, pp. 89–90, 115–16.

within the clinics. Throughout her career, Sanger used similar advisory councils to generate public support, legitimacy, and funding, but she always resisted the intrusion of advisors into the clinics' practices. With respect to white physicians and scientists, Sangerists resisted the dominance of clinic practices by those socially more powerful groups. Unlike the professionals who advised the CRB, however, the Harlem Council members were not socially more powerful than white Sangerists. Their stance toward the Harlem Advisory Council, while consistent with that which they held to all advisors, nonetheless manifested their underlying racial thinking: Sangerists hoped African-American supporters would be reliable. Like their assessment of the Harlem Council, Sangerists' representation of the project as meeting a need that "the race did not recognize" for itself announced their assent to dominant racial ideology.[57]

Sangerists began the clinic with the belief that African-Americans had a special need for and a special difficulty with birth control. In their view, African-Americans in particular needed birth control because their greater fertility and more precarious economic status led to their higher rates of maternal and infant mortality. Like all other women, African-American women deserved the right to use this tool of racial health and betterment. Yet Sangerists anticipated that African-American women would have special problems with birth control. Like many white Americans in the 1930s, Sangerists believed that the "Negro race" contained many incompetent people who were guided by superstition rather than by scientific reasoning. Given this presumed greater incompetence, African-Americans would probably have greater difficulty using "scientific" birth control techniques and initially would especially need the clinic's expert guidance and instruction. Sanger was willing to provide African-American women with equal access to birth control as their right, but because of her racial maternalism she did not expect many to take advantage of that opportunity without special educational efforts to convince them that fertility control existed and was useful.[58] Racial maternalism initially

[57] Letter of Margaret Sanger to Julius Rosenwald, 9 October 1929, MSP-LC; Hannah Stone, Advisory Council meeting, minutes, 23 March 1932, MSP-SSC.

[58] Letters of Margaret Sanger to Julius Rosenwald, 9 October 1929; of Morris Waldman to Jacob Billikopf, 21 June 1929; of Margaret Sanger to Morris Waldman, 21 June, 21 July, and 7 October 1929; and of Margaret Sanger to the New York Foundation, 20 November 1929, MSP-LC. Margaret Sanger in a letter to Edwin Embree, 10 May 1930, MSP-SSC, comments with surprise that black women seemed to use birth control with more care.

blinded white Sangerists to the legitimacy of race-suicide fear; they misinterpreted it as low-interest. Given this perspective, they were not surprised by the low level of interest in the clinic; it fit with their racial expectations. Thus although the clinic represented an effort to give African-American women access to contraception, white Sangerists assumed a position of racial superiority, envisioning the clinic as granting the gift of reproductive self-control to African-American women.

I do not want to overstate the racial prejudice in Sanger's perspective; she would not tolerate bigotry among her staff. When the white manager of the CRB expressed her unwillingness to take on the management of a clinic in Harlem, she was sharply admonished by Sanger for her prejudice and threatened with dismissal.[59] When Sanger became aware of the Advisory Council's feeling that Hannah Stone's racial attitudes obstructed the Harlem clinic's work, Sanger replaced her with Marie Levinson, who the Council felt worked well in an interracial context.[60] She also disputed the ideology of racial degeneracy expressed in the belief that African-Americans were incapable of using birth control. She hoped, in part, that the Harlem clinic would demonstrate to white America that black women wanted contraception and would, if given proper instruction, use it effectively, and she publicized the clinic's work to that end.

Annual reports of the clinic's activities and its patient profiles were carefully constructed within a discourse of racial equality that contested the dominant ideology of inherent differences between the races. Again and again the similarity between African-Americans' and whites' interest in, need for, and use of birth control was stressed in such reports. In the 1934 *Annual Report,* for instance, the patient profiles clearly stated that African-American and white women came to the clinic after a similar number of years of marriage (seven years), and both groups had a similar number of living children (three for whites, four for blacks). It clearly stated that black and white couples had simi-

[59] Letters of Marjorie Prevost to Margaret Sanger, 19 January 1932; of Margaret Sanger to Marjorie Prevost, 27 January 1932, and of Margaret Sanger to Antoinette Field, 8 December 1930, MSP-LC.

[60] One of the problems the Council had with Stone was that she wanted to require patients to see only doctors of the same race. Letters of M. O. Bousfield to Michael Davis, 9 April 1932; of Margaret Sanger to Hannah Stone, 23 April and 26 May 1932; and of Hannah Stone to Margaret Sanger, 26 April 1932; "Report on Dr. Levinson's Lecture at the National Urban League," 17 January 1933; letter of S. A. Allen to Margaret Sanger, 8 February 1933, MSP-LC; Advisory Council meeting, minutes, 25 January and 31 May 1933, MSP-LC.

lar sexual habits and that both groups of women had tried "make-shift" methods before attending the clinic. But most important, the profiles showed that both "Negro and white women learned and applied the clinic's birth control methods equally well with 95 percent success. . . ."[61] When differences were noted, they were attributed to economic rather than biological differences. The comparison of family size stressed the higher infant mortality among African-Americans and attributed it to their greater unemployment rates. Also, this comparison was constructed in a way that obscured any differential total fertility rate between the two groups of patients. The exact sentence read, "There were an average of four living children and 47% dead per Negro family, and three living children and 23% dead per white family."[62] This awkward phrasing makes the higher infant mortality among African-Americans quite obvious but requires readers to calculate for themselves the total pregnancies for each group before a difference in fertility rates is visible.

Despite her assumed superiority, Sanger would not abide bigotry or the refusal to work within interracial projects. The racial expectations that Sanger displayed in managing the Harlem clinic places her well within 1930s race liberalism. Even race liberals assumed that, although they were similar, African-Americans were in some degree inferior to whites. The key was that race liberals believed that their inferiority, not biologically inevitable, was remediable.[63] And Sangerists, like other race liberals in the thirties, worked in coalition with African-Americans to uplift the race.[64] Yet given the posture of superiority, why did the Council members respond to Sanger's proposed closing of the clinic in 1932 with a vigorous effort both to generate greater community support for the clinic and to convince Sanger to keep the clinic open?[65] In part, the Council continued to work with the CRB because

[61] Marie Warner, "Birth Control and the Negro," HBBCCRB, pamphlet, 1934, pp. 4–5. Warner is Marie Levinson's married name.

[62] Ibid., p. 4.

[63] See Kirby, *Black Americans*, pp. 76–96, 231–32. See also Peter Kellog, "Northern Liberals and Black America."

[64] On the relationship between African-Americans and white reformers in the infant and maternal welfare movement, see Muncy, *Creating a Female Dominion*, pp. 117–18; and Meckel, *Save The Babies*, pp. 132, 142.

[65] There was a spate of activity in the community, including speeches and editorials, and letters to Sanger stressing the clinic's importance in late 1932 and early 1933. See Lucien Brown, "Keeping Fit," *New York Amsterdam News*, 28 November 1932; Willa Murray, "Report—Tea for Social Workers in Harlem," 18 January 1933; and letter of Alonzo Smith to Margaret Sanger, 28 March 1933, MSP-LC.

it was the only clinic available to provide birth control services. African-American physicians and nurses did not receive training in contraception any more than did whites. Also, many of the Council members were active in other efforts to integrate medical care. That they should continue to press for inclusion of African-Americans in this particular health service was consistent with their political activity in general.[66] Finally, the Advisory Council, although it insisted on equal opportunity, simultaneously expressed pejorative attitudes toward the poor of their community that were not so dissimilar from Sanger's.

Like that of any members of an oppressed population, the Council members' consciousness consisted of a contradictory mix of opposition and adherence to ideological elements of the dominant culture. Northern-born blacks and older southern migrants regarded the new migrants of the twenties with some disdain and often complained that their low standards of behavior caused the increasing racial hostilities in the North. Middle-class African-Americans often complained that they were unfairly judged by the behaviors of the race's lowest elements. The National Urban League's social uplift program to aid new migrants from the South adjust to urban life was two-edged. It provided needed instruction in the use of urban housing and employment technologies to rural migrants. But it also promoted "accepted standards" of cleanliness, appearance, and comportment for those who were ignorant of urban customs.[67]

With regard to proper standards of birth control, the rhetoric of African-American birth control advocates likewise had a double edge. It both opposed racism and described the poorer segments of the race in disparaging terms reminiscent of eugenics. These middle-class African-Americans opposed eugenic appraisals of the Negro race as a race. Yet their rhetoric reprised eugenic idioms when it came to assessing the implications of fertility patterns within their community. Ironically, these eugenic echoes appeared most frequently in statements opposing the belief that birth control meant race suicide. Du Bois observed in 1932 that "the increase among Negroes, even more than the increase

[66] Beardsley, *A History of Neglect*, pp. 80, 90–93, on the other activities of African-American physicians. M. O. Bousfield, "Reaching the Negro Community," pp. 209–15, forthrightly discusses what whites must do to include African-Americans. See Darlene Clark Hine, *Black Women in White*, pp. 115–21, 128–29, on African-American nurses.

[67] Nancy Weiss, *The National Urban League, 1910–1940*, pp. 117–25, 171–73. This program included tip sheets on appearance and public behavior. See also Osofsky, *Harlem*, pp. 131–35, on African-American nativism, and pp. 42–45, on antipathy to recent southern migrants.

among whites, is from that part of the population least intelligent and fit, and least able to rear their children properly."[68] He was not alone. Others observed as well the differential pattern of fertility where "the Negro who, in addition to the handicaps of race and color, is shackled by mental and social incompetence serenely goes on his way bringing into the world children whose chances of mere existence are apparently becoming more and more haphazard."[69] Such disparaging comments went hand in hand with indictments of the racial politics that produced the "Negro incompetence."

The combination of clear insight into the consequences of racism and condescension toward the poor can be seen in a 1932 editorial written by Lucien Brown in the African-American *New York Amsterdam News*. The editorial extolled the "vital importance" of birth control to Harlem residents, saying that "it offers one definite means of raising [the Negro] to a higher standard of physical fitness, mental capacity and financial stability." Noting low attendance at the clinic, Brown attempts to explain the "apparent indifference" of the community to the clinic. "Certainly, it isn't that he doesn't need much help along birth control lines. On the contrary, his low position in the economic scale of life, which to a marked degree is responsible for the high infant mortality, should recommend this group for even special consideration along these lines." He concludes by saying, "The preponderance of backwardness in the race is too great a handicap and must be taken care of if it expects to enjoy the full measure of respect and opportunity from others."[70]

In addition, African-American Sangerists agreed that poor blacks needed the guidance of scientific health professionals to utilize contraceptive technologies most effectively. Here, again, the double edges of resistance to racism and deprecation of the masses is evident. Support-

[68] Du Bois, "Black Folk," p. 166. Gordon's conclusion that the DNS was conservative is based on the statements in this article, which include: "The mass of ignorant Negroes still breed carelessly and disastrously. . . ." Gordon mistakenly attributes these statements to Sanger, p. 332. Valenza provides valuable documentation of the numerous cases in which Kennedy and Gordon misquote Sanger's views on race and eugenics (pp. 44–46).

[69] Carter, "Eugenics for the Negro," p. 169. See also Garvin, "The Negro Doctor's Task," p. 169; and E. Franklin Frazier, "The Negro and Birth Control," p. 70.

[70] Lucien Brown, "Keeping Fit," *New York Amsterdam News*, 28 November 1932. As one can see by Brown's use of the masculine pronoun in the quotations here, birth control was not exclusively a women's issue but rather a community issue, and in the 1930s among both African-Americans and whites the terms *community* and *the Negro* were generically male.

ers explicitly opposed the situation in which African-American women, who had no access to clinics, were left to seek relief from "grossly inadequate quacks." But calls for greater access to reliable contraceptive services also often disparaged the poor as those who "do greater violence than good to themselves through reliance upon dangerous folk measures."[71]

The Advisory Council disputed the racial thought of white Sangerists. Yet they held a similar posture of superiority toward the poor that provided common ground for their continued support of the Harlem clinic. Where they differed from Sanger, the Advisory Council was able effectively to influence her management of the clinic, as was evident in the changes of name, location, and staff. The Council's effective influence is apparent as well in clinic pamphlets that, after 1932, took care to address suspicions that the clinic promoted race suicide and experimentation. Although the main clinic's materials defined birth control as a "method of avoiding conception by preventing the union of the male sperm and the female ovum," the Harlem clinic's pamphlet prefaced this definition with the word "harmless." It then went on to explain that birth control "is merely a temporary means of preventing undesired pregnancies. It never affects the ability of the mother to have children when she so desires."[72] Also, while all clinic pamphlets distinguished birth control from abortion, the Harlem clinic's materials also distinguished birth control from sterilization, thus reiterating the temporary and voluntary nature of the birth control offered in the Harlem clinic.[73]

The sensitivity in the clinic pamphlets to race suicide and experimentation fears, and the rhetoric of racial equality in general publications demonstrate that the Council did influence Sanger and her associates' racial perspective. I do not, however, want to give the impression that the Harlem clinic experience riveted Sanger's commitment to African-American reproductive self-determination. It did not. The fragile nature of her commitment and of the coalition behind the Harlem clinic became obvious in 1935. As the depression worsened it be-

[71] Carter, "Eugenics for the Negro," p. 169; and Johnson, "A Question," p. 169. See also Du Bois, "Black Folk," p. 167; Alexander, "Birth Control for the Negro," p. 38; and Constance Fisher, "The Negro Social Worker Evaluates Birth Control," pp. 174–75.

[72] Marie Warner, "Birth Control and the Negro," HBBCCRB, pamphlet, 1934, p. 2.

[73] See Rodrique, "The Black Community," p. 338, on African-Americans' opposition to compulsory sterilization in the 1930s.

came increasingly difficult to fund the clinic. Sanger did not want to see the clinic closed and hoped to get the clinic to a point where the community would take over its management and fundraising.[74] The New York City Committee of Mothers' Health Centers, formerly the Junior Committee of the ABCL, had been quietly organizing contraceptive centers in existing settlement houses, day nurseries, and health centers since 1930; and early in 1935 the Committee approached the CRB about taking over its Harlem branch.[75] Saying that they had received funding to open a clinic in Harlem, they proposed to assume management of the existing clinic rather than duplicate efforts in a time of financial crisis. Despite the enormous friction between Sanger and the ABCL during this period, Sanger agreed because she was increasingly hard-pressed to fund both clinics. But she stipulated that the same principles of cooperation should be maintained and that she, Stone, and the Advisory Council be retained as members of the new clinic Advisory Board.[76] Although the takeover plans appear to have been made without their input, the Advisory Council concurred with the plan because they were to remain as the advisors to the New York City Committee clinic, which would be a free clinic with firm financial backing.[77]

The New York Committee took over the Harlem clinic in June, and the animosity between the CRB and the ABCL immediately spilled over into the management of the Harlem clinic. The new Board of Directors drastically cut back the clinic's hours and ignored the ex-

[74] Letters of Margaret Sanger to Michael Davis, 9 December 1932; of Mabel Staupers to Margaret Sanger, 13 March 1935; and of Hazel Zborowski to Margaret Sanger, 15 March 1935, MSP-LC.

[75] These centers were not independent clinical services; they merely added contraceptive prescription for several hours a week to each agency's existing health care services. The individual agencies donated the space, and the New York Committee provided the nursing staff and supplies. See Carol Nash, "Planned Families for New York Mothers," pp. 128–29.

[76] Letters of Margaret Sanger to Mabel Staupers, 7 August 1935, to Frances Ackerman, 10 May 1935, and to Carrie Fuld, c. 10 May 1935; and of Florence Rose to Edwin Embree, 8 January 1936, MSP-LC. About the Committee offer, see letters of Margaret Sanger to James Hubert, NUL, 11 June 1935, and to Allison Moore, 21 June 1935, MSP-SSC.

[77] The ABCL clinic was to be a free clinic, with donations of more than ten cents gratefully accepted. The CRB was a fee-for-service clinic in which fees were waived if a woman was unable to pay. Joint meeting ABCL, CRB, and NUL, minutes, 28 May 1935; letters of Margaret Sanger to James Hubert, 11 June 1935, and to Allison Moore, 21 June 1935, MSP-SSC; letter of Percy Clark to Margaret Sanger, 18 September 1936, MSP-LC.

isting Council, Stone, and Sanger.[78] Mabel Staupers criticized these actions, pointing particularly to their implied paternalism:

> I resent the attitude of the New York Committee toward the Advisory Council when they assumed control of the Clinic. . . . If the Birth Control Association wishes the cooperation of Negroes, especially in the nursing profession, I feel that we should be treated with the proper courtesy that is due us and not with the usual childish procedures that are maintained with any work that is being done for Negroes. I feel that if any work is being done for Negroes in any community, Negroes should share in the planning and in the expense to the best of their ability.
>
> I shall always have faith in the Birth Control Movement and do everything in my power to cooperate, but sincerely hope that you and your associates will discontinue the practice of looking on us as children to be cared for and not to help decide how the caring should be done.[79]

Sanger expressed her shock at the Committee's actions and attempted to dissociate herself from attitudes implied by them. She wrote,

> It is needless perhaps of me to say that I am utterly shocked at what you tell me regarding the situation of the Harlem Birth Control Clinic. You must know what my own attitude is towards negroes and how much I deplore the sort of thing that you mention. I think the records of the Clinical Research Bureau will speak for the fullest and most wholehearted cooperation between the negroes and the birth control work since first we established our clinic in Harlem.

Sanger concludes,

> I especially emphasized to the members of the Committee that the most cordial relations had always existed between our own Clinic and the Clinic in Harlem. I was assured that this would be continued because . . . all of the Committee members I spoke with expressed a

[78] Letters of Margaret Sanger to Allison Moore, 21 June 1935; and of Allison Moore to Dr. Stone, 1 February 1936, MSP-SSC; Board meeting, minutes, CRB, 6 December 1935 and 6 January 1936, and letter of Florence Rose to Edwin Embree, 8 January 1936, MSP-LC.

[79] Letter of Mabel Staupers to Margaret Sanger, 2 April 1935, MSP-LC. Despite her anger at this incident, Mabel Staupers continued to work with Sangerists for many years after the Harlem clinic changed hands. Letter of Florence Rose to Carrie Fuld, 17 November 1941, FRP-SSC, refers to Mabel Staupers's work over the years.

keen interest in the advancement and progress and welfare of the colored people. So naturally I felt that the little clinic in Harlem could be given over in good hands.[80]

Although Sanger deplored the Committee's actions, the racial maternalism articulated in her own management of the "little clinic in Harlem" was not much different. Sanger's cordiality to the Advisory Council was the largess of a patron toward a diminutive affiliate. Her exchanges with the ABCL to redress Staupers's complaints merely degenerated into a squabble over which group was to blame for the difficulties.[81] The CRB did nothing else to redress the services lost to African-American women. It is unclear whether the New York Committee actions were intentionally patronizing to the Advisory Council or if the Council was snubbed as a result of the friction with Sanger. It is telling, in any case, that the Committee made no immediate effort to maintain good relations with the existing Advisory Council.[82] In later years Sanger accused the New York Committee of killing the Harlem clinic, although it hobbled along until at least 1940, when a tenth-anniversary celebration was held.[83]

The history of the Harlem clinic reveals the complexity of racial maternalism within the birth control movement, in which opportunity was both granted and denied. The experience did make Sanger more sensitive to African-American concerns about birth control and about the need to involve African-Americans in projects in their communities. However, white birth control advocates continued to be the arbiters of African-American concerns and involvements, as became evident in

[80] Letter of Margaret Sanger to Mabel Staupers, 7 August 1935, MSP-LC.

[81] The ABCL accused Sanger of trying to get rid of the clinic because it was not making a profit; Sanger accused them of misrepresenting their intentions for the clinic. See joint ABCL, CRB, and NUL meeting, minutes, 28 May 1935; and letters of Margaret Sanger to Allison Moore, 21 June 1935, MSP-SSC, and to Hazel Zborowski, 20 May 1935, MSP-LC.

[82] Eight months after it took over the Harlem clinic, the ABCL tried to set up a new Harlem Council in response to Stone's prodding. Staupers was contacted about it. Letters of Hannah Stone to Allison Moore, 29 January 1936, MSP-LC; and of Allison Moore to Hannah Stone, 1 February 1936, MSP-SSC, and to Mabel Staupers, 28 February 1936; and Board meeting minutes, ABCL, 21 November 1935, MSP-LC.

[83] The Harlem clinic did continue, closing briefly in 1936. But after the transfer, it was represented as the innovation of the New York Committee alone. See handwritten notation, in Sanger's handwriting, on letter of Robert L. Dickinson to Margaret Sanger, ca. 1937, MSP-SSC; invitation, New York City Committee on Mother's Health, commemoration of ten years of service in Harlem, 1945, FRP-SSC; and roundtable, minutes, 30 December 1936, p. 7, MSP-LC.

Planned Parenthood's Division of Negro Service, where the pattern of interracial interaction followed in Harlem was repeated.

The Division of Negro Service[84]

Beginning in the midthirties, the birth control movement began to focus on winning state financing of contraceptive clinics. In part this was a response to declining contributions. In part it was a response to renewed public commitment to maternal and infant health. Sangerists organized this effort by drawing on an extensive national network of support for the National Committee on Federal Legislation for Birth Control (NCFL) to encourage local, state, and county health services to request funding for contraceptive clinics under New Deal health legislation. This effort was not very successful, as will be discussed in Chapter 6. But in venturing into southern states in 1937, fieldworkers began to pay particular attention to the problem of organizing local clinics in segregated communities. Confronted by the exclusion of African-Americans from the existing white medical or social welfare institutions, the movement saw again the great need for funding especially earmarked for an educational project among southern blacks. Such funds would allow the national organization to subsidize any birth control clinics in African-American communities by providing informational literature, physician training, and especially contraceptive supplies.[85]

After several years of effort, Sanger's canvassing of philanthropic resources paid off in December 1938 with a grant of $20,000 from Albert Lasker. Lasker, who had not previously been involved with the movement, was initially troubled by the racial specificity of the project and wrote to Sanger: "It does occur to me that a good many of the poor white people are no better off than a good many of the Negroes down there and is it fair just to confine the work to Negroes?"[86] Sanger

[84] This name was coined by Paul Cornely, professor of preventative medicine and public health, Howard University, and member of the DNS National Advisory Committee. "Biographical Data Concerning Key Negroes Attending Washington Meeting," 17 January 1942, FRP-SSC.

[85] Hazel Moore, field reports, 1937 and 1938, MSP-SSC; letters of Willa Murray to Margaret Sanger, 22 March 1933; and of Margaret Sanger to Hazel Moore, 18 October 1935, and to Edwin Embree, 22 June 1937; Edna McKinnon, field reports, February 1937, MSP-LC; and Florence Rose, report on National Medical Association meeting, 8 September 1941, FRP-SSC.

[86] Letter of Albert Lasker to Margaret Sanger, 3 November 1939, MSP-SSC. Letter of Florence Rose to Fannie Hurst, 12 March 1942, FRP-SSC, refers to Sanger's years of

responded that Lasker was "right in assuming" that poor southern whites were "not much better off than the Negroes," but, she noted, "there has been at least a start in several states to help the poor white." As for African-Americans, "They are just left out of the service in most states. That is why I was anxious to have a special fund directed for the Negroes."[87]

Sanger envisioned that the grant would be used to finance an educational campaign among southern blacks. She wanted to hire two African-Americans to carry out the same kind of organizing work that white fieldworkers had been doing. "After one year of education agitation among the colored people, we could then support a practical campaign for supplying the mothers with contraceptives."[88] But the other leaders of the BCFA had different ideas about the project. Clarence Gamble, the Proctor & Gamble heir, who was instrumental in securing this grant from Lasker and had championed projects designed to disseminate low-cost birth control to the poor throughout the 1930s, proposed that the Lasker grant be used to set up a demonstration project in which a birth control clinic for "needy Negroes" would be financed for two years.[89]

These two proposals addressed very distinct audiences. Sanger's proposed campaign would address African-Americans, enabling them to meet their own community's needs. It would train black physicians and nurses to provide contraceptive services in their communities and would stimulate the organization of local clinics. The Federation's plan would be addressed primarily to southern, and thus white, state officials. The goal was to demonstrate to those officials that contraceptive clinics for African-Americans would be valuable additions to existing

---

effort to secure such funds before the Lasker grant. Lasker's future wife, Mary Reinhardt, was an active member of the Birth Control Federation and was responsible for convincing Lasker to make the donation. By this time the American Birth Control League and the Birth Control Clinical Research Bureau had reconciled their differences and reunited into the Birth Control Federation of America. The merger of these two organizations and the resultant changes in style and strategies are discussed here in Chapter 6.

[87] Letter of Margaret Sanger to Albert Lasker, 12 November 1939, MSP-SSC.

[88] Letter of Margaret Sanger to Clarence Gamble, 26 November 1939, MSP-SSC.

[89] Letter of Clarence Gamble to Mary Reinhardt, 1 November 1939, CJG-CL. Gamble had given such supplemental funds to various birth control clinics between 1935 and 1940. This practice of Gamble's caused conflict between Gamble and the BCFA. See especially, letters of Allison Moore to Clarence Gamble, 10 March 1937; of Clarence Gamble to Allison Moore, 8 April 1937, CJG-CL; and of D. Kenneth Rose to Clarence Gamble, 20 February and 3 March 1942, CJG-CL. For biographical information on Gamble see Reed, *The Birth Control Movement*, pp. 252–56.

state health programs. Studies would be done in connection with the clinic to show 1) that African-Americans could be taught to use birth control; 2) that birth control was useful in reducing maternal and infant mortality; and 3) that birth control was useful in reducing the number of people dependent upon relief.[90]

Sanger strenuously objected to a demonstration clinic and struggled over it for several months with Gamble, Lasker, and the Federation. Since there were already several clinics nationwide that served African-Americans and were hard-pressed for resources, a new demonstration clinic was redundant.[91] When in early 1939 North and South Carolina, both of which already had white-only birth control clinics, were proposed as sites for the African-American demonstration project, Sanger objected, noting that "naturally one would ask why North and South Carolina does [*sic*] not already give such information and supplies to their colored people." Besides the objectionable segregation in the plan, she did not believe that "this project should be directed or run by white medical men." Instead, "the Federation should direct it with the guidance and assistance of the colored group."[92] Such organizing was the first step, in Sanger's view: "Someone in the office must be familiar with conditions, not only from the Southern viewpoint, but from the point of view of the leaders among the Negroes. This is most essential; otherwise people in the office are just writing at random without direction, without vision and knowledge." The demonstration clinic exemplified this lack of vision. It would be too small to meet the needs of the wider African-American population, and it would do little to dispel their fears of birth control. Her reason for supporting an educational campaign was precisely to provide a means to cope with the sensitivities of the African-American community to the subject.[93]

From her experience in the Harlem clinic, Sanger knew that projects designed *for* African-Americans without input *from* African-Ameri-

[90] Letters of Clarence Gamble to Margaret Sanger, 25 January 1940 and 2 December 1939, MSP-SSC; of Woodbridge Morris to John Overton, 6 February 1940; and of Clarence Gamble to Florence Rose, 26 January 1940, CJG-CL. Gamble's objectives in the DNS were comparable to those of other projects he funded. See Reed, *The Birth Control Movement*, pp. 248–56.

[91] See Hazel Moore, field reports, 1937–39; "Virginia Project Possibilities," 1939, MSP-SSC; and Edna McKinnon, field reports, February 1937, MSP-LC.

[92] Letters of Margaret Sanger to Clarence Gamble, 26 November 1939. See also letter of Margaret Sanger to Clarence Gamble 10 December 1939, MSP-SSC.

[93] Letter of Margaret Sanger to Clarence Gamble, 17 December 1939, MSP-SSC. See also letters of Margaret Sanger to Cecil Damon, 24 November 1939, FRP-SSC, and to Robert Seibels, 12 February 1940, CJG-CL.

cans were destined to fail. Most blacks would be suspicious of a birth control program provided and endorsed solely by whites. She did not want thoughtless and careless organizing to create an erroneous suspicion of genocide that would limit the effectiveness of DNS programs. Beyond the suspicions generated by an all-white staff, which would keep many women away, the Harlem clinic had shown her that African-American women were more willing to "lay their cards on the table, which means their ignorance, superstitions and doubts," if they were dealing with a doctor of their own race.[94] Mabel Staupers concurred with these observations at a 1942 PPFA meeting to discuss continuing outreach to African-American leaders. Staupers argued that without the support of these leaders "there will be difficulty in having families absorb such knowledge; but if it comes to them through people in whom they already have confidence, their natural eagerness to stay well will provide the necessary stimulus."[95]

Ultimately, Sanger lost the internal struggle over how to do birth control work among African-Americans. In January 1940 Albert Lasker vetoed all educational work in favor of two demonstration projects. He wanted his grant to provide contraception directly to African-Americans. Lasker's goal was not, however, strictly to provide a service to black women. He wanted the grant to produce "a piece of birth control work which would be so striking that it could be used to convince leaders everywhere of the fundamental importance of birth control."[96] Between 1940 and 1942 two city clinics in Nashville, Tennessee, and clinical programs in several rural counties of South Carolina were operated by white physicians as demonstration clinics.

John Overton, the city health officer who had supervised the Nashville Health Department's white-only contraceptive clinic since it

[94] Letter of Margaret Sanger to Clarence Gamble, 10 December 1939, MSP-SSC. Gordon quotes Sanger as saying, "We do not want word to get out that we want to exterminate the Negro population," as evidence to substantiate Sanger's racism. Replacing this quotation into its context of the full letter and the series of which it is part demonstrates that Sanger's concern was to hire African-Americans in order to try to avoid the erroneous impression that the DNS's motives were genocidal. Sanger's position consistently opposed a few demonstration clinics run by white doctors as suggesting race suicide. See Gordon, *Woman's Body*, p. 332. See also Valenza, "Was Margaret Sanger a Racist?" pp. 44–46; and letters of Margaret Sanger to Cecil Damon, 24 November 1939, FRP-SSC, to Clarence Gamble, 26 November 1939, MSP-SSC, and 17 December 1939, FRP-SSC, and 4 February 1940, and to Florence Rose, 8 March 1941, MSP-SSC.

[95] Mabel Staupers, quoted in National Negro Advisory Council meeting, minutes, PPFA, 11 December 1942, MSP-SSC.

[96] BCFA, annual report, 1939, MSP-SSC. See also letters of Clarence Gamble to Margaret Sanger, 25 January 1940, and to Woodbridge Morris, 26 January 1940, CJG-CL.

opened in 1937, was persuaded by the BCFA to supervise two demonstration clinics for African-Americans. The first clinic was opened in a black settlement house, Bethlehem Center, on 15 February 1940. In July, the second clinic was opened at Fisk University. Initially this project was not enthusiastically received by the black community. Clinic attendance and contraceptive usage increased in the project's second year, however, when African-American public health nurses were trained in providing contraceptive instruction.[97] In South Carolina the BCFA convinced Robert E. Seibels, chairman of Maternal Welfare for the South Carolina Medical Association, to supervise a project specifically for African-American women that would be added to the white-only county health contraceptive service. Seibels organized the birth control services into a general health program that also gave women free anemia treatments. Because of the rural character of the region, no clinic was established. Instead, women were instructed individually in their homes by one of the two African-American nurses hired by the project. In twenty-one months, the project provided 1,008 women with contraceptives. The presence of African-Americans on the field staff may account for the fact that the project's test population was larger than that in Nashville. But the supervising physician, who had to prescribe birth control in each case, was white, and the dropout rate in South Carolina was greater than that in Nashville. Altogether, the demonstration clinics served fewer than 3,000 women in the entire two-year period. As Sanger predicted, the case loads in these clinics were very low.[98] While the clinics were featured in *Life Magazine* in 1940, there is no evidence that any public or private clinic was opened as a direct result of the demonstration projects.[99]

[97] John Overton, "A Birth Control Service among Urban Negroes," pp. 97–101, esp. p. 98. Kathryn Trent, field report, 1940, PPFA-SSC. These nurses gave birth control information and clinic appointments during postpartum home visits. Women had to be eligible for health-department care to use the clinics. Thus, only the poorest women had access to these services. In the two-year period 638 women were served by the clinic.

[98] Letter of Margaret Sanger to Cecil Damon, 24 November 1939; Robert Seibels, "Maternal Welfare in a Rural Project," comments on annual report of the Berkeley County Demonstration Project, 1 April 1940–30 March 1941 (typescript); Dorothy Ferebee, "Planned Parenthood as a Public Health Measure for the Negro Race," pp. 7–10. Dorothy Ferebee project reports presented at the BCFA 1942 meeting, MSP-LC. Letter of Woodbridge Morris to John Overton, 6 February 1940, CJG-CL.

[99] "Birth Control: South Carolina Uses It for Public Health," *Life Magazine*, 6 May 1940, pp. 64–68. The clinics were also featured in a *Look Magazine* layout in August 1942; reprint, FRP-SSC.

Meanwhile, Sanger, who was angered but undaunted by Lasker's decision, began to solicit funds for the educational campaign she had envisioned.[100] Sanger's former secretary, a white woman named Florence Rose who ran the educational campaign, began by organizing a National Negro Advisory Council to give advice and support to the project.[101] Her report on these early organizing activities gives insight into the developing relationship between the BCFA and the African-American community. "Of course I find extreme sensitivities on the subject; but once they are convinced of our motives, as expressed in the idea of a Negro Advisory Council, their whole attitude changes."[102] Acting on the advice of Council members, Rose focused on enlisting the support of African-American medical professionals, so that when funds were obtained for educational work among the general public, medical professionals would be available to provide the necessary services.

The bulk of the DNS educational activities involved the distribution of pamphlets and exhibits at African-American professional conferences. Any black health professional, teacher, minister, or social worker who expressed an interest in doing birth control work in her or his local community was given exhibits and pamphlets in large quantities. Many were used during National Negro Health Week. Negro nurses were contacted through Mabel Staupers, and many state and local nursing organizations offered cooperation. By 1942 the Federation hired Mae McCarroll, a black physician, to travel to various meetings of African-American professional organizations. After she attended the 1942 annual meeting of the National Medical Association, it endorsed the DNS's birth control work.[103]

[100] She solicited old friends of the movement, such as Mrs. Fuld, who contributed $2,000, and sent letters to the previous Harlem Clinic Council requesting funds. Funding appeal letter signed by Sanger, 30 October 1940, FRP-SSC.

[101] Florence Rose, who began working with Sanger in 1932, was the person through whom Sanger was able to continue to have a demonstrable effect upon the organization after the 1939 merger with the ABCL. The National Negro Advisory Council members included W. G. Alexander, Claude Barnett (Ida B. Wells's son), Michael J. Bent, Mary McLeod Bethune, M. O. Bousfield, Paul Cornely, W. E. B. Du Bois, Crystal Fauset, E. Franklin Frazier, Dorothy Ferebee, Charles Hubert, Charles S. Johnson, John Lawlah, Peter Marshall Murray, Rev. A. Clayton Powell, Jr., Ira DeA. Reid, Bishop David A. Sims, Mabel Staupers, Mary Church Terrell, and Walter White.

[102] Letter of Florence Rose to Clarence Gamble, Old Year's End 1939, MSP-SSC.

[103] DNS, "News," Christmas 1941, p. 2; Margaret Sanger to Mary Lasker, 18 February 1941; Negro Project organizational chart, BCFA, c. 1939–40, Sanger plan; National Negro Advisory Council meeting, minutes, 11 December 1942, MSP-SSC. Fundraising

But endorsements for birth control did not come only from African-American professionals. In October 1941, the National Council of Negro Women became the first national women's organization officially to endorse the practice of contraception. Dorothy Ferebee, an African-American physician, had addressed the meeting. As a result of her address, a permanent Committee on Family Planning was formed, and the following resolution was approved:

> We are resolved to urge to the Health Committee of every Negro organization throughout the country the inclusion of all public health programs, especially the less familiar one of Family Planning which aims to aid each family to have *all* the children it can support and afford, but no more—in order to insure better health, greater security and happiness for all.[104]

As with the Harlem clinic, the DNS discourse represented birth control as a means to increase maternal and infant health in the black community. Birth control was needed to ameliorate health conditions of African-American women and children and to secure happiness of family life and a higher standard of living for the race. Health continued to be linked to racial progress, whereas security and happiness were imbued with economic meaning. Sexual independence, as with the Harlem clinic, was not listed among the reasons for blacks to use contraception. African-American supporters reprised versions of this Sangerist rhetoric. Yet for them the issue of race suicide remained conspicuous. It continued to be an issue of concern to women in the clinics and it was explicitly addressed by supporters. As the National Council of Negro Women resolved, family planning should aim to help families have *all* the children they could afford.

Florence Rose carried on educational work until July 1943, when

---

letter, 30 October 1940, signed by Margaret Sanger; letter of Florence Rose to Margaret Sanger (handwritten), c. 31 December 1939; "Preventive Measures in the Solution of Public Health Problems," FRP-SSC. Letters of Paul Cornely to Florence Rose 29 January 1940; and of Florence Rose to Margaret Sanger, 1 February 1940; acceptance list for National Negro Advisory Council, 1 May 1940; Florence Rose, activities report, 30 November–13 December 1941, 1–22 March 1942, and 31 March–7 April 1942, MSP-LC; letter of Florence Rose to Clarence Gamble, 6 May 1940; Executive Committee meeting, minutes, BCFA, 7 July 1942, CJG-CL.

[104] Passed by the National Council of Negro Women, Washington, D.C., 18 October 1941. See DNS, "News," p. 3, MSP-SSC; letter of Dorothy Ferebee to Florence Rose, 29 October 1941, CJG-CL. Mary McLeod Bethune subsequently wrote letters on DNS letterhead to encourage the local chapters to utilize the DNS resources. See DNS form letter of 19 December 1941, signed by Mary McLeod Bethune, FRP-SSC.

she resigned from the BCFA. Rose had for several years been working in tense relationship with the new leadership of PPFA. She was frequently admonished for not adhering to the new procedures established to professionalize the organization, and she finally resigned because she could no longer tolerate the condescending attitude of the professional male leadership toward longtime laywomen activists.[105] In the next chapter, I will examine this issue more closely. Here, I want to note only that a broad-based DNS was one of the casualties of the movement's internal struggle between laywomen and professional men. Florence Rose was a dynamo. She often worked evenings and weekends, devoting her life to the cause. Her tireless efforts were the primary reason for the breadth of African-American organizing and input that did exist. After Rose's resignation, educational work, especially efforts to reach local individuals, shrank considerably. The educational campaign among the general public was never financed, and thus efforts to gain support from national African-American organizations were never followed up.

Although the National Negro Advisory Council overwhelmingly favored continuing educational activities, the Program Committee of PPFA concluded in 1942 that the bulk of this work had already been completed.[106] Some of the educational work that Rose began was continued until 1947 by a "Negro consultant" who was hired to replace her. But a shift in PPFA priorities sharply constricted the range of activities, increasing the distance between PPFA and the African-American community.[107] After 1942 the national organization retreated, leaving state and local Planned Parenthoods to conduct this work. With that decision, African-American birth control needs were consigned to state leagues that varied in size, strength, and concern for African-Americans. Even though PPFA prohibited the hiring of persons with racist attitudes and required affiliates' staff to reflect their region's racial composition, the PPFA's work in African-American

---

[105] Letter of Florence Rose to D. Kenneth Rose, 8 September 1943, FRP-SSC.

[106] Program Committee meeting, minutes, PPFA, 30 December 1942, PPFA-SSC. The minutes attribute the decision to D. Kenneth Rose.

[107] Field Department reports, PPFA, 1944; annual report, PPFA, 1945; Board meeting, minutes, PPFA, 1945, PPFA-SSC. PPFA, "Suggestions on State-National Program for Promoting Pregnancy Spacing among Negroes," 15 January 1943, FRP-SSC. PPFA, "Program to Enlist the Interest and Cooperation of Negroes," January 1944; and M. Schanks, "Progress and Program on Work with Negroes," January 1945, PPFA-SSC. Marie Key, "Report on Work with Minority Groups 1944–1947"; PPFA, "National Program," 1947, pp. 5–6, MSP-LC.

communities was severely limited after the Second World War.[108] In the South, African-Americans' contraceptive needs were consigned to a segregated health system, and many PPFA affiliates refused to abide by the nondiscrimination requirements of the national organization.

The Question of Racism

Several observations about the racial politics in the Harlem clinic and the Division of Negro Service shed light on the larger question of the movement's racism. Neither project simply imposed contraception on an unreceptive population. Since race progressives in both the black and white communities held that the races shared a common culture, it is an oversimplification to conclude that these projects imposed white social controls on the African-American population. Incorporating African-Americans into middle-class culture was part of the goal of racial integration; it did not threaten the integrity of African-American culture, it redressed a historical exclusion. To conclude that the birth control movement imposed social control on the African-American population also ignores the indigenous interest in birth control within the African-American community. Harlem women sought access to contraception in the main branch of the CRB, and community leaders encouraged the CRB to open the Harlem Branch. Movement fieldworkers found many instances of existing African-American community efforts when they ventured south. Judged in the context of racial politics of the 1930s, the birth control movement followed a progressive course of action in attempting to expand its activities and services to the African-American population and in its strategy of interracial project planning. In the terms of the 1930s, it would have been racist not to expand services to include the African-American community or to form interracial committees to administer those services.

The question of whether these projects perpetuated racism is more subtle. Racism was evident not so much in the intentions of whites as in the racial dynamics undergirding the organizing and implementing of these projects. The hierarchies of America's race order were replicated in these projects because white birth controllers delineated the terms of African-American inclusion. The dominant culture's standards of

[108] Gordon, *Woman's Body*, p. 353 and p. 457, n. 35. PPFA, "Program Policies," 17 October 1947, p. 34, PPFA-SSC.

proper family size were prescribed before equal opportunity was offered. As Sanger remarked to Albert Lasker in 1942, anticipating the
coming civil rights movement,

> I believe that the Negro question is coming definitely to the fore in
> America, not only because of the war, but in anticipation of the place
> the Negro will occupy after the peace. I think it is magnificent that
> we are in on the ground floor, helping Negroes to control their birth
> rate, to reduce their high infant and maternal death rate, to main-
> tain better standards of health and living for those already born,
> and to create better opportunities for those who will be born. In
> other words, we're giving Negroes an opportunity to help them-
> selves, and to rise to their own heights through education and the
> principles of a democracy.[109]

The interracial coalition was limited to special projects in the African-American community though. Crossing the color line with regard
to birth control in the 1930s and 1940s was one-directional; whites
could aid African-Americans, but African-Americans could not aid
the "general" movement. No African-Americans were included on the
Advisory Boards of the CRB before the Harlem clinic opened, and
Sanger did not invite the Harlem Council members to join a CRB
Board after they were snubbed by the New York City Committee. Nationally prominent African-Americans were not solicited for membership on any national advisory committee until the Division of Negro
Service was formed, and then they were invited to serve on the Advisory Council of only that Division. The various birth control organizations did tend to include special councils of physicians, scientists,
clergy, and such. All the other councils, however, were defined by members' profession, not by their race.

Finally, the role of African-Americans was limited to one of assistance; they were always brought into projects after the projects were
initiated, thereby implying that their participation was incidental,
rather than essential, to the project. Moreover, bringing African-
Americans into the projects after they were initiated made those projects special cases of the general program and compelled African-
Americans continually to contest the existing structure of such projects. Arguing that if such projects were to succeed they had to be man-

[109] Letter of Margaret Sanger to Albert Lasker, 9 July 1942, MSP-SSC.

aged by community members, African-Americans had to struggle to get themselves and their perspectives incorporated into the programs in their own communities.

That contest can be read in the literature about birth control and "the Negro" authored by African-Americans and whites. African-American authors always explicitly situated the "facts" of Negro disease and poverty in terms of the conditions under which African-Americans were forced to live within a racist society. Striving to clarify that their needs were special only because of racism, authors argued for example that

> wherever birth control may seem to have special aspects among Negroes, it is because they are subject to special social and economic pressure. Tuberculosis, which strongly justifies contraception, is not a Negro disease but a result of bad housing, overcrowding, poor hygiene, malnutrition and neglected sanitation in those districts in which Negroes are forced to live.[110]

Any race would have such needs if faced with the same conditions. They disallowed any notion that naturally greater fecundity caused African-Americans to need birth control by arguing that "people whose economic and health status is lowest have least access to the techniques of planned parenthood."[111] Such arguments also disallowed racial degeneracy as an interpretation of "the facts" and defined African-Americans as oppressed rather than inherently irresponsible. White birth control advocates were not always so careful to contextualize their statements; thus they tended to discuss the problems of "the Negro" without referring to the constraints imposed upon "him" by a racist society. Even when noting high disease and death rates among African-Americans, the white birth controllers did not always place these within a context of racism and segregation. Often high fertility was identified as the cause of high disease rates. Although white birth controllers did not actively blame the victim, their rhetoric did not actively disallow such interpretations, either.[112]

Explanations for the apparent slow progress of birth control among

[110] Roberts, "The Birthright of The Unborn," p. 88. See also Frazier, "The Negro," p. 70.

[111] Ferebee, "Planned Parenthood," p. 7.

[112] "Editorial," *BCR: Special Negro Number* 16 (June 1932): 163–64 is but one example. See, for example, Overton, "A Birth Control Service," pp. 97–101; and Robert Seibels, "A Rural Project in Negro Maternal Health," pp. 42–44.

African-Americans was the other key area of contest between black and white birth control supporters. Throughout these projects whites discounted the racially specific concerns about birth control expressed by African-Americans. Reporting on the DNS clinics, Dorothy Ferebee listed the suspicion that birth control was "a clever bit of machination to persuade them to commit race suicide" and cited fear of impaired function as the chief causes of black women's reluctance to use contraceptives. Whites tended to regard those concerns as irrational fears of a backward race.[113] The racial position of white birth control supporters was willfully blind to the contours of racial history that made such fears rational. At the same time that the movement sought the trust of the African-American community, the U.S. Public Health Service was likewise asking blacks to trust them in the Tuskegee syphilis experiment.[114] To African-American birth control supporters, such fears were real concerns that had to be dealt with forthrightly. The best way to confront them was to utilize "Negro professionals . . . [who] . . . could break down fallacious attitudes and beliefs, elements of distrust and inspire the confidence of the group."[115]

Even though African-American birth control supporters took those concerns seriously, their own pejorative representations of "the poor Negro" undercut the effectiveness with which they contested the racial maternalism of white Sangerists. Both groups justified birth control as a tool of racial betterment by articulating an economic ethic of fertility that linked proper family size to economic standing and racial progress. For African-Americans this economic ethic was to ensure the progress of the African-American community against the barriers imposed by racist America. For whites this sense of justice was largely absent. Instead, there was merely a sense of what was proper. That is, it was proper to match family size to income; and it was proper that all Americans, including African-Americans, should prosper.[116] The clearest aspect of white paternalism—the assessment that the "Negro race contained many backward elements"—was never fully challenged,

[113] Ferebee, "Planned Parenthood," p. 8. She also noted that the women's husbands likewise feared impaired function and that there was a confusion of birth control and abortion. Seibels, "A Rural Project," p. 44. See also Overton, "A Birth Control Service," p. 97.

[114] Jones, *Bad Blood*, pp. 1–16.

[115] Ferebee, "Planned Parenthood," pp. 8–9.

[116] Planned Parenthood was careful to concede that family planning represented only a partial answer to the economic and health needs of African-Americans. They did not claim that birth control was a panacea. See "Better Health," MSP-SSC.

because, however ambivalently, middle-class African-Americans concurred.

Both African-American and white Sangerists particularly represented birth control as a scientific and rational tool to combat superstition and chance. For example, "the mass of Negroes still believe in magic and superstition as cures for disease. Education is the only vaccination against superstition that the world has found. Negroes have come a long way since the civil war, but still have a long way to go toward a knowledge of modern science."[117] To the extent that class and race are conflated in America, the middle-class bias of African-American supporters reinforced Sanger's racial maternalism. The outcome of this contest of meaning is apparent in the health hypothesis discussed at the beginning of this chapter. That hypothesis assumes that poverty accounts more than race for differences in the impact of contraceptive use. That hypothesis however, assumes that low interest in and incompetent use of contraception are based in the culture of poverty, a culture that it assumes is characteristic of the black community. In other words, the low fertility rates in the black community between 1900 and 1945 could not be the result of contraceptive use because poor people who cannot plan effectively cannot use contraception effectively.[118]

This edge of racial maternalism and the one-directional nature of interracial coalition are, I believe, the keys to understanding the racism in U.S. birth control politics. Sanger, and later the Planned Parenthood Federation, did not explicitly exclude African-Americans from the movement. In fact, they included African-Americans in clinics and on advisory councils at a time when complete exclusion was common in professional organizations like the AMA and the American Nurses' Association. But despite the rhetoric of racial similarity and equality, they saw the fertility control needs of African-Americans as a special issue requiring special programs. Sanger did not believe that African-Americans were incapable of using contraception; she believed that if given the opportunity they would practice birth control. But even in defining the needs of African-Americans as special, white Sangerists discounted the racially specific positions from which African-American women confronted the birth control movement. The offer of equal access to this social right was empty when articulated within a context that ignored racism. Birth control movement projects within the Afri-

[117] E. S. Jamison, "The Future of Negro Health," p. 94. See also Garvin, "The Negro Doctor's Task."

[118] Kennedy, *Birth Control in America*, pp. 124–25, offers an example of this argument.

can-American community between 1930 and 1945 were racist, then, because they relegated the fertility control needs and desires of African-American women to a special, secondary cause of the general movement, whose terms were defined from a white perspective by white staff. Moreover, that secondary cause was taken up and then sacrificed at the discretion of whites. Such a perspective left white birth control advocates to identify the need and to provide the opportunity, and it left African-Americans to contest those provisions. More than the men, African-American women, such as Mabel Staupers and Dorothy Ferebee, explicitly objected to the paternalism this perspective embodied. Their objection was not gender-specific; they were not concerned with the effect of this paternalism on African-American women particularly. Rather, their concern was for the black community in general.[119]

Finally, the racial maternalism by which the birth control movement addressed the African-American community is also a key to understanding how the movement's feminism was displaced. It discounted African-Americans' subjective perspective on the racial politics of birth control, but it largely ignored the subjective perspective of African-American women as women. Focused on the community's health, both African-Americans and white birth control advocates represented "the Negro" as generically male. "Tomorrow's Children," the main exhibit distributed by the DNS, represented birth control's promise of racial betterment with a photograph of a black man lifting a black infant above his head toward the limitless sky. The gender-based right of African-American women to contraception was represented only in the need to improve their community's maternal and infant health statistics.[120] This disengagement of contraception from the specific sexual power relations in which African-American women might practice birth control was part of the wider repositioning of women's rights to birth control discussed in the following chapter.

[119] See letter of Mabel Staupers to Margaret Sanger, 7 August 1935; National Negro Advisory Council meeting, minutes, PPFA, 11 December 1942, MSP-SSC; and Ferebee, "Planned Parenthood," pp. 7–8.
[120] "Tomorrow's Children," MSP-LC. This representation of a man and child was unique to the DNS. Parent-child images used by the movement in the white community invariably pictured white women and infants in classic Madonna-and-child poses. See, for instance, "The First Key to Strong National Health—Birth Control," fundraising newspaper advertisement, BCFA, c. 1939, CJG-CL.

CHAPTER SIX

Laywomen and
Organization Men

The Birth Control Federation of America contains a considerable
proportion of men. As children have fathers as well as mothers, so
birth control will gain much from the leadership of men as well as
women.

> —Richard Pierson, 1939 Presidential Address, BCFA

If our New Dealers turn a deaf ear to the cries of the Forgotten
Woman, they are attempting to solve the problem of economic
security without due consideration of the basic human factors
involved in that problem.

> —Margaret Sanger, "National Security and Birth Control"

By the late thirties, the *One Package* decision and the AMA endorsement gave a measure of legitimacy to the birth control movement's
more than 350 clinics across the country.[1] That legitimacy, however,
was not achieved on feminist terms. Like its divorce of birth control
from African-American critiques of racism, the rhetoric of "planned
parenthood" divorced birth control from any feminist critique of male
dominance. During the Great Depression, the proportional weights of
the three main ideological elements of birth control discourse were
recalibrated so that the economic ethic of fertility linked to the ideal of
racial betterment completely overshadowed the rights of women. The
outcome might have been different if not for the political economy of
the depression.

In the 1930s U.S. birth rates fell below replacement levels, height-
ening cultural anxiety about the self-reliance and solidarity of the fam-

[1] ABCL, "Distribution of Clinics by Type and State," January 1938; and Executive
Committee meeting, minutes, CRB, 6 December 1935, MSP-LC. Not all the agencies
that the ABCL counted as clinics were free-standing, extramural clinics solely devoted
to contraception. Many were private physicians or health centers that reserved several
hours weekly for contraceptive appointments.

ily, the backbone of the nation. America could maintain its position in the world no more with a declining population than with a declining economy. This fear of depopulation was incorporated into the "under-consumption" explanation of the depression through the population analyses of Louis Dublin, Metropolitan Life Insurance statistician. In criticizing the movement, Dublin insisted that birth control was already overused.[2] In addition, Roman Catholics, an important constituency of the New Deal coalition, vigorously opposed birth control on moral grounds. Their opposition was voiced in very sectarian terms, but it resonated within the national mood of atonement for the financial and moral excesses of the twenties. As the movement tried to win a place in the New Deal, it reshaped its rhetoric in an effort to counter these depopulation fears and moral opposition. But together, they effectively prevented birth control from being included in the emerging welfare state.

At the same moment that birth control became more difficult to defend ideologically, increased demand for contraception, which underlay declining fertility rates, put great strain on the movement's financial resources. This chapter examines the responses within birth control organizations to the pressures that reshaped birth control discourse and practices in the closing years of the Great Depression. For most of the depression, as discussed in the first section of this chapter, the movement was divided. In 1939, largely because of fundraising constraints, the independent ABCL and Sangerist CRB publicly settled their differences and merged to become the Birth Control Federation of America (BCFA). Three years later the name was changed to the Planned Parenthood Federation of America (PPFA).[3] This name change was symbolic of the organization's internal restructuring that is the focus of the second section of the chapter. With this name change, the fighting words *birth control* were replaced with the less militant rhetoric of *child spacing* and *family planning*. Like economic planning, family planning sounded more reasonable in response to the population crisis. Through its gender neutrality, this rhetoric represented contraception as more than just a woman's issue. In fact, it represented

[2] Louis Dublin, letter in "Birth Selection vs. Birth Control: A Symposium of Comments on Dr. Osborn's Address," *BCR* 16 (October 1932): 233; "Experts Warn Birth Control Danger Exists," *Syracuse Post-Standard*, 11 July 1935; "Drop in Population Feared for Nation," *New York Times*, 28 March 1937, MSP-LC; Gordon, *Woman's Body*, p. 315.
[3] Special membership meeting, minutes, BCFA, 29 January 1942, MSP-SSC.

women's subjective perspective on birth control as too limiting. Instead, contraception became a tool by which families, in both their own and the nation's interests, could delay childbearing until financially appropriate.

Since birth control was no longer merely a women's issue, there was no reason for women to continue to dominate the leadership of birth control organizations. And, with the founding of the BCFA, for the first time in the movement's history men dominated the policy-making positions in a birth control organization.[4] Sanger remained as the only woman in the top leadership, but her position as honorary chairman of the Board of Directors was ex-officio, carrying little power. Initially, several laywomen who were longtime Sangerists continued to work in the BCFA, but they eventually resigned because, under the rubric of professionalism, their experience-based authority was devalued and displaced. The new leadership argued that "new beginnings" called for "new experts" to create "new public support" for the public health agency that PPFA considered itself to be.[5] That newness was masculine, and it eclipsed any feminist perspective on birth control.

Division and Depression

In 1928, Sanger resigned from the ABCL over differences with the acting president, Eleanor Jones, about organizational structure and appropriate strategies. The conflict between Sanger and Jones became so fractious, with Jones accusing Sanger of fanaticism and chaotic leadership and Sanger accusing Jones of playing petty politics and letting the League languish in apathy, that the movement itself was virtually split.[6] Thereafter, supporters of Jones clustered in the ABCL, and

[4] Annual meeting, minutes, BCFA, January 1939, MSP-SSC. Richard N. Pierson was president and chairman of the Board; Robert L. Dickinson, Henry Pratt Fairchild (a sociologist and eugenicist), Frederick Holden, and C. C. Little were vice presidents; and D. Kenneth Rose was managing director of the Federation. Each of these men had previously been an advisor to either the ABCL or CRB.

[5] Letters of Florence Rose to D. Kenneth Rose, 8 September 1943, p. 3, FRP-SSC; and of Mrs. Klein to Mary Lasker, 5 March 1943, PPFA-SSC. Muncy, *Creating a Female Dominion*, pp. 152–57, notes a similar displacement of women by male professionals when infant and maternal welfare was incorporated into mainstream public policy under the 1935 Social Security Act.

[6] Letter of Margaret Sanger to Board of Directors, ABCL, 8 June 1928, MSP-SSC. Board of Directors' meeting, minutes, ABCL, 12 June 1928, and 20 September 1929, MSP-LC. Letters of Margaret Sanger to Eleanor Jones, 17 November 1928 and 12 January 1929, MSP-LC, 31 January 1929, MSP-SSC, and 11 February 1929, PPFA-SSC; of Eleanor Jones to Margaret Sanger, 12 December 1928; and of the executive secretary

Sangerists clustered in the CRB.[7] Over the years, the antipathy of the two groups became more pronounced as they pursued different strategies to advance the cause and repeatedly competed for public recognition, money, and affiliates.

In 1929, Sanger agreed to organize and lead the National Committee on Federal Legislation for Birth Control (NCFL), believing that legal changes were necessary before the network of clinics could expand. "Agitation for legislation" was, in her estimation, the "means" to stimulate "interest in the establishment of clinics." Although the Federal laws were not being vigorously enforced by this time, "public institutions, hospitals, dispensaries," and individual physicians continually used the existence of those laws to refuse to incorporate contraception into their practices. Inconsistency between numerous state and Federal laws also produced confusion about when and where contraceptive prescriptions were legal. Finally, prohibitions on the importation and interstate transport of contraceptive information and devices hindered the ability of clinics to obtain sufficient supplies.[8] Sangerists insisted that repealing the Federal laws would eliminate each of these problems.[9] The new leadership of the ABCL disagreed.

Until the thirties the ABCL had likewise supported legislative reform, but, struggling to survive without Sanger and committed to becoming a responsible public health agency, ABCL leaders changed their position.[10] Although they conceded that the laws would have to

---

of ABCL to the Executive Committee of ABCL, 10 November 1929, PPFA-SSC; and Executive Committee meeting, minutes, CRB, 2 December 1929, MSP-LC.

[7] Discounting the larger differences between the two groups, previous accounts focus on Sanger's personality and attribute the 1928 split and subsequent problems primarily to her need for dominance. See Reed, *The Birth Control Movement*, pp. 109, 258, 264; Kennedy, *Birth Control in America*, pp. 103–5, 256–57; and Gordon, *Woman's Body*, pp. 271–72. Cf. Chesler, *Woman of Valor*, pp. 238–39, 391–92, who provides a more balanced account.

[8] Letter of Margaret Sanger to Alice Boughton, 11 April 1932, MSP-LC; and Margaret Sanger, "National Security and Birth Control," p. 139. On NCFL organizing see also letters of Margaret Sanger to Eleanor Jones, 22 November 1928 and 18 November 1929; Board meeting, minutes, CRB, 2 December 1929 and 5 August 1932; and Robert L. Dickinson, "Memo on Cooperation between Organizations Interested in Birth Control and Allied Subjects," 2 December 1929, MSP-LC.

[9] Although their efforts failed, the NCFL carried out eleven campaigns to change the laws, which included five Congressional hearings on NCFL bills. See Reed, *The Birth Control Movement*, p. 264; and Dienes, *Law, Politics, and Birth Control*, p. 104. The history of the NCFL is given in detail by Chesler, *Woman of Valor*, pp. 339–54; and Kennedy, *Birth Control in America*, pp. 227–43.

[10] As noted in Chapter 3, in 1924 the ABCL had briefly attempted to change Federal laws. As late as 1929 it sponsored a doctors-only bill in New York State. See Eleanor

be changed eventually, they thought the crisis of the depression made the work of organizing clinics more pressing, and controversy would undermine that organizing effort.[11] Although Sanger had turned away from anarchist tactics, she still practiced agitation. She believed that "what some call fanaticism" was "never dangerous to the life" of the movement; it raised people's interest in and fervor for the cause.[12] The ABCL argued, however, that controversy generated by NCFL publicity actually scared physicians and public welfare officials away from the movement. Moreover, they argued, Sanger overstated the impact of the Federal law, insisting that they knew of no case in which it had hampered a clinic's operations. They concluded that the NCFL efforts just reinforced "psychological barrier[s]" to the movement's progress.[13]

The new ABCL leadership did have a serious problem, though. They believed that the ABCL was the definitive, responsible birth control organization and that Sanger's "individual" enterprise was prone to overstatement and emotionalism. But Sanger was a cultural hero, and her name was so closely linked with birth control that the ABCL had considerable difficulty gaining public recognition of its distinction from her.[14] The increasing vehemence with which the League pronounced its differences from Sanger may well have resulted from their frustration of being overshadowed by someone they saw as disruptive. By 1934, the ABCL began publicly to criticize the NCFL and agitation associated with it, suggesting that the "contributing public" would be better served by supporting the ABCL's work of quietly organizing a national network of clinics, whose existence would eventually nullify

Jones, "Birth Control in 1929," p. 18; and ABCL fundraising letter, 22 March 1929, MSP-LC.

[11] Eleanor Jones, ABCL form letter criticizing NCFL, 2 January and 20 May 1931, MSP-LC, and "Editorial," *BCR* 15 (January 1931): 4.

[12] Letter of Margaret Sanger to Board of Directors, ABCL, 8 June 1928, p. 2, MSP-SSC.

[13] Letters of Marguerite Benson to Mrs. Bassett, 12 August 1936; of Allison Moore to Stella Hanau, 6 March 1936; and of Marguerite Benson to Charles Scribner, 30 March 1936; ABCL, annual report, 1934, p. 10, MSP-LC. Contrary to the ABCL claim, birth control advocates became involved in sixteen court cases in which the Federal law had been used to stop the importation and distribution of contraceptive information or devices in the early thirties. See Reed, *The Birth Control Movement*, pp. 114, 121, 337; and Dienes, *Law, Politics, and Birth Control*, pp. 108–55.

[14] See "Margaret Sanger Celebrates a Birth Control Victory," *Life Magazine*, 11 January 1937, pp. 18–21; and Margaret Sanger, "This Is Why I Fight for Birth Control," *Look Magazine*, 15 August 1939. See also Executive Committee meeting and Board meeting, minutes, CRB, 7 January 1931; memo of Willa Murray and Hazel Zborowski, report of meeting with ABCL, 9 February 1933, letter of Elsie Wulkop to Catherine Bangs, 17 October 1934, MSP-LC; and Marguerite Benson, "A Public Trust," pp. 1–2.

the Federal laws.[15] As one supporter noted, the ABCL conduct in the thirties was "something of a crusade . . . to demonstrate that birth control [was] now out of the hands of its propagandist pioneers."[16] But even though the ABCL had great difficulty gaining sufficient recognition of its independence, the ABCL emphasized different goals for the movement, which were articulated in its alliances with eugenicists, social workers, and physicians.

After 1928 a rigidly hereditarian view of racial betterment through birth control was the keynote rhetoric expressed by the ABCL. Eleanor Jones, president of the ABCL until 1935, thought that "bad heredity," which she identified as the primary cause of "social unfitness," posed an "insurmountable obstacle to the achievement of social welfare." However, the ABCL was "demonstrating that philanthropy [could] gradually overcome this obstacle by the promotion of birth control among the socially inadequate." Reduced birth rates among those "handicapped by bad heredity" underpinned the ABCL's rhetoric that represented birth control as a valuable tool for reducing the cost of relief babies to American taxpayers. Jones characterized the crisis of the depression as the "dysgenic multiplication of the unfit," whom she defined as "paupers," "morons" and "degenerates." "For the good of the race," she concluded, "people of poor stock—incompetent and sickly—should have few or no children.[17] That is why the ABCL favored clinic organizing over legislative agitation; clinics would have an immediate impact on the fertility of the socially unfit. And, Jones in-

[15] Letter of Marguerite Benson to Charles Scribner, 30 March 1936, MSP-LC. See also letters of Catherine Bangs to Jessie Ames Marshall, 31 July 1934; and of Eleanor Jones to C.-E. A. Winslow, 10 January 1934; Hazel Moore, memo on meeting with ABCL Executive Committee, 18 June 1934; letter of Mabel Wood to Stella Hanau, 6 January 1935; Board meeting, minutes, ABCL, 31 October 1935; letters of Marguerite Benson to Margaret Judson, 15 January 1936; and of Mabel Wood to Zelda Franklin, editor of *Health and Hygiene*, 23 April 1936, MSP-LC. In mid-1933 the ABCL recast the *Review* to report only on the League's activities. Thereafter the ABCL refused to publicize the NCFL activities, arguing that as the house organ of the League the *Review* was not obligated to report on the activities of other organizations. See letters of Margaret Sanger to Allison Moore, 13 May 1935; and of Allison Moore to Stella Hanau, 6 March 1936, MSP-LC.

[16] Letter of Percy Clark to Margaret Sanger, 18 September 1936, MSP-LC. See also letters of Marguerite Benson to Mrs. Beeson, c. 1936, PPFA-SSC; and of Stella Hanau to Margaret Sanger, 12 July 1935, MSP-LC.

[17] Letter of Eleanor Jones to Charles Vickrey, Golden Rule Foundation, 18 May 1934; Eleanor Jones, ABCL fundraising form letter, 20 May 1931, MSP-LC; Eleanor Jones, "Birth Control—First-Aid in Social Work," p. 218, and see also Eleanor Jones "A New Era in Social Service," p. 209; letter of Catherine Bangs to Sheldon Glueck, 3 January 1936; Eleanor Jones, ABCL fundraising form letter, 2 April 1934, MSP-LC; and Chesler, *Woman of Valor*, pp. 215–17, 344.

sisted, coercion was not necessary, because "luckily," the socially inadequate did not want to have children.[18]

For the good of the movement, in 1933, Eleanor Jones proposed merging the ABCL and American Eugenics Society (AES), each of which was suffering financially. Jones's proposal was not carried out, in part because she refused to consider including Sanger. Nonetheless, a continuing close association of the two organizations reshaped ABCL policy.[19] Having by this time revised the extreme hereditarianism of its early years, the AES began to support birth control.[20] Still, eugenicists insisted that a positive program of encouraging the fit to have more children was necessary to balance birth control's negative program. In 1934, the ABCL amended its program accordingly, adding the aim of "encourag[ing] desirable reproduction, so that there may be more well-born children" to its existing goal of "perfecting clinical instruction of the socially inadequate to effect a more substantial reduction in their fertility." A year later the two organizations began a joint campaign to persuade officials that relief recipients should be referred to contraceptive clinics.[21]

Too impoverished to support the expense of extramural clinics, the ABCL concentrated instead on convincing local public health and wel-

[18] Jones, "First-Aid," p. 318. When confronted about bias of this rhetoric, the ABCL softened its position and reasserted that birth control was voluntary. See letters of Ruth Topping to Dwight Cushman, 3 February 1934; of Margaret Lamont to *BCR*, 20 June 1934; of Margaret Woodbury to Margaret Lamont, 4 July 1934; of Eleanor Jones to Margaret Lamont, 11 September 1934; of Marguerite Benson to Robert Kelso, Colorado State Emergency Relief Administration, 13 March 1935; and of Elmira Coutant to Frances Goldberg, 9 May 1936, MSP-LC.

[19] Within two years the Council on Population Policy, consisting of the AES, NCMH, ABCL, NCFL, Human Betterment Foundation, American Genetics Association, and Population Association of America, was formed to facilitate the sharing of information between the organizations concerned with birth control. See executive secretary, ABCL, report, 1933, PPFA-SSC. ABCL, Executive Committee meeting, minutes, March, June, and November 1933, PPFA-SSC; ABCL, annual report, 1934, p. 19; and letter of Frederick Osborn to Margaret Sanger, 16 October 1935, MSP-LC.

[20] See, for example, the responses of eugenicists to Henry Fairfield Osborn's indictment of birth control as inherently dysgenic in "Birth Selection vs. Birth Control: A Symposium of Comments on Dr. Osborn's Address," pp. 232–35, 254–55; and H. J. Muller, "The Dominance of Economics," pp. 236–38. See also Reed, *The Birth Control Movement*, p. 136; and Kevles, *In the Name of Eugenics*, pp. 172–75, on the new generation of AES leaders in the thirties.

[21] Annual meeting, minutes, ABCL, 1934, PPFA-SSC; Executive Committee meeting, minutes, ABCL, 10 January 1935, PPFA-SSC; and Gordon, *Woman's Body*, pp. 304–5. A year earlier, the ABCL had passed a resolution encouraging its affiliates to work to pass laws compelling sterilization in cases of serious hereditary defect. See annual meeting, minutes, ABCL, 1933, PPFA-SSC.

fare agencies to incorporate birth control services into their existing practices.[22] To this end, the League cultivated a relationship with the National Conference of Social Work, becoming a "kindred group" of the Conference in 1929. Thereafter, yearly attendance at the Conference served as the primary route by which the League developed relationships with local relief agencies. The Conference did not endorse the practice of birth control. Nevertheless, the League declared that its acceptance as a kindred group of the Conference proved that birth control was "considered a sound scientific movement for social betterment."[23] The ABCL demonstrated its commitment to social workers' professional standards in its growing disdain for Sangerist agitation and emotionalism. By the thirties, the social work profession declared that the age when "great leaders heroically blazed the way" had passed. The profession argued that its scientific casework techniques would rationalize the functions of New Deal agencies, supplanting the emotionalism of volunteers with the objectivity of professionals. The expansion of democracy in the emerging welfare state depended, the profession insisted, upon their expertise in the science of efficient bureaucracy.[24] Likewise, the ABCL declared that the movement had "progressed beyond the stage of 'rugged individualism.'" It was now a "public trust." Its "professional workers" encouraged clinics and state birth control leagues to "adopt recognized social work procedures," which included, first and foremost, maintaining "the highest possible standards of administration and public relations."[25]

The League's most ambitious effort to become a professional public

[22] Eleanor Jones, ABCL fundraising form letter, 20 May 1931, MSP-LC; and "Editorial," *BCR* 15 (March 1931): 69.

[23] Jones, "First-Aid," p. 217. In deference to the objections of the Conference's Roman Catholic members, the League's participation in the Conference was limited to a yearly display booth and occasional presentation of workshops by social workers supportive of the movement. See National Conference of Social Work files, NCFL; and National Catholic Welfare Conference, "The Question of Birth Control," pp. 1–13, c. 1925, MSP-LC; "Editorial," *BCR* 12 (June 1928): 170.

[24] Roy Lubove, *The Professional Altruist,* pp. 158, 159–71. See also Muncy, *Creating a Female Dominion,* pp. 66–79, 152–57. Muncy argues that changes in the social work profession during the 1930s reflect the ascendence of masculine definitions of the profession over feminine definitions.

[25] Letter of Marguerite Benson to Mrs. Beeson, c. 1936, PPFA-SSC; Marguerite Benson, "A Public Trust," pp. 1–2; letter of Ruth Topping to Henry Lurie, director of the Bureau of Jewish Social Services, 2 March 1934, MSP-LC. See also letter of Annie Porritt to Kitty Marion, 23 January 1930, MSP-LC. Marion had been selling the *BCR* on New York City streets for many years. In this letter she was told to stop that practice because the *Review* was no longer a propaganda magazine but a scientific one.

health agency, its 1935 clinic certification program, brought proper medical supervision to contraceptive clinics. Begun in response to the growth of "commercial clinics" operated by contraception manufacturers, ABCL certification deferred to the standards of clinic practice that Robert Dickinson had long championed. Although the CMH refused any official linkage with the ABCL, Robert Dickinson and Clarence Gamble both personally advised the ABCL as it developed standards for this program. Through it, clinics were inspected to ensure that they offered only scientific, medically supervised contraception free to the needy. If a clinic passed the inspection, it received a certificate of membership and authorization by the League, enabling it to demonstrate that it was a reputable agency. Whether a clinic was extramural or organized within an existing agency, the ABCL required it to be supervised by a medical advisory board, which was to have sole authority for determining all the clinic policy, including referral policy, entrance requirements, examination and prescription procedures, and even hours of operation.[26] The program also deferred to physicians' professional interests in maintaining fee-for-service medicine by requiring its affiliates to provide service only to charity patients.[27]

Despite progress in establishing itself as a responsible public health agency, the ABCL continued to languish in the NCFL's shadow.[28] The ABCL did not even have a monopoly on clinic organization. Although they gave less attention to clinic organizing than to legislation, Sangerists did help organize clinics throughout the depression. While most clinics were affiliated with the ABCL, those that found its requirements too limiting could instead become affiliated with the CRB, and several did.[29]

[26] Letters of Eric Matsner to Clarence Gamble, 9 May 1935, CJG-CL; and of Marguerite Benson to Ruth Hamilton, 13 May 1936, MSP-LC; ABCL, "The Next Step Forward," pp. 10–14, CJG-CL; "Editorial," *BCR* 15 (January 1931): 3; and Marguerite Benson, "A Public Trust," p. 1. Dickinson and the CMH were here again concerned about the impact of a lay organization on the profession's domain. See Executive Committee meeting, minutes, CMH, 11 June 1929; NCMH, annual report, 1930–31, p. 3; Board meeting, minutes, NCMH, 25 April 1935; and NCMH, annual report, 1940, NCMH-CL.

[27] One source of conflict between the ABCL and Sangerists was that the CRB charged some patients a fee, which in the League's eyes meant it was not a charity clinic. Letter of Marguerite Benson to Mrs. Beeson of the Minnesota Birth Control League, c. 1936, PPFA-SSC.

[28] John Price Jones, "Survey on Plans for Fund-Raising for the American Birth Control League," 1938, pp. 85, 90–91, MSP-LC.

[29] The number of clinics increased from 28 in 1929 to 374 by 1938. Of these, at least 70 were affiliated with the CRB. ABCL, "Prospect and Retrospect," *BCR* 13 (February 1929): 57, 60; ABCL, "Distribution of Clinics by Type and State," January 1938; CRB,

This problem of establishing independence cut both ways, though. Linked with Sanger in the public's mind, the ABCL's desire to limit the higher fertility of the socially inadequate was often attributed to her. Roman Catholic opponents, in particular, repeated the ABCL's hereditarian rhetoric to discredit the NCFL's legislative efforts.[30] Thus Sangerists, as well, were unable to dissociate themselves from the ABCL.

Although Sanger did link birth control and relief babies, she maintained her strong opposition to hereditarian interpretations of fitness. The keynotes of NCFL rhetoric emphasized democratizing birth control in the interests of improving maternal and infant health. Legalizing birth control and including it in national recovery programs would end the existing arbitrary conditions in which only the poor were effectively denied access to effective contraception. The limited historical record makes it difficult to determine if in fact only poor women were denied access to effective contraception. The one national study of contraceptive practices among women of childbearing age during the thirties, which was conducted in 1978, demonstrates that middle-class, urban women were more likely to use contraception. Eighty-three percent of the middle-class women in the sample used contraception, compared to only 70 percent of working-class women and 65 percent of farm women. But all of the women were more likely to rely on contraceptive methods that did not require a doctor's prescription. Condoms, withdrawal, and douches were each used at some time by 45–50 percent of the sample. Only 20 percent of the women ever used diaphragms or cervical caps. It is impossible to determine to what extent these data reflect women's personal preferences or the accessibility of the various methods. These data do tend to indicate, however, that even urban, middle-class women had limited access to effective female-controlled methods.[31]

"Suggestions for the Establishment of a Clinic," 26 January 1932; and Executive Committee meeting, minutes, CRB, 6 December 1935, MSP-LC. The League's autocratic control of clinic procedures caused several of its affiliates and clinics to defect to the CRB, including the thirteen New York City Committee's clinics. See Willa Murray and Hazel Zborowski, report, 9 February 1933; letter of Elsie Wulkop to Catherine Bangs, 9 December 1934; J. P. Jones, survey, 1938, p. 86, MSP-LC; and Executive Committee and Board of Trustees meeting, minutes, CRB, 11 November 1938, p. 2, PPFA-SSC.

[30] Chesler, *Woman of Valor*, pp. 341–48, 556; and Kennedy, Birth Control in America, pp. 235–40, on the 1934 NCFL hearings. The failure to distinguish the positions of Sanger and the ABCL is replicated in historical accounts. See Gordon, *Woman's Body*, pp. 304–7, 313–15; and Kennedy, *Birth Control in America*, pp. 108–26.

[31] See Dawson, Meny, and Ridley, "Fertility Control," pp. 79–80. See also Ray and Gosling, "American Physicians," p. 399.

The economic crisis made legalized birth control even more important, according to Sangerists, because thousands of women were dying each year from trying to end unwanted pregnancies. In the crisis of national economic collapse, "there could be no justification for violating the right of every married woman to decide when and how often she would undertake the physical and far-reaching responsibilities of motherhood."[32] In contrast to the ABCL, whose primary concern was the cost of relief, Sangerists argued that contraceptive clinics should receive public funding because health was one of the specified rights of the New Deal, and birth control was essential to protect women's health. But for Sangerists this program of "family planning" was also essential for New Deal economic planning to be effective. Without ready access to contraception, unwanted pregnancies would stymie the efforts of individual families to recover financially, and unregulated reproduction would undercut the nation's economic recovery.

The public confusion about the differences between the two organizations not only undercut the success of each group's programmatic efforts, it also affected their financial stability. Throughout the 1930s the ABCL was a much-weakened organization that had tremendous difficulties raising enough money to maintain its programs. Its leaders wanted to dissociate the League from Sanger's agitation, but they found it difficult to raise money without her efforts or her name.[33] Even though it had the advantage of greater recognition, the CRB had financial problems as well. The NCFL raised a lot of money. But as the number of patients who were unable to pay any fee increased and raising money privately became more difficult, the CRB was confronted with deficits. Stock market losses devastated J. Noah Slee, and Sanger could no longer count on his money to cover the CRB expenses.[34] Also,

[32] Margaret Sanger, "An Open Letter to Social Workers," p. 141, and "National Security and Birth Control," pp. 140–41, quoting the CMH-supported study by Fred Taussig, *Abortion: Spontaneous and Induced,* which determined that there were eight hundred thousand induced abortions a year in the United States of which seventeen thousand resulted in the woman's death.

[33] After 1928 J. Noah Slee and others revoked their financial support of the League. See letter of Dorothy Dick to Eleanor Jones, 28 November 1929; executive secretary, monthly reports, 1930; "ABCL Preliminary Recommendations on Next Steps for the League," 30 April 1938, PPFA-SSC. Board meeting, minutes, ABCL, 13 February 1929; Juliet Rublee to ABCL Board, 11 February 1929, MSP-LC. See also Reed, *The Birth Control Movement,* p. 264; and Kennedy, *Birth Control in America,* pp. 105–6.

[34] On NCFL fundraising see Reed, ibid. and p. 117, who puts the figures as $150,000 raised between 1932 and 1936. Chesler, *Woman of Valor,* pp. 291–93, argues that the clinic's budget actually grew during these years and that it had no deficits, but my reading of clinic records indicates that Sanger was continually concerned in these years with

corporate foundations cut back their programs. The Bureau of Social Hygiene, through which the movement had received its largest grants, was absorbed into the Rockefeller Foundation, which favored basic research, not social causes. The Milbank Memorial Fund, which began to support population studies in the 1930s, gave some money to the CRB, but it preferred to underwrite clinical studies rather than basic patient services.[35] Thus, with their access to large donations limited, both the ABCL and the CRB suffered under the depression's constraints on charitable giving. Competition between them for what little money was available further limited each group's ability to fund their programs.[36] In the economic hard times, although they each tried to demonstrate that their program was uniquely deserving of financial support, both were pressured by donors and allies to resolve their differences and cooperate in order to avoid duplicating their efforts.[37]

After the *One Package* decision, Sanger disbanded the NCFL and turned the full attention of its nationwide network of supporters to the tasks of organizing clinics and pressuring public health officials to include birth control in their programs.[38] The prospect of the New

the effort to raise sufficient money to make the clinic self-supporting. See Board meeting, minutes, CRB, 11 June 1930, and 19 May and 18 November 1931; and the numerous letters in the Board of Trustees files, 1931–33 and 1936, MSP-LC. The CRB's financial woes followed the depression-era pattern of health care expenditures. See Daniel Fox, *Health Policies*, pp. 70–76.

[35] Reed, *The Birth Control Movement*, p. 283; and Borell, "Biologists," pp. 78–81. The Milbank Memorial Fund began its public health philanthropy in 1925 but did not support birth control until it began to underwrite the Population Association of America in 1930. The Fund supported many of the demographic studies cited in Chapter 4. "Milbank Memorial Fund," *BCR* 9 (January 1925): 22; and Milbank Memorial Fund files, 1931–38, NCFL, MSP-LC. See Chapter 5 regarding the Rosenwald Fund.

[36] This was especially a problem in and around New York City, where the ABCL, CRB, NCFL, New York City Committee, and the New York State Birth Control League all canvassed the same supporters for donations.

[37] Some of those who urged coordination served on the Boards or Advisory Councils of both groups. See Robert L. Dickinson, "Memo on Cooperation between Organizations in Birth Control and Allied Subjects," 2 December 1929; Board meeting, minutes, ABCL, 23 May 1935, MSP-LC; ABCL, preliminary recommendations on next steps, 10 April 1938; Robert L. Dickinson to ABCL, c. 1937, PPFA-SSC; Henry Pratt Fairchild to Marguerite Benson, c. April 1936, MSP-SSC; Board meeting, minutes, ABCL, 31 October 1935; letters of Mrs. Edward Cornish to Robert L. Dickinson, 18 April 1937; of Margaret Sanger to Clarence Gamble 21 April 1939, CJG-CL; of Mrs. Henry deRham to Margaret Sanger, 16 October 1936; of Margaret Sanger to Hazel Moore, 24 September 1936; of C. C. Little to Marguerite Benson, 13 June 1936, and to Allison Moore, 14 January 1936; and of Marguerite Benson to C. C. Little, 30 March 1936, MSP-LC.

[38] Letter of Margaret Sanger to NCFL membership, 2 May 1937, MSP-LC. See also Edna Rankin McKinnon, activity reports, 24 November 1936, 9 January–13 April 1937, MSP-LC.

Deal welfare state taking up responsibility for contraception promised to provide wider access to contraception and to ease the movement's financial burdens. With this shift in emphasis, however, differences between the CRB and ABCL agendas became even less apparent to the larger public, and the pressure on both groups to reunite increased.

Reunion and Reframing

Sanger's increased intrusion into its privileged domain of clinic organizing produced a crisis for League officials, who believed that the CRB's fieldwork already interfered with their more "conservative" efforts.[39] Although the number of clinics had increased dramatically, this expansion was slow and costly. Public officials continued to cite the threat of public controversy in explaining their reluctance to incorporate contraception into public health and welfare agencies.[40] To the ABCL, which continued to blame Sangerists' agitation for provoking the fear of controversy, increased activity by the CRB nationally would only exacerbate its problems. But while the League blamed Sangerists for scaring public officials, the culture of the depression itself had impeded birth control's progress.

Its most vocal opponents, the Roman Catholic Church, denounced birth control on sectarian religious grounds. Yet the tenor of their moral opposition resonated with moral anxieties of the dominant culture. The nation may have embraced the New Deal's economic experiments, but it rejected the social experiments of the twenties, represented by the flapper and gin, and returned to traditional family values as a spiritual guide to survival in hard times. In response to declining rates at which new families were being formed and increasing instability of existing families, New Deal ideology and practice enshrined social support for the traditional family roles of both genders. Eligibility requirements for Unemployment Insurance and Old Age Insurance structured social security on the assumption that those served by the program would be male breadwinners. Women entered the New Deal only as mothers, who were eligible for public support when their role was threatened by ill-health or by the loss of the family breadwinner

[39] Allison Moore, Board meeting, minutes, ABCL, 23 May 1935, MSP-LC; and letter of Cecil Damon to Allison Moore, 3 December 1937, PPFA-SSC.

[40] See letter of John Rice, New York City Health Commissioner, to Mary Reinhardt, 27 May 1940, MSP-LC, which explicitly refers to depopulation as the reason that his office would not support contraceptive clinics.

through death or desertion. The immense public disapproval of married women who worked was embodied in the National Recovery Act, whose provisions prohibited their employment. Also, throughout the decade, the dominant cultural images, many of which were produced by New Deal agencies, represented women as vulnerable mothers who deserved the nation's protection. Demands for women's individual rights, which implicitly challenged their traditional roles, became increasingly suspect. Women reformers who won a measure of power in Roosevelt's administration eschewed both the label of feminism and any suggestion that they gave special consideration to women. Instead, they represented themselves as concerned with the welfare of all of humanity.[41] In such an atmosphere it is not surprising that relief officials shied away from a technology that was popularly connected both to moral excess and to the "bias" of feminism. The ABCL's conclusion that Sangerist agitation maintained the image of birth control militancy may have been accurate, but moral and political anxiety undergirding the New Deal made birth control ideologically tenuous anyway.

The resurgence of traditional family values also hindered fundraising. At the end of 1936, facing greater competition with Sanger and a budget deficit, the League's financial prospects seemed no better for 1937. The recurrence of a recession in 1937, which lasted through 1938 and actually produced a more rapid decline of the national economy than had occurred in 1929, only made the ABCL's financial position more precarious.[42] Hoping that professional fundraising assistance would surmount its problems, the League turned to the John Price Jones Corporation to plan its 1938 fundraising campaign.

Surveying the field from the League's perspective, the Jones Corporation complimented it as the "largest and oldest" national birth control agency.[43] Through its "insistence on minimum clinic standards

[41] On the gendering of New Deal Policy see Mink, "Lady," pp. 109–12; Mimi Abramowitz, *Regulating the Lives of Women*, pp. 215–37; and Linda Gordon, ed., *Women, The State, and Welfare*. On gender imagery during the depression see Wendy Kozol, "Madonnas of the Fields," pp. 1–23; and James Curtis, "Dorothea Lange," pp. 1–20. And on the perspective of women reformers see Susan Ware, *Beyond Suffrage*, pp. 14–17, 117–20; and Cott, "What's in a Name," pp. 821–23.

[42] On the 1937–38 recession and its impact on New Deal reforms see Richard Polenberg, "The Decline of the New Deal," pp. 255–58.

[43] Jones, "Survey," 1938, pp. 58 and 42. This survey was in part a sales pitch to convince the League to use the Jones Corporation's services. As such it appealed to the League's sense of its own importance. The John Price Jones Corporation was one of several firms that organized professional fundraising drives for a variety of charitable organizations

and on the establishment of medical advisory boards in connection with all clinics," the League had kept the movement on the "proper levels" of professional decorum. This conduct, the survey deduced, was "largely responsible" for the interest and support that birth control had already won among public health and welfare professionals. However, noting that Sanger's "early work had made her name almost synonymous with birth control," the survey concluded that the League had "a real job" ahead to "win wide acceptance" as the leading birth control agency.[44] In delineating a long-term financing policy to meet this challenge, the Jones Corporation advised that the ABCL's first priority had to be ending the confusion and the duplication of effort with Sangerists. The sense that there was "dissension within the ranks of birth control advocates" hindered fundraising. The League, whose professionalism led it to eschew "militant controversy," was the "logical organization to take the lead in bringing about better coordination of effort" between the birth control agencies.[45]

Beyond coordination with Sangerists, the financing plan proposed several other changes to make the League attractive to a wider audience of potential donors. Acknowledging the valuable assistance of women volunteers to past fundraising efforts, the plan suggested that "particular attention should be paid to . . . enlisting men workers," who would be more effective in raising the large sums of money needed by the League. Including men would also help the League present its case "in relation to the whole social and economic picture," which, by limiting its appeal to women, the movement had so far failed to do.[46] Instead of assessing the culture of the depression as a hin-

---

in the 1920s. In this capacity it helped advance the professional culture of social work. See Lubove, *The Professional Altruist*, pp. 215–19.

[44] Jones, "Survey," 1938, pp. 64, 90–91, 89. The Jones Corporation had conducted a similar survey in 1930 for Sanger's CRB and NCFL. Many of the recommendations it made in 1938 repeated those of the 1930 survey. See Jones, "Survey," 1930, pp. 97, 108, 151, on its earlier conclusion that Sanger should not continue to dominate the movement. These recommendations were largely based on the opinions of Sanger's opponents within the birth control movement.

[45] Jones, "Survey," 1938, pp. 175, 144. See also p. 85, which notes that there was an internal struggle on the ABCL Board about its relationship to Sanger. In particular, C. C. Little who had become the League's president in 1937, wanted greater cooperation although he was largely inactive.

[46] Ibid., pp. 161, 47, 150. See also p. 170, where it is noted that controversy would make it difficult to enlist men. This repeated its 1930 recommendation that a man should head the organization and the name should be changed. See Jones, "Survey," 1930, p. 151, 103–4.

drance to the cause, the survey argued that "renewed emphasis on the home and family as the key institution of society" gave the League a unique "opportunity . . . to advance their cause materially." But in taking advantage of this opportunity, the financing campaign should highlight only certain aspects of birth control. In its professional experience, the Jones Corporation had found that successful fundraising depended upon an organization's articulation of the big ideas behind its cause. The ideas best suited to the League's campaign were those aspects of birth control that promoted "the physical, social, and moral well-being of the people," such as "betterment of the human race; the promotion of public health; [and] raising the standard of living." Each of these big ideas was phrased in terms of family values, not women's rights. Women were represented in the plan only in terms of birth control's impact on maternal health; sexuality was represented only in terms of the impact of marital adjustment on the family's mental hygiene. By focusing on the benefit of birth control to the family, the League could effectively counter the "greatest obstacle" to public acceptance of birth control, the "moral issue," expressed in the contention that birth control would increase promiscuity and thereby would undermine the family.[47] These recommendations, which the ABCL followed in conducting its 1938 fundraising campaign, became the blueprint for both the movement's reorganization and its reframing of birth control into planned parenthood.

In late 1937, as a demonstration of the unity among birth control advocates, the ABCL asked Sanger to serve as a sponsor of the Jones-inspired financial campaign, the Citizens' Committee for Planned Parenthood.[48] To Sangerists, this request was a self-serving gesture to appear to be cooperative. Earlier in 1937, when they had organized a joint committee of League and CRB officials to air interorganizational conflicts, the League had summarily dismissed Sangerist proposals for cooperation on movement publications and fieldwork.[49] With a budget

[47] Ibid., pp. 55, 1, 9, 144. See also pp. 12, 138–42.

[48] Letter of C. C. Little, president of the ABCL, to Margaret Sanger, 14 December 1937 and 20 January 1938, MSP-LC.

[49] The joint committee, the Birth Control Council of America, was formed in late 1936. It collapsed after only a few meetings, when the League refused to consider either a joint publication or a mobile clinic to serve rural areas. By this point the *BCR* was largely defunct, and there was no regular birth control magazine. See memo, CRB, 30 November 1936, MSP-LC; and Birth Control Council of America meeting, minutes, 14 May 1937, MSP-SSC, and 22 June 1937, CJG-CL. See also Kennedy, *Birth Control in America*, p. 257, who, in his usual sarcastic tone, blames Sanger for the squabbling and notes that "fortunately" the "cooler heads" that prevailed "belonged to men."

of their own to raise, Sanger and her staff felt that her name should be reserved for the CRB's sole use, at least until there was real cooperation from the League. So, believing the League simply wanted to cash in on her name, Sanger, with the full approval of the CRB staff, declined the invitation to become a sponsor.[50]

Even without Sanger's participation, the League's fundraising campaign was moderately successful. Yet the effort involved in raising the money reaffirmed that the ABCL would not "get widespread public support and substantial financial support until [it was] in a position to merge" the efforts of the ABCL and CRB or to explain why that could not be done. The Citizens' Committee recommended that the League form a joint committee with CRB representatives to assess the feasibility of merging the two organizations.[51] Sanger, who had left the door open for such discussions in her refusal to serve on the Citizens' Committee, agreed to participate. Over a ten-month period in 1938, during which the national recession continued, the Joint Committee of the CRB and ABCL tried to reconcile the conflicting agendas that each group brought to the merger negotiations.

The League hoped that a merger would finally solve their "Sanger problem." With a merger, the professional-minded League might increase its authority over birth control programs nationally, depending on Sanger's role within the new organization. At least clinics and supporters would no longer be able to defect to the CRB if they objected to the League's procedures. Moreover, a merger could give League members the ability to rein in what they saw as irresponsible propaganda.[52] Sangerists, who believed that success in gaining state support of birth control would require a concerted effort, wanted the merger to provide a united front for the movement in the education, fieldwork, and fundraising needed to organize new clinics. They also hoped a merger would put an end to the League's constant criticism. Sanger, who was nearly sixty and whose husband was ill, had spent twenty-five years in the front lines of the birth control movement. She was ready

[50] Letters of Florence Rose to Margaret Sanger, 4 January 1938, MSP-SSC; of Cecil Damon to Clarence Gamble, 10 December 1937; of Clarence Gamble to Cecil Damon, 11 December 1937, CJG-CL; and of Margaret Sanger to Mrs. Lewis Delafield, 30 December 1937, and to C. C. Little, 30 December 1937, MSP-LC, and 1 January 1938, CJG-CL.

[51] "Preliminary Recommendations on Next Steps for the League, Part III: Settling the Sanger Problem," 30 April 1938, PPFA-SSC.

[52] Ibid. For instance, Clarence Gamble simply took his projects (and his money) to the CRB if the League disapproved of them. See Clarence Gamble, notes on ABCL Board meeting, 8 April 1937, CJG-CL; and Reed, *The Birth Control Movement*, pp. 257–65.

to step back from its daily operation, especially the constant effort of fundraising.[53]

Yet Sangerists, who continued to define women as the subject of birth control, were not willing simply to capitulate to the League's perspective. The CRB objective for the new organization was to democratize birth control as a woman's right, and they objected to the terms in which the League articulated that the new goal should be making contraception available to "the medically and economically indigent." In the CRB statement of its objectives for the merger, Sanger noted that the "attempt to capture the uninformed reactionary opposition by camouflaging birth control" under "the so-called 'positive' side" was a "grave error." More would be lost than would be gained if the new organization were to "submerge its identity and activities into other channels."[54] Moreover, Sangerists did not intend to relinquish practical management of the CRB to the merged organization. Because it ran the "only clinic in New York City where anyone can come and receive information regardless of class, color, creed or anything else," Sangerists thought it was important to maintain the CRB's independence. Retaining administrative control was the only way to "keep the clinic as it is, free of all medical authority, interference or interruption."[55] By 1938 the CRB was the leading national clinic. It had conducted the most extensive research on methods, and it had set up a number of specialized services to meet women's diverse needs. Through its marital advice clinic, women who were engaged to be married could obtain contraceptives. The "over-due clinic" provided pregnancy testing to women whose menstrual cycles were delayed and provided therapeutic abortions, in some cases, if the women were in fact pregnant. A "safe-period" clinic studied "menstrual periodicity" among patients whose "religious convictions" precluded the use of "artificial methods." And a marriage counseling clinic provided sexual counseling to women.[56]

[53] Letters of Margaret Sanger to Penelope Huse, 25 September 1938, MSP-SSC, and to Henry Pratt Fairchild, 14 October 1938, MSP-LC; and Executive Committee and Board meeting, minutes, CRB, 11 November 1938, p. 1, PPFA-SSC.

[54] Joint committee, report, 3 October 1938, pp. 11, 6; and Margaret Sanger, "Aims and Objectives," preamble to the Bureau statement to the joint committee, n.d., CJG-CL.

[55] Executive Committee and Board of Trustees meeting, minutes, CRB, 11 November 1938, p. 3, PPFA-SSC. The Executive Committee and Board agreed unanimously with her.

[56] By this time more than 65,000 women had used the CRB. Joint committee, report, p. 12. The Marital Advice Clinic was established in October 1931. See CRB, progress report, 1933, p. 8, MSP-LC. On the practice of providing therapeutic abortions, see

Led by D. Kenneth Rose, whom the ABCL hired as a mediator, the Joint Committee developed a plan for merging birth control fieldwork, education, and fundraising that accounted for the concerns of each group, at least in part. When the merger was formalized in January 1939, Sanger was elected honorary chairman of the Board. This position limited her day-to-day involvement in the new organization, but it was intended to retain "the value of her past and present leadership."[57] In addition, the CRB, renamed the Margaret Sanger Clinical Research Bureau, remained independent. It would be funded by the BCFA and would serve as a teaching and research center, but the existing Board would continue to manage it.[58] The task of blending the philosophies and activities of the ABCL and CRB into a united effort fell to D. Kenneth Rose, who was appointed as managing director. However, under Rose's leadership, the Federation not only combined the two organizations but also restructured the movement according to the recommendations that the John Price Jones Corporation had been urging.[59]

The words *birth control* were initially retained in the new organization's title, but because agitation was no longer thought to be appropriate, its rhetoric was reshaped. Birth control propaganda, the new leaders argued, had actually limited the movement's progress because birth control, often confused with abortion, evoked an image of avoiding motherhood, and it "tend[ed] to limit support to women." As a practical matter, the BCFA needed to appear to be more friendly to men's concerns because men controlled the agencies from which the

---

Diagnostic Clinic, monthly reports, 1933–36, MSP-LC; and Chesler, *Woman of Valor*, pp. 300–303. On marriage counseling see Gordon, *Woman's Body*, pp. 368–90.

[57] Although D. Kenneth Rose promised that the honorary chairmanship was not an effort to "shelve" Sanger, the CRB insisted that she also be given a place on the Executive Committee of the BCFA. D. Kenneth Rose convinced ABCL officers that this arrangement was necessary to generate sufficient financial support. See Executive Committee meeting, minutes, CRB, 10 October 1938; joint meeting of the Executive Committee and Board of Trustees, minutes, CRB, 11 November 1938, p. 1; joint committee meeting, minutes, 9 January 1939, PPFA-SSC; letters of Clarence Gamble to Margaret Sanger, 22 November 1938 and 14 January 1939, CJG-CL.

[58] The Margaret Sanger Clinical Research Bureau remained in operation through the early seventies and still tested and prescribed diaphragms. Petchesky, *Abortion and Woman's Choice*, pp. 196, 204. The New York City Committee also retained independent management of its clinics, which it had likewise insisted on before agreeing to join the new organization. See Executive Committee meeting, minutes, BCFA, 31 January 1939, CJG-CL.

[59] The Jones Corporation recommendations, which Rose had drafted in 1938, would reorganize the Federation to conform with the general principles of professional organization in voluntary social services. See Lubove, *The Professional Altruist*, pp. 215–18.

BCFA sought support.[60] To broaden its appeal, the new organization emphasized the gender-neutrality of its cause, saying that it sought to win public "acceptance of Planned Parenthood through birth control" and "the inclusion of birth control services in the programs of all private and public health services." Planned parenthood, the true goal of the movement, was as relevant to men as it was to women.[61]

At the same time, Rose argued, building a professional organization was essential to making the BCFA more effective, and, for leadership, the new organization needed to hire a "man of outstanding administrative ability" to serve as its president.[62] But in the interim, as managing director, Rose instituted new procedures that emphasized rational administration of the organization's functions over charismatic leadership and individual efforts.[63] He reorganized the various activities of the Federation staff into discrete subdivisions, each of which was supervised by trained experts in an administrative hierarchy that Rose presided over.[64] With authority centralized in upper management, longtime staff members were prohibited from undertaking any work

[60] Summary of Recommendations to Joint Committee of ABCL and CRB, 10 October 1938, PPFA–SSC; and National Referendum on the Name to be Adopted by State Leagues, Affiliated Committees, and Federations, 17 April 1941, as quoted by Reed, *The Birth Control Movement,* p. 265. See also Chesler, *Woman of Valor,* pp. 391–93; Gordon, *Woman's Body,* pp. 341–45; and Kennedy, *Birth Control in America,* pp. 257–71.

[61] In the three-page announcement of the merger, the word *women* appeared only in the opening title and in the closing paragraph requesting funds. The term *racial betterment* was also replaced by *public welfare.* See "A Statement of National Importance to All Those Men and Women Who Have Supported Local and National Efforts to Improve the Quality of the American People," c. January 1939, pp. 2, 1, PPFA-SSC. See also annual meeting, minutes, BCFA, 1939, pp. 6–7, MSP-SSC.

[62] Ibid.; and "Recommendations of Joint Committee," 10 October 1938, PPFA-SSC. See also Executive Committee meeting, minutes, ABCL, c. November 1936, MSP-LC. C. C. Little had been the League president since 1936. At this meeting, in an effort to convince him to stay on, the Committee stated that birth control was not a woman's movement.

[63] D. Kenneth Rose, "A Report with Recommendations to the Board of Directors of the BCFA," 18 May 1939, pp. 1–2, CJG-CL; letters of D. Kenneth Rose to Florence Rose, 11 January 1943, FRP-SSC; and of Sidney Goldstein to Margaret Sanger, 10 January 1941, MSP-LC. Rose was not continuously employed by the BCFA in this period, in part because he suffered from tuberculosis. See letter of D. Kenneth Rose to Clarence Gamble, 9 October 1940, CJG-CL.

[64] The three main divisions were a regional organization department, a medical department, and a public information department. Rose also tried unsuccessfully to persuade the NCMH to enter the merged organization. The NCMH remained independent, but it did become the agency through which research money was funneled to the Federation. See Executive Committee meeting, minutes, NCMH, 3 November and 1 December 1938; letter of Raymond Squirer to D. Kenneth Rose, 16 December 1938, NCMH; annual report, 1940; annual meeting, minutes, NCMH, 1942, NCMH-CL.

without prior approval. Staff members were often prohibited from engaging in activities deemed by Rose to be outside the purview of the departments to which they had been assigned. These rules were implemented through an elaborate system of time sheets that allowed Rose to keep close track of how staff members used their time.[65]

In addition to restructuring internal procedures, Rose imposed a formalized relationship between the Federation and its Board of Directors. All communication with the Board was to go through his office; direct contact between staff and Board members was prohibited. This policy was deemed necessary to establish efficient management. The standards of professional social service required that the activities of volunteers be subordinated to the agency's professional administrators.[66] With all communication routed through Rose, initiatives made by Board members, all of whom were volunteers, were subject to review by professional administrators. However, his actions were also an effort to contain Sanger's influence in the new organization. Removing Sanger from a position of administrative authority would go a long way toward eliminating militant, and thus irresponsible, agitation. Yet as the honorary chairman of the Board, she was still located in a position to support the new professional organization, because she could continue to engage in the fundraising for which she was considered indispensable.[67]

Sanger soon felt squeezed out by the reorganization and even contemplated resigning in 1943. Because of her indispensability as a fundraiser, Rose convinced her to stay.[68] But many of the longtime Sangerist

[65] Letters of Florence Rose to D. Kenneth Rose, 8 September 1943, FRP-SSC; of Florence Rose to Mrs. Hadley, chairman of the Executive Committee, BCFA, 10 September 1943, MSP-LC; and of Woodbridge Morris to Edna Rankin McKinnon, 1 June 1939, CJG-CL.

[66] See Lubove, *The Professional Altruist*, pp. 157–63; and Muncy, *Creating a Female Dominion*, pp. 120–21, who discuss the containment of voluntarism as social work professionalized.

[67] The restrictions on Board members was made to contain both Sanger and Clarence Gamble. See letters of Margaret Sanger to Clarence Gamble, 8 February 1943; of Clarence Gamble to D. Kenneth Rose, 27 November 1941, and 20 February and 15 July 1942, and to Edna Rankin Mckinnon, 17 May 1939; and of D. Kenneth Rose to Clarence Gamble, 3 March 1942, CJG-CL; and to Margaret Sanger, 7 February 1944, MSP-LC. See also Reed, *The Birth Control Movement*, pp. 137, 269–71.

[68] The ease with which D. Kenneth Rose accomplished the name change is the best example of Sanger's powerlessness in the new organization. Sanger despised the new name, calling it appeasing and weak. See letters of Margaret Sanger to Mary Lasker, 8 January 1943, MSP-SSC; of Mrs. Mali to Margaret Sanger, 8 February 1943; of D. Kenneth Rose to Margaret Sanger, 7 February 1944, MSP-LC; of Clarence Gamble to Margaret Sanger, 2 December 1939 and 30 September 1942; and of Margaret Sanger to

staff women, who likewise resented Rose's reorganizing efforts, did resign from the Federation. Hazel Moore, who came to the movement in 1931 from the American Red Cross, had been the principal lobbyist for the NCFL before 1936 and a dedicated fieldworker traveling around the country organizing local clinics for several years thereafter. She resigned in mid-1939 after Rose tried to restrict her lobbying efforts. Edna Rankin McKinnon, whose sister, Jeannette Rankin, was the first woman elected to Congress, resigned in 1940 because of the new organization's constraints on her activities. The most tragic loss came in 1941, when Hannah Stone, who had been the CRB Medical Director since 1924, died suddenly of a heart attack. Cecil Damon remained the longest as Rose's assistant, but by 1949 she too left the National Federation and moved over to become director of the still semi—independent Margaret Sanger Research Bureau.[69]

In the more informal administration of Sanger's organizations these women had been used to a good deal of autonomy in their work. What supervision they did receive occurred in the context of their close personal relationships to Sanger. In contrast, Rose's management style was remote, and his procedural restrictions were dictatorial. Most irritating, however, was the prohibition against discussing their work with Board members. When Florence Rose, who was among the last of Sanger's former assistants to leave the Federation, resigned, she wrote a long letter detailing her dissatisfactions with the Federation. Her basic complaint was that the administration had become more concerned with the structure and procedures of the organization than

---

Clarence Gamble, c. October 1942, 10 December 1939, and 8 February 1943, and 29 March 1946, CJG-CL, and 23 March 1943, FRP-SSC; and to Sidney Goldstein, 16 January 1941, MSP-LC.

[69] Edna McKinnon went on to become the executive director of the Chicago Planned Parenthood Association from 1946 to 1958. There is no record of Hazel Moore's subsequent activities. Penelope Huse, who had been the ABCL secretary until 1928 and then had worked for the CMH, also resigned. Huse eventually went to work for the Ortho-Gynol company. Allison Moore and Marguerite Benson resigned from the League. See obituary, *New York Times*, 11 July 1941, MSP-LC; letters of Hazel Moore to D. Kenneth Rose, 24 March 1939; of Edna Rankin McKinnon to Clarence Gamble, 23 March, 4 April, 6 June, 3 August 1939, and 11 and 26 January 1940; of Hazel Moore to Florence Rose, 2 February 1939, and to D. Kenneth Rose, 24 March 1939; Executive Committee meeting, minutes, BCFA, 27 April 1939, CJG-CL; letters of Penelope Huse to Margaret Sanger, 1 July 1949; of Mary Compton to Penelope Huse, 20 July 1949, MSP-LC; and of Florence Rose to D. Kenneth Rose, 8 September 1943, FRP-SSC; and Wilma Dykeman, *Too Many People*, pp. 85–87, 106.

with birth control. In this concern, she felt the new leadership belittled the work and experience of longtime laywomen workers.[70]

D. Kenneth Rose's perspective on what a good organization required was based on gender stereotypes that did dismiss the experience of longtime birth control advocates—both paid staff members and volunteers. As part of restructuring the organization, Rose sought to hire male experts to oversee BCFA programs. Hiring a male president was not enough; six months after the merger, Rose recommended hiring "two men," one to serve as medical director and one to serve as director of public information.[71] Rose did not consider the female staff to be sufficiently professional to be promoted to these positions. As Sanger told Florence Rose in 1943, "Go ahead, darling, get kicked around— you will never get kicked upstairs."[72] In fact, Sanger was correct. From Rose's perspective, men were needed to compensate for weakness caused by the general character of the staff. "The women workers" were "too emotionally concerned with the birth control problem and too little equipped with the experience, techniques and skill to do an objective job." The emotionalism of the female staff contributed to a continuing "lack of sufficient masculine support" for the Federation.[73]

Rose's perceptions set up an intolerable working situation for the staff women. In early years of the reorganization, men were brought in at considerable expense, while longtime staff women were denied promotions or raises. Moreover, these men, while they were experts in public health or public relations, generally had little experience in the field of birth control. Thus, the experienced staff women were con-

[70] Moore and McKinnon also expressed anger about the way in which the new leadership belittled their experience. See Dykeman, *Too Many People*, pp. 85–87; letters of Hazel Moore to D. Kenneth Rose, 24 March 1939, and to Florence Rose, 2 February 1939, CJG-CL. Florence Rose, originally a social worker, eventually went to work for Meals on Wheels. Letters of Florence Rose to D. Kenneth Rose, 8 September 1943, pp. 2–3, FRP-SSC; of Florence Rose to Mrs. Hadley, 10 September 1943; of Penelope Huse to Margaret Sanger, 1 July 1949; and of Mary Compton to Penelope Huse, 20 July 1949, MSP-LC. See also Chesler, *Woman of Valor*, pp. 287–309, who describes Sangerist organizations as a community of women.

[71] Rose, report with Recommendations, p. 2. By this recommendation, Rose was ignoring Hannah Stone, who was still alive at this point and had the longest continuous record of any physician in the field.

[72] Florence Rose, personal notes, 2 May–25 May 1943, MSP-SSC. Chesler, *Woman of Valor*, pp. 392–95, notes the masculinization of the leadership and attributes it in part to the lack of a female successor. However, this ignores the fact that if Sanger was a problematic leader, then neither her compatriots nor her subordinates would have been seen as professional enough to lead the new organization.

[73] Rose, report with recommendations, p. 3.

tinually put in the position of having to train those people who would become their supervisors. Since the men tended not to stay with the organization for very long, the whole process of hiring and training had to be repeated several times. Not surprisingly, there was much turnover among the female staff and, with it, a considerable loss of practical experience.[74]

D. Kenneth Rose hoped that these changes in image, organization, and staff would enable the Federation to influence public policy where previous efforts had failed. Even as the merger was being negotiated, Sangerists were engaged in a vigorous but unsuccessful campaign to persuade Federal officials to fund contraceptive clinics.[75] They focused in particular on the maternal and infant health program authorized by the 1935 Social Security Act.[76] In January 1938, the Children's Bureau, which administered part of the program, sponsored a "National Conference on Better Care for Mothers and Babies" to highlight the problems of maternal and infant deaths.[77] Although the Children's Bureau investigation focused on the inadequacies of health care for pregnant women and newborns, it also revealed that 25–30 percent of maternal deaths occurred as a direct result of illegal abortions. The death rate from abortion was highest among the poorest women.[78] To Sangerists,

[74] Letters of Florence Rose to D. Kenneth Rose, 8 September 1943, pp. 3–4, FRP-SSC, and to Mrs. Hadley, 10 September 1943, which lists the men who had come and gone from the Federation and claims that the administrative staff averaged less than one year's employ with the organization.

[75] Throughout 1938 and 1939, health reformers believed that passage of a national health insurance program was imminent. But although Senator Robert Wagner did introduce a bill, the Roosevelt Administration did not back it, and it was never enacted. See Fox, *Health Policies*, pp. 79–93.

[76] Letters were also sent to the Public Health Service and to President Roosevelt. See Public Progress Committee, summary, 15 January 1939, pp. 1, 3, MSP-LC, which indicates that over 1,100 letters were sent to the Children's Bureau, and 530 were sent to the Public Health Service. See also letter of Margaret Sanger to Public Progress Committee, June 1938, CJG-CL.

[77] The Conference took place in Washington, D.C., 17–18 January 1938. Representatives of the CRB were initially invited to attend the Conference. They were prohibited from making any statements during the meeting, however, and were refused membership in the association that grew out of this Conference. See letters of Hazel Moore to Florence Rose, 7 and 8 January 1938; of Helen Sachs Strauss, secretary of the National Committee on Better Care for Mothers and Babies, to Margaret Sanger, 17 May 1938; and of Margaret Sanger to Helen Sachs Strauss, 14 June 1938; Hazel Moore, report, 6 October 1938, MSP-LC; letter of and Hazel Moore to Clarence Gamble, 24 January 1938, CJG-CL.

[78] On abortion mortality statistics see Children's Bureau, "Facts about Maternal and Early Infant Care," 1 March 1938, p. 3; and letter of Margaret Sanger to Public Progress Committee members, June 1938, CJG-CL.

these statistics provided their best argument for government support of birth control. With universal access to reliable contraception, women—especially poor women—would no longer be compelled to risk their lives to control their fertility. More than one thousand letters, however, did not persuade Federal officials to include birth control in Federal health programs. Katherine Lenroot, Chief of the Children's Bureau, steadfastly refused to make any policy statement on birth control, citing the dangers of depopulation and political controversy.[79]

Immediately after the merger, Rose tried to squash this letter-writing effort. He preferred that the Federation carry out a more discreet and less political campaign, using the euphemisms of "planned parenthood" and "child spacing," to persuade the government to utilize the BCFA's contraceptive services unofficially.[80] Federation Board member Mary Lasker, who ignored Rose's admonishments to be discreet, prevailed upon her friend Eleanor Roosevelt to break her silence on the topic and use the influence she had with government officials.[81] As First Lady, Eleanor Roosevelt, who had been a Board member of the ABCL in 1928, refused to comment on birth control until January 1940. When she did announce her support of birth control she did so tentatively, saying that she was not "opposed to the planning of children."[82] In 1940 Roosevelt also began to use her influence to convince Federal agencies to meet with the Federation. But, despite her efforts, little of substantive value came out of the Federation's efforts to get public funding for family planning. The Children's Bureau maintained its distance and refused to initiate any activity concerned with contraception. As well, the Public Health Service, although it agreed to let state officials use some of their existing grants under the 1939 Venereal Disease Act for contraceptive clinics, refused to initiate any

[79] The Public Health Service likewise refused to make a policy statement. See letters of Thomas Parran to George Lake, 4 June 1938, CJG-CL; and of Katherine Lenroot to Emeth Tuttle Cochran, 14 March 1938; and Public Progress Committee, summary, pp. 1–3, 4–5, MSP-LC.

[80] Curtailment of the Public Progress Committee led Hazel Moore to resign. See D. Kenneth Rose, memo, 24 February 1939, pp. 2–3; BCFA, annual report, 1939, p. 7, MSP-SSC; BCFA, annual report, 1940, p. 1, CJG-CL; "Procedures for Gaining Acceptance by Public Health Officials," 17 June 1942; and memo of D. Kenneth Rose to Florence Rose, 15 January 1939, MSP-LC. See also Chesler, *Woman of Valor*, p. 394.

[81] Letter of Margaret Sanger to Clarence Gamble, 8 February 1943, CJG-CL.

[82] "Mrs. Roosevelt Is 'Not' Opposed to Practice of Birth Control," *New York Herald Tribune*, 17 January 1940; and "Birth Control Endorsed by First Lady," *Washington Herald*, 16 January 1940; MSP-LC. See also letter of Hazel Moore to Clarence Gamble, 22 January 1940, MSP–LC.

programs.[83] Thus D. Kenneth Rose's efforts to reframe birth control rhetoric and reorganize the movement did not produce the results he had hoped they would. By 1945, the PPFA was a respectable organization in terms of its procedures and staff, but it did not hold much sway with policymakers. Privately financed, extramural clinics continued to provide the great majority of clinical contraceptive services.[84]

However, moral opposition and concern for depopulation, which Federal agencies cited in refusing to support contraceptive services, did become the solvent of feminist demands embodied in the birth control movement itself. Over the objections of Sangerists, the BCFA's efforts to accommodate its opposition displaced women as the subjects of birth control. Women's perspectives, dismissed as emotional and personal, and thus not objective, no longer defined the organization or its rhetoric. By 1945 the only remnant of the earlier feminist basis of the PPFA was Margaret Sanger's name on the organization's letterhead. Framing contraception as a public health issue, Planned Parenthood was no longer concerned with freeing women from the "tyranny" of "man-made laws"; rather, it focused on childspacing as the means to fit family size to family income.[85] Thus the movement succeeded practically by organizing more than eight hundred clinics in which women could legally obtain reliable contraceptives.[86] But at the same time, women's perspectives and women's organizations were eclipsed from the discourse and institutions sustaining those clinics. Moreover, even the movement's practical achievements were compromised: without either public money or a cadre of vigorous laywomen advocates

[83] Florence Rose, activities report, December 1941, p. 8, MSP-SSC, reports on a White House meeting of the BCFA, Children's Bureau, Public Health Service, and Agriculture Department, 8 December 1941; letters of C. C. Pierce to D. Kenneth Rose, 2 February 1942; and of Thomas Parran to Eleanor Roosevelt, 6 January 1942; Warren Draper to C. C. Pierce, 11 February 1942; surgeon general to district offices, draft, 13 February 1942; annual meeting, minutes, PPFA, 1942, p. 2, CJG-CL; letter of D. Kenneth Rose to Katherine Lenroot, 12 December 1941, MSP-LC. See also Kennedy, *Birth Control in America*, pp. 260–71, who overstates the success of this meeting, and Chesler, *Woman of Valor*, pp. 389–91.

[84] Ray and Gosling, "American Physicians," pp. 406–7. There was public support for government funding of contraception. A 1940 Gallup poll found that 77 percent of those surveyed approved of the distribution of contraceptives to married persons in government health clinics. See letter of BCFA, Public Progress Committee to members, 24 January 1940, MSP-LC.

[85] Sanger, "Shall We?"

[86] PPFA, "Organization, Objectives, Services," p. 3.

and staff to support it, the PPFA stalled in the 1940s and 1950s. In those years, the number of its clinics did not increase.[87]

Conclusion

The birth control movement represents a case in which a social movement, while remaining controversial, nonetheless legitimated some of its claims within the dominant culture. It did so only by forging alliances with middle-class, primarily white, professional groups, who themselves remained reluctant supporters of birth control. Women's groups, particularly welfare feminists, avoided birth control because the sexual controversy it engendered threatened to undermine their political authority. Court-mandated medical authority over contraception founded an uneasy relationship between the birth control movement and a medical profession that objected to laywomen defining the scope of acceptable contraceptive practice. Although jealous of their professional domain, physicians as a group also were reluctant to support birth control because of its sexual implications. In their struggle against a medical hegemony, Sangerists turned to eugenicists, whose statistical expertise and commitment to social and economic indicators for birth control gave scientific legitimacy to the movement. In particular, eugenicists articulated a socially respectable language that divorced contraception from sexual controversy. This eugenical language muted the sexual controversy of contraception by abstracting it from the sexual context in which women made contraceptive decisions. Thus the language divorced questions of women's sexuality from debates about contraception altogether. In so doing, it undercut the claims to women's sexual self-determination articulated in earlier Sangerist rhetoric. In the absence of a rhetoric of women's sex rights, the only position left to women in birth control rhetoric was that of responsible maternity.[88]

Continuing to champion individual rights, Sangerists resisted the more invidious elements of eugenic ideology and practice. Nonetheless, their own racially maternalist perspective limited their rejection

[87] Chesler, *Woman of Valor,* pp. 394–95, points out that the number of clinics it operated actually declined by 1960.

[88] Although sex counseling continued through the forties and fifties, particularly in the Margaret Sanger Research Bureau, it was focused on helping women adjust to traditional marriage. Thus the counseling functioned primarily as an aid to responsible maternity. On this counseling see Gordon, *Woman's Body,* pp. 378–90.

of the racial perspective underlying eugenics. This racial maternalist stance, in which the economic ethic of fertility was represented as a means of racial uplift, was most clearly enacted in the tentative alliance of Sangerists and African-Americans. Here, again, questions of women's sexuality were muted. Sangerists, positioned as patrons, granted African-Americans equal access to contraception as a means of promoting maternal and infant health. Although African-American supporters struggled against Sangerists' definition of the terms of that opportunity, their own ideological linkage of poverty and ignorance limited the effectiveness of that resistance.

The fatal aspect of all these relationships was that, through them, concerns other than social justice for women came to dominate the ideology and practices of the contraceptive institutions. During the depression, women's increased demand for contraception coupled with economic constraints on private fundraising put enormous strains on the movement. In the context of such constraints, the movement reorganized to accommodate both the moral opposition and the fear of national depopulation that were expressed by its allies and foes alike. In replacing the "fighting words" *birth control* with the rhetoric of "planned parenthood" through "child spacing," Planned Parenthood eclipsed the movement's core of woman-centered ideology and practice. Under the guise of objectivity, PPFA's perspective instead defined contraception as a tool for improving family health and national well-being.

PPFA's perspective required a balanced approach to fertility control, which it provided by developing services for those families who "should have more children."[89] To the extent that contraception gained social acceptance before the 1960s, the economic ethic of fertility provided the grounds upon which it was legitimated. This ethic, distinguishing responsible and irresponsible fertility, owed more to the politics of race than to the principles of gender equity. Explicit references to racial betterment were discarded in the wake of revelations about Nazi use of eugenics.[90] The economic ethic, however, was still implicitly linked to racial politics through the continuing cultural conflation of poverty and race in definitions of who should have more children. Planned Parenthood's balanced program recommended numerous, well-spaced chil-

[89] PPFA, "Organization, Objectives, Services," p. 6. See also annual meeting, minutes, BCFA, 1939, MSP-SSC.

[90] Letter of Mrs. Klein to Mary Lasker, 5 March 1943, PPFA-SSC.

dren for middle-class, white families and prescribed fewer, well-spaced children for poorer families and families of color.

Yet restructuring its organizations and reframing its rhetoric did not sanitize PPFA's image. These alterations did not dispel the taint of immorality that clung to contraception. The Federation's retirement from politics in favor of being a modern public health agency was always undercut by a feminist past that the organization could not live down.[91] Sanger continued to be a cultural hero whose name was synonymous with birth control. But it was not Sanger's direct or personal influence that undermined PPFA's respectability. Sanger popularly represented the implicit challenge to gender hegemony embodied in diaphragms. Female-controlled contraceptives allowed women some ability to determine both their sexual lives and their reproductive lives for themselves. Although submerged in its program and rhetoric, Planned Parenthood presented a challenge to gender conventions that professional organization and discreet publicity could not eliminate. Muting the underlying demands for women's sexual and reproductive self-determination did not eliminate moral opposition to contraception; it only displaced women's subjective perspectives from the debates about contraceptive practice.

Although beyond the scope of this study, the ways in which the dynamics underlying the birth control movement between 1916 and 1945 have continued to shape reproductive politics should be noted. In the 1960s, with the renewal of feminist challenges, the political dynamics underlying PPFA in 1945 reemerged in debates about birth control and abortion. A new generation of feminists contested the restrictions on women's sexual and reproductive freedom, but, as was the case earlier in the century, gender equity was only one aspect of these debates.[92] At the same time, the economic ethic of fertility was rearticulated to justify contraceptive and abortion practices in an overpopulated world. In fact, within a dominant culture that was hardly more receptive to women's sexual and reproductive independence than it had been earlier in the century, the economic ethic of fertility became the principal argument legitimating the right to privacy in reproductive decision-making. This economic ethic of fertility could legitimate reproductive privacy because of its ongoing conflation with race. The specter of a growing and increasingly rebellious population of color

[91] Chesler, *Woman of Valor,* p. 395, also makes this point.
[92] See Gordon, *Woman's Body* (1990), pp. 402–51, for a detailed account of reproductive rights struggles in the 1970s.

lurked beneath this vocabulary of private (and largely economic) choice in the 1970s. This specter remains compelling today.[93]

While the (white) feminist underpinnings of the pro-choice movement remained solid in the face of the intense opposition of the 1980s, the hazards to which PPFA succumbed during the 1930s remain, particularly in regard to abortion rights. The election of Bill Clinton should halt the erosion of women's reproductive rights that occurred in the eighties, but a great deal has already been lost. Recent Supreme Court decisions in *Webster v. Reproductive Health Services* and *Planned Parenthood v. Casey* have widened the range of restrictions that states can impose on women's abortion rights. In particular, both decisions allow states to abandon neutrality in reproductive policy and to "influence" women's choices.[94] At the same time, the ongoing conservative assault on feminist principles of reproductive choice, under the guise of family values, continues to pit women as sexual individuals against the family and the nation. Although it did not win a second term for George Bush, the family values rhetoric remains potent. Clinton contested Republican definitions of who could count as an American family, but he did not challenge the primacy of family values, particularly as they refer to heterosexual propriety.

The polemical appeal of the family values rhetoric in reproductive politics derives from deeply felt social concerns. As Rosalind Petchesky has noted, the conundrum of reproductive politics is that in its "very nature," reproduction "is social and individual at the same time." The individual dimensions are, of course, that reproduction occurs "within and upon women's individual bodies." Thus feminists have argued, as Sanger did, that women have a fundamental right to decide when and if they will engage in sexual and reproductive activities. At the simplest level, the social dimension of reproduction is that the continuity of any human group depends upon women's sexual and reproductive activities. Beyond that, however, the social dimension of reproduction consists of the cultural context, relationships, and institutions in which women's individual sexual and reproductive activities are organized.

[93] See Dienes, *Law, Politics, and Birth Control*, pp. 254–65, 293–96, 300–303; and Luker, *Abortion*, pp. 175–86. Although neither author employs the concept of economic ethic of fertility as developed here, both cite historical evidence consistent with it. Luker, in particular, illuminates its interconnections with women's rights rhetoric in the pro-choice worldview of the period. Dienes, and Petchesky, *Abortion and Woman's Choice*, pp. 101–37, also note the specter of race within this debate.

[94] At the moment this right to influence women's choices is limited to the pro-natalist encouragement of childbirth over abortion. See *Webster v. Reproductive Health Services* 109 S. Ct. 3040 (1989); and *Planned Parenthood v. Casey* 112 S. Ct. 2791 (1992).

At stake in reproductive politics are not just women's abstract individual rights but also the configuration of the social relationships in which those rights are exercised.[95] Feminist demands for women's reproductive autonomy embody a deep challenge to the terms of women's participation in the heterosexual, maternal, and familial relationships by which our culture has organized the social aspects of reproduction. In labeling feminist demands as selfish promotions of promiscuity, Republicans and the pro-life movement have tapped the deep cultural anxiety about how such social needs might otherwise be met.[96]

The family values rhetoric has in the past effectively deflected what are essentially political questions about women's autonomy into a debate about sexual morality. As the analysis here reveals, feminists must not lose sight of this basic aspect of reproductive rights: it is a political contest about the terms of women's participation in sexuality on the one hand and family life on the other. Between 1916 and 1945, access to contraception separated, in practice, sex and reproduction, but they could not be separated in the politics of the period. Nor can sexuality and reproduction be separated in contemporary politics. The current "problem" of teenage pregnancy, where the crisis of family values is most potent, is really a problem of premarital sexuality. Like the first birth control clinics, "the local abortion clinic represents the existence of [young white women's] sexual identity independent of marriage, of parental authority, perhaps of men. . . . The clinic symbolically threatens white patriarchal control over 'their' young women's sexual 'purity.'"[97] Avoiding this moral controversy, as PPFA did in the period studied here, will not strengthen individual reproductive rights against moral backlash. The moral controversy signifies the underlying challenge that abortion and contraception pose to conventional controls of women's sexuality; it is unavoidable.

The analysis offered here also reveals the inadequacies of white feminist demands for abstract individual rights in the face of the cross-cutting race politics shaping the social dimensions of reproduction. The most ominous manifestation of contemporary racial politics are

[95] Petchesky, *Abortion and Woman's Choice*, p. 2. My observations are indebted to Petchesky's analysis which remains the definitive feminist analysis of this tension between the individual and social aspects of reproductive politics.

[96] Relying on Petchesky, Gordon, *Woman's Body* (1990), pp. 452–53, also makes this point.

[97] Rosalind Petchesky, "Abortion Politics in the '90s," p. 733. This moral debate has focused most sharply on teenage sexuality, although teen pregnancy rates have in fact been declining. See also Gordon, *Woman's Body* (1990), pp. 454–65, and Petchesky, *Abortion and Woman's Choice*, pp. 210–14, 231–32.

expressed in welfare reform measures. Renewing the rhetoric of responsible fertility, various state legislatures are considering coercive applications of the economic ethic of fertility to poor women. Proposals to cut off welfare benefits to women who have additional children or to give paltry economic bonuses to poor women who "voluntarily" use Norplant constitute two examples of such coercive applications. Although such proposals are offered to promote responsible fertility among the poor, they are imbued with racial meaning.[98] With poverty rates among African-Americans and Hispanic-Americans twice that of whites, such measures would delay the recently predicted end of white numerical supremacy in the United States.[99] In a society that effectively denies poor women access to basic health care—including contraception and abortion—and that offers them few routes out of poverty, punishment for economically imprudent childbearing effectively curtails poor women's sexual and reproductive choices. At the same time, rewarding poor women for refraining from having children until they can afford it, without providing them with any real means to obtain financial independence, effectively makes sex and procreation economic privileges.[100] Because poverty rates are so much higher among women of color, these women will bear the brunt of such coercive applications of the economic ethic of fertility.

Although the impact is differentiated by race, underlying racial politics cut the ground out from under sexual and reproductive self-determination for every group of women. If sisterhood is not a compelling enough reason for white women to be clear about these racial politics, and historically it has not been, then white women need to see that their own reproductive rights are also compromised by racism. Racism justifies the social regulation of white women's sexuality and fertility in the service of maintaining white supremacy. As one example, curtailment of abortion rights, which white women practice in higher proportions, will also slow the current decline of white numerical dominance.[101]

[98] Maryland, New Jersey, and Arizona were among states considering such proposals in 1993. In the international context, with Clinton's reestablishment of foreign aid for family planning, the unresolved race politics of the population control programs of the 1970s could also reemerge. For an example of recent population control programs see Nafis Sadik, *The State of World Population*, 1990.

[99] See William Henry, "Beyond the Melting Pot," pp. 28–31. This article reports the Census Bureau prediction that, if current growth rates continue, by 2056 Americans of European descent will constitute less than 50 percent of the total U.S. population.

[100] Pro-choice women of color are quick to make this point. See Laura Fraser, "After Roe v. Wade," pp. 47–49, esp. 48.

[101] About two-thirds of the women getting abortions each year are white. Petchesky, "Abortion Politics in the '90s," p. 732.

Although we must reject the racism underlying such proposals, it is impossible to reject all social determinants of reproduction in favor of defending women's abstract individual rights.[102] Given the inevitable tension between the social and individual dimensions of reproductive politics, women, as a diverse social group, must continue to contest the social arrangements in which, as individuals, they exercise the fundamental right to control their bodily processes. Thus reproductive rights advocates must not only defend the individual right of choice but also contest the conditions in which those choices are made. In the next several years, numerous occasions for contesting these conditions will arise as the nation considers health care reform. Feminists must insist, as Sangerists did during the depression, that proposals to provide basic health care to all Americans include concrete access to the full range of reproductive health care for all women.

Such political contests will continue to be rooted in the institutions of reproductive health care that women have built over the course of this century. The extramural birth control clinics in the twenties and thirties were built by women for women. Women provided the staff, the clients, and the financial backing. Those institutions were revitalized by the women's health movement of the 1960s and 1970s. With an African-American president in the 1980s, PPFA increasingly reflected the diversity of women's perspectives.[103] Just as it was earlier in the century, control of these institutions is what is at stake in the 1990s.[104]

While legally sanctioned assaults on clinics continue to threaten their very existence, recent judicial decisions have curtailed the practices within clinics.[105] On the second day of his administration, President Clinton revoked the gag rule, the absolute ban on abortion counseling and referral in agencies that received Federal funding. The *Casey* decision, however gave legal sanction to similar restrictions on clinic practices.

---

[102] Petchesky, *Abortion and Woman's Choice*, pp. 13–14, 387–89, has persuasively argued that there will always be some level at which the individual and social dimensions of reproduction are irreconcilable.

[103] On this increasing diversity see Gordon, *Woman's Body* (1990), pp. 442–51.

[104] See Faye Wattleton, "Planned Parenthood and Pro Choice: Sexual and Reproductive Freedom," a speech delivered to the Columbus Metropolitan Club and Planned Parenthood of Central Ohio, Columbus, Ohio, 9 March 1992. See also Gordon, *Woman's Body* (1990), p. 451, who notes PPFA's increasingly militant response to pro-life attacks on clinics.

[105] As of 1993, there were no abortion services available to women in 83 percent of U.S. counties. Forced to travel great distances to obtain abortion services, women also encounter tremendous harassment by pro-life protestors when they arrive at clinics. See Stanley Henshaw and Jennifer Van Vort, "Abortion Services in the United States,"

A self-contradictory decision, *Casey* both affirmed abortion as women's right and weakened their claim to that right. Using a version of the economic ethic, the Court found that "the ability of women to participate equally in the economic and social life of the Nation has been facilitated by their ability to control their reproductive lives."[106] But by weakening the standard used to review the legality of antiabortion legislation, the *Casey* decision severely undermined the right to choose.[107] Among the restrictions upheld in the decision, the Court legitimated the right of states to legislate the content of counseling for "informed consent" to abortion. States may now dictate the language that physicians must use in counseling women seeking abortions. The Pennsylvania law upheld by *Casey* requires the use of language designed to dissuade women from choosing abortion. Similar "biased counseling" laws existed in half a dozen states before the *Casey* decision, and nearly a dozen states began to consider such legislation after *Casey*.[108] Many of these biased counseling laws also require physicians to give the counseling. This requirement makes abortion more expensive and curtails the authority of nurses and laywomen staff within the clinics.[109] In the 1916–45 period, proper medical supervision eclipsed feminists and their perspective on birth control within clinics. Today, legislative regulation of counseling practices could likewise eclipse feminist perspectives on reproductive choice in abortion clinics. If that were to happen, an important institution from which to contest the terms of women's participation in sexual and reproductive relationships would again be weakened.

---

p. 106; and Stanley Henshaw, "The Accessibility of Abortion Services," pp. 246–63, esp. 249–50.

[106] 112 S. Ct. at 2809, as quoted in the Center for Reproductive Law and Policy, "An Analysis of *Planned Parenthood v. Casey*," p. 5.

[107] Ibid., pp. 5–6. Abortion is no longer a fundamental right. States no longer have to demonstrate that a particular restriction furthers its "compelling interests." Rather, women and physicians must now prove that a particular restriction places an "undue burden" on them.

[108] On biased counseling legislation see the Center for Reproductive Law and Policy, *Reproductive Freedom News*, 5 February and 19 February 1993.

[109] The Center for Reproductive Law and Policy, "An Analysis," pp. 10–11.

Chronology of Events in the U.S. Birth Control Movement

1873
Congress amends the U.S. Postal Code to prohibit the distribution of obscene materials, including contraceptive information and devices. Called the Comstock Act, these laws carry the name of their author, Anthony Comstock, director of the New York Society for the Suppression of Vice.

1883
Sir Francis Galton first employs the term *eugenics* to describe his science of racial improvement through controlled breeding.

1891
Francis Walker, director of the 1870 and 1880 U.S. Census, advances the concept of "race suicide" to describe the statistical differential between immigrant and old-stock growth rates.

1900s
The infant welfare movement emerges to fight the nation's high rates of infant mortality.

1906
The American Breeders' Association forms the first eugenics organization in the United States. Charles Davenport is elected as the secretary of its Committee on Eugenics.

1907
National hysteria develops over the white-slave trade, the purported practice of abducting young white women into prostitution.

Indiana enacts the nation's first compulsory sterilization law.

1910s

Obstetricians begin to define pregnancy as a medical condition that always has the potential for pathology.

Leftist intellectuals begin to articulate a new morality, which values heterosexual expression.

1910

In reaction to hysteria about the white-slave trade, Congress passes the Mann Act, which prohibits interstate transport of women for immoral purposes.

1912

Margaret Sanger works for Lillian Wald's Visiting Nurses' Association on the Lower East Side of New York City. The death of women, particularly Sadie Sachs, from illegal abortions inspires Sanger to fight to legalize contraception.

Henry Goddard publishes the first modern eugenics genealogy, *The Kallikak Family.*

Congress creates the U.S. Children's Bureau to "investigate and report upon all matters pertaining to the welfare of children and child life among all classes of our people."

1913

Women begin to use the term *feminist* to describe their political commitment to economic, political, and sexual rights for women.

The Children's Bureau publishes its first advice pamphlet for mothers, *Prenatal Care.* Contraception is not mentioned in the pamphlet.

1914

Margaret Sanger coins the phrase *birth control* to refer to contraception.

Sanger publishes nine issues of the magazine *The Woman Rebel* to publicize birth control. Arrested on charges of obscenity and incitement to murder and riot, she flees to Europe.

Sanger publishes *Family Limitation*, the first pamphlet to provide concrete and reliable birth control information since the passage of the Comstock Act.

The Children's Bureau publishes its second advice pamphlet for mothers, *Infant Care*. Again, birth control is not mentioned.

1915

In Margaret Sanger's absence, the National Birth Control League forms to pursue the legalization of contraception.

Margaret Sanger receives contraceptive training in Dutch birth control clinics.

William Sanger, entrapped by Comstock, is prosecuted for violating the New York state law prohibiting the distribution of contraceptive information and devices.

Margaret Sanger returns from Europe to face trial.

Anthony Comstock dies.

1916

In February the charges stemming from Sanger's publication of *The Woman Rebel* are dropped.

In April Sanger begins a national speaking tour promoting birth control.

In October Sanger, Ethel Byrne, and Fannie Mindell open the first U.S. contraceptive clinic in the Brownsville section of Brooklyn. The clinic remains open for ten days, and 488 women are fitted with pessaries. Sanger, Byrne, and Mindell are arrested.

William Robinson, a Socialist physician, publishes *Birth Control or the Limitation of Offspring*, in which he elaborates on eugenic benefits of birth control.

1917

The National Birth Control League introduces the first open bill to repeal the New York State prohibition on contraception.

Sanger and Byrne are convicted for dispensing contraceptive devices in the Brownsville clinic. Mindell is convicted for distributing obscene information. Each serves a thirty-day prison sentence.

Sanger begins publishing the *Birth Control Review.*

1918
The New York Court of Appeals upholds Sanger's 1917 conviction for dispensing contraception. Judge Crane's decision widens the physicians' exemption in the law, allowing greater latitude in contraceptive prescription for the cure and prevention of disease.

1919
The U.S. Supreme Court refuses to hear Sanger's appeal of her 1917 conviction.

The National Birth Control League disbands.

Mary Ware Dennett forms the Voluntary Parenthood League to pursue repeal of the Federal Comstock Act.

1920
Mary Ware Dennett resigns from the editorial board of the *Birth Control Review* because of its militantly feminist tone.

At its organizing convention, The League of Women Voters refuses to include birth control on its agenda.

1921
In November Margaret Sanger sponsors the First American Birth Control Conference in New York. Just before the conference, Sanger formally establishes the American Birth Control League. Police arrest speakers at the Conference's closing event, a mass meeting held at Town Hall. The police claim to have acted at the request of the archbishop Patrick Hayes. Charges are later dropped, and the local precinct captain is held solely responsible after an investigation fails to reveal any formal proof of the archbishop's involvement. The event is rescheduled and occurrs without further incident.

The American Birth Control League rents rooms for a birth control clinic. However, Lydia DeVilbiss, the doctor hired to run the clinic, backs out, and the clinic does not open.

At the organizing convention of the National Woman's Party (formerly the Congressional Union), Alice Paul prevents the issue of birth control from being introduced on the convention floor.

Congress passes the Sheppard-Towner Act.

Congress passes an emergency Immigration Restriction Act.

1922
The American Birth Control League's application for a dispensary license to operate a birth control clinic is denied by the New York State Board of Charities.

W. E. B. Du Bois gives his public endorsement to birth control.

1923
In January the Birth Control Clinical Research Bureau opens in New York City. The clinic operates without a license. Dorothy Bocker is the physician in charge, and Hannah Stone is a volunteer.

In March Robert Dickinson establishes the Committee on Maternal Health.

The American Birth Control League meets with the National Woman's Party but fails to convince the Party's leaders to support birth control legislation.

1924
In January Robert Dickinson and George Kosmak conduct a surprise inspection of the Clinical Research Bureau, and Dickinson publishes a harsh criticism of its work.

Sangerists try unsuccessfully to introduce birth control as a study item in the League of Women Voters' Citizenship Committee. The Citizenship Committee decides to study a separate proposal for sterilization as a measure to reduce degeneracy among the citizenry.

The American Birth Control League makes its first attempt to introduce a doctors-only bill into Congress. This bill would exempt physicians from the Comstock Act and allow them to prescribe birth control for any reason.

Hannah Stone is forced to resign her hospital affiliation because of her work in the Clinical Research Bureau.

Congress passes a permanent Immigration Restriction Act.

1925
The American Birth Control League and the Committee on Maternal
Health agree to form a joint council, the Maternity Research Council,
to seek a dispensary license for the Clinical Research Bureau.

Hannah Stone becomes director of the Clinical Research Bureau.

The Clinical Research Bureau Board rejects "proper medical supervision" until a license is obtained.

The Bureau of Social Hygiene gives $10,000 to the Clinical Research
Bureau.

1926
The Maternity Research Council application for a dispensary license
is denied by the New York State Board of Charities.

The American Birth Control League tries unsuccessfully to introduce
birth control into the League of Women Voters' Child Welfare and
Social Hygiene Committees.

The Voluntary Parenthood League disbands.

1927
The Supreme Court decision in *Buck vs. Bell* condones compulsory
sterilization to prevent the spread of feeblemindedness. The Court
equates the procedure with compulsory vaccination.

The Committee on Maternal Health calls for the study of maternal
and infant mortality to determine if "child spacing" is a medically legitimate use of contraception.

Congress renews the Sheppard-Towner Act for two years.

1928
Hannah Stone publishes the first study of contraceptive effectiveness
based on Clinical Research Bureau patient records.

The American Birth Control League tries once again to introduce
birth control into the League of Women Voters' Child Welfare and
Social Hygiene Committees. Once again the proposal is rejected.

Sanger resigns from the American Birth Control League over differences with the acting president, Eleanor Jones. Sanger retains control over the Clinical Research Bureau.

Grace Abbott publicly reiterates that the Children's Bureau will take no part in birth control activities.

1929
On 15 April the Clinical Research Bureau is raided by New York City police. The raid causes an uproar in the medical community because physicians' files are seized. All charges are later dropped.

In October the Social Workers' Club of Harlem publicly endorses the Clinical Research Bureau's plan to open a branch clinic in Harlem.

In November the Clinical Research Bureau Board rejects Dickinson's plan to turn the Bureau into a hospital-affiliated, fee-for-service clinic.

Sanger agrees to lead the National Committee on Federal Legislation for Birth Control, which pursues doctors-only legislation in the Congress.

The American Birth Control League is accepted as a Kindred Group by the National Conference of Social Work.

Twenty-eight birth control clinics exist nationwide.

The Sheppard-Towner Act lapses.

1930
The Harlem Branch of the Clinical Research Bureau opens. The clinic is partially funded by the Rosenwald Fund.

The *Young's Rubber Co. vs. C. I. Lee and Co.* decision offers the first reinterpretation of the Comstock Act. The judge in the case suggests that obscenity is located in the intent of contraceptive users and not in the devices themselves.

1931
The Senate Judiciary Committee holds hearings on a doctors-only bill that the National Committee for Federal Legislation on Birth Control sponsors. The bill is defeated in Committee.

1932

The Harlem Branch Clinic is moved to the New York Urban League building, a more central location, and African-Americans are added to the clinic's staff.

The House Ways and Means Committee and Senate Judiciary Committee hold hearings on a doctors-only bill that is sponsored by the National Committee on Federal Legislation for Birth Control. Both proposals are defeated in Committee.

1933

Eleanor Jones proposes a merger of the American Birth Control League and the American Eugenics Society. The merger is rejected, but the two groups continue to work together closely.

In *Davis vs. United States* the court rules that conviction under the Comstock Act requires evidence of a defendant's intent to distribute contraception for immoral purposes.

1934

The Senate and House Judiciary Committees hold hearings on another National Committee for Federal Legislation–sponsored bill. The bill is squashed in the full Senate.

Eugenicist Raymond Pearl's research shows that the single greatest factor in the differential birth rate is knowledge of and access to birth control.

1935

In June the New York City Committee of Mothers' Health Centers takes over the Clinical Research Bureau's Harlem Branch.

The American Birth Control League begins a clinic certification program similar to that championed by Robert Dickinson.

1936

In *One Package of Japanese Pessaries*, a case brought by Sangerists, the U.S. Court of Appeals rules that medical prescription of contraception for the purpose of saving a life or promoting well-being is not a condemned purpose under the Comstock Act.

The American Medical Association Committee on Contraception issues a report indicting all contraception and the lay organizations that sponsor it.

1937
The American Medical Association Committee on Contraception reverses its 1936 statement and gives tentative endorsement to contraception.

The national organization of African-American physicians, the National Medical Association, endorses birth control with the stipulation that it be regulated and supervised by physicians.

1938
The Clinical Research Bureau's invitation to participate in the National Conference on Better Care for Mothers and Babies is revoked. The Conference is organized by the Children's Bureau.

The Children's Bureau releases a report revealing that 25–30 percent of maternal deaths occur as a direct result of illegal abortions.

Three hundred seventy-four birth control clinics exist throughout the country.

1939
In January the American Birth Control League and the Clinical Research Bureau reunite and become the Birth Control Federation of America. Sanger is elected honorary chairman of the Board. D. Kenneth Rose is appointed executive director.

The Birth Control Federation of America organizes a Division of Negro Service to coordinate efforts to provide contraceptive information and services to the African-American community. Sanger obtains a $20,000 grant from Albert Lasker for this work.

1940
In January Albert Lasker vetoes educational work in the Black South in favor of two southern white-run demonstration clinics.

In February the first Division of Negro Service demonstration clinic opens in the Bethlehem Center, a black settlement house, in Nashville, Tennessee.

In April the Division of Negro Service Rural Demonstration Project begins in Berkeley County, South Carolina.

In July a second Division of Negro Service clinic opens in Nashville at Fisk University.

First Lady Eleanor Roosevelt announces publicly that she does not oppose the planning of children.

Katherine Lenroot of the Children's Bureau gives begrudging support to the principle that states can use Federal maternal health funds for birth control clinics.

1941
In July Hannah Stone, medical director of the Clinical Research Bureau since 1924, dies suddenly of a heart attack.

In October the National Council of Negro Women becomes the first national women's organization officially to endorse the practice of contraception.

1942
The National Medical Association endorses the work of the Division of Negro Service.

The Birth Control Federation of America changes its name to the Planned Parenthood Federation of America.

The U.S. Public Health Service decides quietly to allow states to finance contraceptive clinics using funds from the 1939 Venereal Disease Control Act.

1943
Florence Rose is among the last Sangerists to resign from the Planned Parenthood Federation of America.

1945
More than eight hundred birth control clinics exist nationwide.

Works Cited

Archival Collections

Clarence James Gamble Papers, Francis Countway Library, Boston Massachusetts.

National Committee on Maternal Health Papers, Francis Countway Library, Boston, Massachusetts.

Planned Parenthood Federation of America Records, Sophia Smith Collection, Smith College, Northampton, Massachusetts.

Florence Rose Papers, Sophia Smith Collection, Smith College, Northampton, Massachusetts.

Margaret Sanger Papers, Library of Congress, Washington, D.C.

Margaret Sanger Papers, Sophia Smith Collection, Smith College, Northampton, Massachusetts.

Printed Primary and Secondary Sources

Specific citations to judicial decisions, newspaper articles, and all unsigned editorials in the *Birth Control Review* are given in the footnotes.

Abramowitz, Mimi. *Regulating the Lives of Women*. Boston: South End Press, 1988.

Alcoff, Linda. "Cultural Feminism versus Poststructuralism: The Identity Crisis in Feminist Theory." *Signs* 13 (Spring 1988): 405–36.

Alexander, W. G. "Birth Control for the Negro . . . A Fad or a Necessity." *Journal of the National Medical Association* 24 (August 1932): 34–39.

Allen, Garland. "Genetics, Eugenics, and Class Struggle." *Genetics* 79 (supplement, June 1975): 29–45.

——. *Life Sciences in the Twentieth Century*. New York: John Wiley and Sons, 1975.

Andersen, Kirsti. *Creation of the Democratic Majority, 1928–1936*. Chicago: University of Chicago Press, 1979.

Andersen, Margo. *The American Census*. New Haven: Yale University Press, 1988.

Antler, Joyce, and Daniel Fox. "The Movement toward a Safe Maternity:

Physician Accountability in New York City, 1915–1940." *Bulletin of the History of Medicine* 50 (1976): 569–95.

Arney, William. *Power and the Profession of Obstetrics.* Chicago: University of Chicago Press, 1982.

Baker, Paula. "The Domestication of Politics: Women and American Political Society, 1780–1920." *American Historical Review* 89 (June 1984): 620–47.

Beardsley, Edward. *A History of Neglect: Health Care for Blacks and Mill Workers in the Twentieth-Century South.* Knoxville: University of Tennessee Press, 1987.

Benson, Marguerite. "A Public Trust." *Birth Control Review,* N.S. 4 (September 1936): 1–2.

"Birth Selection vs. Birth Control: A Symposium of Comments on Dr. Osborn's Address." *Birth Control Review* 16 (October 1932): 231–5 and 252–4.

Borell, Merriley. "Biologists and the Promotion of Birth Control Research, 1918–1938." *Journal of the History of Biology* 20 (Spring 1987): 51–87.

Bousfield, M. O. "Reaching the Negro Community." *American Journal of Public Health* 24 (1934): 209–15.

Brandt, Allan. *No Magic Bullet.* New York: Oxford University Press, 1985.

Brickman, Jane Pacht. "Public Health, Midwives, and Nurses, 1880–1930." In *Nursing History: New Perspectives, New Possibilities,* ed. Ellen C. Lagemen, pp. 65–78. New York: Teachers College Press, 1983.

Brown, Dorothy M. *Setting a Course: American Women in the 1920s.* Boston: G. K. Hall, 1987.

Buhle, Mary Jo. *Women and American Socialism, 1870–1920.* Urbana: University of Illinois Press, 1983.

Carlson, Elof Axel. "R. L. Dugdale and the Jukes Family: A Historical Injustice Corrected." *BioScience* 30 (August 1980): 535–39.

Carter, Elmer. "Eugenics for the Negro." *Birth Control Review* 16 (June 1932): 169–70.

Center for Reproductive Law and Policy. "An Analysis of *Planned Parenthood v. Casey.*" *Reproductive Freedom in Focus.* New York, 1993.

——. *Reproductive Freedom News,* 5 and 19 February 1993.

Chesler, Ellen. *Woman of Valor: Margaret Sanger and the Birth Control Movement in America.* New York: Simon and Schuster, 1992.

Copelon, Rhoda. "What's Missing from the Abortion Debate." *Ms.* September–October 1992, pp. 86–87.

Costin, Lela. *Two Sisters for Social Justice: A Biography of Grace and Edith Abbott.* Urbana: University of Illinois Press, 1983.

Cott, Nancy. *The Grounding of Modern Feminism.* New Haven: Yale University Press, 1986.

——. "What's in a Name? The Limits of 'Social Feminism,' or, Expanding the Vocabulary of Women's History." *Journal of American History* 76 (December 1989): 809–29.

Cowan, Ruth Schwartz. "Francis Galton's Statistical Ideas: The Influence of Eugenics." *ISIS* 63 (1972): 509–28.

Curtis, James. "Dorothea Lange, Migrant Mother, and the Culture of the Great Depression." *Winterthur Portfolio* 21 (Spring 1986): 1–20.

Cutright, Phillips, and Edward Shorter. "The Effects of Health on the Completed Fertility of Non-White and White U.S. Women Born between 1867 and 1935." *Journal of Social History* 13 (1979): 191–97.

Davenport, Charles. *Heredity in Relation to Eugenics.* New York: Henry Holt, 1913.

Davis, Angela. *Women, Race, and Class.* New York: Random House, 1981.

Dawson, Deborah A., Denise J. Meny, and Jeanne Clare Ridley. "Fertility Control in the United States before the Contraceptive Revolution." *Family Planning Perspectives* 12 (March–April 1980): 76–86.

Debs, Eugene. "Freedom Is the Goal." *Birth Control Review* 2 (May 1918): 7.

Decotte, Ben E. "Six Arguments against Sangerism." *Catholic World* 5 (November 1940): 51–54.

Dennett, Mary Ware. *Birth Control Laws: Should We Keep Them, Change Them, or Abolish Them?* New York: Frederick Hitcock, 1926.

Diamond, Irene, ed. *Families, Politics, and Public Policy: A Feminist Dialogue on the State.* New York: Longman Press, 1983.

Dickinson, Robert L. "Contraception: A Medical Review of the Situation: First Report of the Committee on Maternal Health of New York." *American Journal of Obstetrics and Gynecology* 8 (November 1924): 583–605.

——. "Suggestions for a Program for American Gynecology." *Transactions of the American Gynecological Society* 45 (October 1920): 1–13.

Dienes, C. Thomas. *Law, Politics, and Birth Control.* Urbana: University of Illinois Press, 1972.

Dublin, Louis. "The Health of the Negro." In *The American Negro,* Annals of the American Academy of Political and Social Science, vol. 140 (November 1928): 77–85.

Du Bois, W. E. B. "Black Folk and Birth Control." *Birth Control Review* 15 (June 1932): 166–67.

——. "Opinion." *Crisis* 24 (1922): 247–53.

——. "Race Relations in the United States." In *The American Negro,* Annals of the American Academy of Political and Social Science, vol. 140 (November 1928): 6–10.

Dykeman, Wilma. *Too Many People, Too Little Love: Edna Rankin McKinnon, Pioneer for Birth Control.* New York: Holt, Rinehart, and Winston, 1974.

East, Edward M. *Mankind at the Crossroads.* New York: Charles Scribner's Sons, 1926.

Eastman, Crystal. "Birth Control in the Feminist Program." In *Crystal Eastman: On Woman and Revolution,* ed. Blanche Wiessen Cook, pp. 46–48. New York: Oxford University Press, 1978.

——. "Now We Can Begin." In *Crystal Eastman: On Woman and Revolution,* ed. Blanche Wiessen Cook, pp. 52–57. New York: Oxford University Press, 1978.

Eisenstein, Zillah. *Feminism and Sexual Equality: Crisis of Liberal America.* New York: Monthly Review Press, 1983.

Engerman, Stanley. "Changes in Black Fertility, 1880–1940." In *Family and Population in Nineteenth Century America,* ed. Tamara Haraven and Maris Vinovskis, pp. 126–53. Princeton: Princeton University Press, 1978.

Estabrook, Arthur. *The Jukes in* 1915. Carnegie Institute of Washington, 1916.

Farrall, Lyndsay. "Controversy and Conflict in Science: A Case Study of the English Biometric School and Mendel's Laws." *Social Studies of Science* 5 (1975): 269–301.

Femia, Joseph. *Gramsci's Political Thought.* London: Oxford University Press, 1981.

Ferebee, Dorothy. "Planned Parenthood as a Public Health Measure for the Negro Race." *Human Fertility* 7 (January 1942): 7–10.

Fisher, Constance. "The Negro Social Worker Evaluates Birth Control." *Birth Control Review* 16 (June 1932): 174–75.

Foucault, Michel. *History of Sexuality,* vol 1. New York: Vintage Books, 1980.

Fox, Daniel. *Health Policies, Health Politics.* Princeton: Princeton University Press, 1986.

Fraser, Laura. "After Roe v. Wade." *Mother Jones* (July–August 1992): 47–49.

Frazier, E. Franklin. "Birth Control for *More* Negro Babies." *Negro Digest* 3 (July 1945): 1–4.

——. "The Negro and Birth Control." *Birth Control Review* 17 (March 1933): 68–70.

——. "The Negro Family." In *The American Negro,* Annals of the American Academy of Political and Social Science, vol. 140 (November 1928): 44–51.

Fredrickson, George. *The Black Image in the White Mind.* Middletown: Wesleyan Press, 1971.

——. *White Supremacy.* New York: Oxford University Press, 1981.

Freedman, Estelle. "The New Woman: Changing Views of Women in the 1920s." In *Decades of Discontent: The Women's Movement, 1920–1940,* ed. Lois Scharf and Joan Jensen, pp. 21–44. Boston: Northeastern Press, 1987.

———. "Separation as Strategy: Female Institution Building and American Feminism, 1870–1930." *Feminist Studies* 5 (Fall 1979): 512–29.

Fullinwider, S. P. *The Mind and Mood of Black America.* Homewood, Ill.: Dorsey Press, 1969.

Galton, Francis. *Inquiries into Human Faculty.* New York: Macmillan, 1883.

Garrett, Elizabeth. "Birth Control's Business Baby." *New Republic* 77 (January 1934): 269–72.

Garvin, Charles H. "The Negro Doctor's Task." *Birth Control Review* 16 (November 1932): 269–70.

Gaulard, Joan. "Woman Rebel: The Rhetorical Strategies of Margaret Sanger and the American Birth Control Movement, 1912–1938." Ph.D. dissertation, Indiana University, 1978.

Giddings, Paula. *When and Where I Enter: The Impact of Black Women on Race and Sex in America.* New York: William Morrow, 1984.

Gilman, Charlotte Perkins. "Back of Birth Control." *Birth Control Review* 6 (March 1922): 31–33.

Glazer, Penina Migal, and Miriam Slater. *Unequal Colleagues: The Entrance of Women into the Professions, 1890–1940.* New Brunswick: Rutgers University Press, 1987.

Goddard, Henry Herbert. *The Kallikak Family: A Study in the Heredity of Feeblemindedness.* 1912. Reprint. New York: Macmillan, 1923.

Goldman, Emma. *Living My Life.* New York: Alfred Knopf, 1931.

Goldstein, David. *Suicide Bent: Sangerizing Mankind.* St. Paul: Radio Replies Press, 1945.

Gordon, Linda. "What's New in Women's History." In *Feminist Studies/Critical Studies,* ed. Teresa de Lauretis, pp. 20–39. Bloomington: Indiana University Press, 1986.

———. "Why Nineteenth-Century Feminists Did Not Support 'Birth Control' and Twentieth-Century Feminists Do: Feminism, Reproduction, and the Family." In *Rethinking the Family,* ed. Barrie Thorne, pp. 40–53. New York: Longman Press, 1982.

———. *Woman's Body, Woman's Right.* 1976. Revised ed. New York: Penguin, 1990.

———, ed. *Women, The State, and Welfare.* Madison: University of Wisconsin Press, 1990.

Gossett, Thomas. *Race: The History of an Idea.* New York: Schocken Books, 1965.

Gould, Stephen Jay. *The Mismeasure of Man.* New York: W. W. Norton, 1981.

Gramsci, Antonio. *Selections from the Prison Notebooks.* Ed. Quintin Hoare and Geoffrey Nowell Smith. New York: International Publishers, 1972.

Gray, Madeline. *Margaret Sanger.* New York: Richard Marek Publishers, 1979.

Works Cited

Grether, Judith. "Sterilization and Eugenics: An Examination of Early Twentieth-Century Population Control in the United States." Ph.D. dissertation, University of Oregon, 1980.

Grossberg, Lawrence. "History, Politics, and Postmodernism: Stuart Hall and Cultural Studies." *Journal of Communication Inquiry* 10 (Summer 1986): 61–77.

Haber, Samuel. *Efficiency and Uplift.* Chicago: University of Chicago Press, 1964.

Hall, Stuart. "Gramsci's Relevance for the Study of Race and Ethnicity." *Journal of Communication Inquiry* 10 (Summer 1986): 5–27.

——. "On Postmodernism and Articulation: An Interview with Stuart Hall (edited by Lawrence Grossberg)." *Journal of Communication Inquiry* 10 (Summer 1986):45–60.

——. "The Toad in the Garden: Thatcherism among the Theorists." In *Marxism and the Interpretation of Culture,* ed. Cary Nelson and Lawrence Grossberg, pp. 35–57. Chicago: University of Illinois Press, 1988.

Haller, Mark. *Eugenics: Hereditarian Attitudes in American Thought.* New Brunswick: Rutgers University Press, 1963.

Harley, Sharon. "For the Good of Family and Race." *Signs* 15 (Winter 1990): 336–49.

Hays, Samuel. "The Politics of Reform in Municipal Government in the Progressive Era." In *American Political History as Social Analysis,* ed. Samuel Hays, pp. 205–32. Knoxville: University of Tennessee Press, 1980.

Henry, William. "Beyond the Melting Pot." *Time Magazine,* 9 April 1990, pp. 28–31.

Henshaw, Stanley, and Jennifer Van Vort. "Abortion Services in the United States, 1987 and 1988." *Family Planning Perspectives* 22 (1990): 106.

——. "The Accessibility of Abortion Services in the United States." *Family Planning Perspectives* 23 (1991): 246–63.

Higham, John. *Strangers in the Land.* New Brunswick: Rutgers University Press, 1955.

Hill-Collins, Patricia. *Black Feminist Thought: Knowledge, Consciousness, and the Politics of Empowerment.* Boston: Unwin Hyman, 1990.

Hine, Darlene Clark. *Black Women in White.* Indianapolis: Indiana University Press, 1989.

Jamison, E. S. "The Future of Negro Health." *Birth Control Review,* N.S. 6 (May 1938): 94.

Jensen, Joan. "All Pink Sisters: The War Department and the Feminist Movement in the 1920s." In *Decades of Discontent: The Women's Movement, 1920–1940,* ed. Lois Scharf and Joan Jensen, pp. 199–222. Boston: Northeastern Press, 1987.

———. "The Evolution of Margaret Sanger's 'Family Limitation' Pamphlet, 1914–1921." *Signs* 6 (Spring 1981): 548–55.

Johnson, Charles S. "The Changing Economic Status of the Negro." In *The American Negro,* Annals of the American Academy of Political and Social Science, vol. 140 (November 1928): 128–38.

———. "A Question of Negro Health." *Birth Control Review* 16 (June 1932): 167–69.

Jones, Eleanor. "Birth Control in 1929." *Birth Control Review* 13 (January 1929): 227–43.

———. "First-Aid in Social Work." *Birth Control Review* 13 (August 1929): 217.

———. "A New Era in Social Service." *Birth Control Review* 16 (July–August 1932): 209.

Jones, James H. *Bad Blood: The Tuskegee Syphilis Experiment.* New York: Free Press, 1981.

Kellog, Peter. "Northern Liberals and Black America: A History of White Attitudes, 1936–1952." Ph.D. dissertation, Northwestern University, 1971.

Kennedy, Anne. "History of the Development of Contraceptive Materials in the U.S." *American Medicine* 41 (1935): 159–61.

Kennedy, David. *Birth Control in America: The Career of Margaret Sanger.* New Haven: Yale University Press, 1970.

Kevles, Daniel. *In the Name of Eugenics: Genetics and the Uses of Human Heredity.* Berkeley and Los Angeles: University of California Press, 1985.

Kirby, John. *Black Americans in the Roosevelt Era.* Knoxville: University of Tennessee Press, 1980.

Kiser, Clyde. "Fertility and Harlem Negroes." *Milbank Memorial Fund Quarterly* 13 (1935): 273–85.

Kolbert, Kathryn. "*Webster v. Reproductive Health Services*: Reproductive Freedom Hanging by a Thread." *Women's Rights Law Reporter* 11 (1989): 153–62.

Kopp, Marie. *Birth Control in Practice.* New York: Robert McBride, 1933.

Kozol, Wendy. "Madonnas of the Fields: Photography, Gender and the 1930s Farm Relief." *Genders* 2 (Summer 1988): 1–23.

Kraditor, Aileen. *The Ideas of the Woman Suffrage Movement, 1890–1920.* New York: W. W. Norton, 1981.

Ladd-Taylor, Molly. *Raising a Baby the Government Way.* New Brunswick: Rutgers University Press, 1986.

Lasch, Christopher. "Mary Ware Dennett." In *Notable American Women,* vol. 3, ed. Edward T. James and Janet Wilson James, pp. 463–65. Cambridge: Harvard University Press, 1971.

Laughlin, H. H. "Eugenists on the Place of Birth Control: The Two Aspects of Control." *Birth Control Review* 10 (January 1926): 7.

Works Cited

Leavitt, Judith Walzer. *Brought to Bed: Childbearing in America, 1750–1950.* New York: Oxford University Press, 1986.

Lemons, Stanley. *The Woman Citizen: Social Feminism in the 1920s.* Urbana: University of Illinois Press, 1975.

Lichtman, Allan. *Prejudice in the Old Politics.* Chapel Hill: University of North Carolina Press, 1979.

Lindemen, Edward. *Wealth and Culture: A Study of 100 Foundations and Community Trusts during the Decade 1921–1930.* New York: Harcourt, Brace, 1936.

Lipsitz, George. *A Life in the Struggle: Ivory Perry and the Culture of Opposition.* Philadelphia: Temple University Press, 1988.

Little, C. C. "Another View." *Birth Control Review* 10 (January 1926): 7–34.

——. "Unnatural Selection and Its Resulting Obligations." *Birth Control Review* 10 (August 1926): 243–57.

——. "Will Birth Control Promote Race Improvement?" *Birth Control Review* 13 (December 1929): 343–45.

Lorimer, Frank, and Frederick Osborn. *Dynamics of Population: Social and Biological Significance of the Changing Birth Rates in the U. S.* New York: Macmillan, 1934.

Lubove, Roy. *The Professional Altruist: The Emergence of Social Work as a Career, 1880–1930.* New York: Atheneum, 1977.

Ludmerer, Kenneth. *Genetics and American Society.* Baltimore: Johns Hopkins University Press, 1972.

Luker, Kristin. *Abortion and the Politics of Motherhood.* Berkeley and Los Angeles: University of California Press, 1984.

McAdam, Doug. *Political Process and the Development of Black Insurgency, 1930–1970.* Chicago: University of Chicago Press, 1982.

McFalls, Joseph, and George Masnick. "Birth Control and the Fertility of the U. S. Black Population, 1880 to 1980." *Journal of Family History* 6 (Spring 1981): 89–106.

McLaren, Angus. *Birth Control in Nineteenth-Century England.* New York: Holmes and Meier, 1978.

Malthus, Thomas. *An Essay on the Principles of Population.* New York: Ward Lock, 1890.

Manning, Kenneth. *Black Apollo of Science: The Life of Ernest Everett Just.* New York: Oxford University Press, 1983.

Matsner, Eric. "Contraceptives and the Consumer." *Consumers Defender,* December, 1935, pp. 9–10.

——. *The Technique of Contraception.* Baltimore: Williams and Wilkins, 1936.

Meckel, Richard. *Save the Babies: American Public Health Reform and the Prevention of Infant Mortality, 1850–1929.* Baltimore: Johns Hopkins University Press, 1990.

Michel, Sonya, and Robyn Rosen. "The Paradox of Maternalism: Elizabeth

Lowell Putnam and the American Welfare State." *Gender and History* 4 (Autumn 1992): 364–85.

Miller, Lawrence G. "Pain, Parturition, and the Profession: Twilight Sleep in America." In *Health Care in America,* ed. Susan Reverby and David Rosner, pp. 19–44. Philadelphia: Temple University Press, 1979.

Mink, Gwendolyn. "The Lady and the Tramp: Gender, Race, and the Origins of the American Welfare State." In *Women, the State, and Welfare,* ed. Linda Gordon, pp. 92–122. Madison: University of Wisconsin Press, 1990.

——. *Old Labor and New Immigrants in American Political Development: Union, Party, and State.* Ithaca: Cornell University Press, 1986.

——. *The Wages of Motherhood: Maternalist Social Policy and Women's Inequality in the Welfare State,* 1917–1942. Ithaca: Cornell University Press, forthcoming.

Moore, Ronald, and Gloria Moore. *Margaret Sanger and the Birth Control Movement: A Bibliography.* Metuchen, N.J.: Scarecrow Press, 1986.

Morantz-Sanchez, Regina. *Sympathy and Science: Women Physicians in American Medicine.* New York: Oxford University Press, 1985.

Muller, H. J. "The Dominance of Economics." *Birth Control Review* 16 (October 1932): 236–38.

Muncy, Robyn. *Creating a Female Dominion in American Reform, 1890–1935.* New York: Oxford University Press, 1991.

Nash, Carol. "Planned Families for New York Mothers: An Evaluation of Neighborhood Center Programs, 1930–1938." *Birth Control Review,* N.S. 6 (November 1938): 128–29.

New York Association for Improving the Condition of the Poor. *Health Work for Mothers and Children in a Colored Community.* New York, 1924.

Omi, Michael, and Howard Winant. *Racial Formation in the United States: From the 1960s to the 1980s.* New York: Routledge, 1986.

Osborn, Henry Fairchild. "Birth Selection versus Birth Control." *Science* 76 (August 1932): 174–79.

Osofsky, Gilbert. *Harlem: The Making of a Ghetto.* 2d ed. New York: Harper and Row, 1971.

Overton, John. "A Birth Control Service Among Urban Negroes." *Human Fertility* 7 (August 1942): 97–101.

Palmer, Rachel, and Sarah Greenberg. *Facts and Frauds in Woman's Hygiene.* New York: Garden City Publishing, 1938.

Pearl, Raymond. "Contraception and Fertility in 4,945 Married Women." *Human Biology* 6 (May 1934): 355–401.

——. "Contraception and Fertility in 2,000 Women." *Human Biology* 4 (1932): 306–407.

——. "The Differential Birth Rate." *Birth Control Review* 9 (October 1925): 278–300.

——. "Second Progress Report on Family Limitation." *Milbank Memorial Fund Quarterly* 11 (July 1934): 248–69.

Petchesky, Rosalind. "Abortion Politics in the '90s: Giving Women a Real Choice." *The Nation,* 28 May 1990, pp. 732–36.

——. *Abortion and Woman's Choice.* Boston: Northeastern University Press, 1985.

Polenberg, Richard. "The Decline of the New Deal, 1937–1940." In *The New Deal,* vol. 1, ed. John Braeman et al., pp. 246–66. Columbus: Ohio State University Press, 1975.

Popenoe, Paul. "Birth Control and Eugenics." *Birth Control Review* 1 (March 1917): 6.

——. *Conservation of the Family.* Baltimore: Williams and Wilkins, 1926.

Porritt, Annie. "An Opponent of Birth Control." *Birth Control Review* 10 (December 1926): 375–76.

Ray, Joyce, and F. G. Gosling. "American Physicians and Birth Control, 1936–1947." *Journal of Social History* 18 (1985): 399–411.

Reed, James. *The Birth Control Movement and American Society: From Private Vice to Public Virtue.* Princeton: Princeton University Press, 1983.

——. "Doctors, Birth Control, and Social Values: 1830–1970." In *The Therapeutic Revolution,* ed. Morris J. Vogel and Charles E. Rosenberg, pp. 109–33. Philadelphia: University of Pennsylvania Press, 1979.

"Report of Reference Committee on Executive Session." *Journal of the American Medical Association* 106 (1936): 1910–12.

"Report of Reference Committee on Executive Session." *Journal of the American Medical Association* 108 (1937): 2217–18.

Roberts, Carl. "The Birthright of the Unborn." *Birth Control Review,* n.s. 6 (May 1938): 87–89.

Robinson, Caroline Hadley. *Seventy Birth Control Clinics.* Baltimore: Williams and Wilkins, 1930.

Robinson, William. *Birth Control or the Limitation of Offspring.* 1916. Reprint. New York: Eugenics Publishing, 1926.

Robinson, Winnafred Corwin. "One Way to Run." *Birth Control Review* 4 (May 1920): 13.

Rodgers, Daniel T. "In Search of Progressivism." *Reviews in American History* 10 (December 1982): 113–32.

Rodrique, Jessie. "The Black Community and the Birth Control Movement." In *Unequal Sisters,* ed. Carol DuBois and Vicki Ruiz, pp. 333–44. New York: Routledge, 1990.

Roosevelt, Theodore. *The Foe of Our Own Household.* New York: George Doran, 1917.

——. "Race Decadence." *Outlook,* 8 April 1911, pp. 763–68.

Sadik, Nafis. *The State of World Population 1990.* New York: United Nations Population Fund, 1990.

Works Cited

Sanger, Margaret. "An Answer to Mr. Roosevelt." *Birth Control Review* 1 (December 1917): 13.

——. "Birth Control and Racial Betterment." *Birth Control Review* 3 (February 1919): 11–12.

——. "Contraception: A Medical Review of the Situation." Book reviews, *Birth Control Review* 9 (January 1925): 20–21.

——. "Editorial." *Birth Control Review* 9 (March 1925): 67–68.

——. "The Eugenic Value of Birth Control Propaganda." *Birth Control Review* 5 (October 1921): 5.

——. *Margaret Sanger: An Autobiography.* New York: W. W. Norton, 1938.

——. *My Fight for Birth Control.* New York: Farrar and Rinehart, 1931.

——. "National Security and Birth Control." *The Forum* 93 (March 1930): 139–41.

——. "An Open Letter to Social Workers." *Birth Control Review* 17 (June 1933): 140–41.

——. *Pivot of Civilization.* New York: Brentano's, 1922.

——. "Shall We Break this Law?" *Birth Control Review* 1 (February 1917): 4.

——. *Woman and the New Race.* New York: Brentano's, 1920.

Sassoon, Anne Showstack, ed. *Approaches to Gramsci.* London: Writers and Readers Publishing Cooperative, 1982.

Schuyler, George. "Quantity or Quality." *Birth Control Review* 16 (June 1932): 165–66.

Schwarz, Judith. *Radical Feminists of Heterodoxy: Greenwich Village 1912–1940.* Revised ed. Norwich, Vt.: New Victoria Publishers, 1986.

Seibels, Robert. "A Rural Project in Negro Maternal Health." *Human Fertility* 6 (1941): 42–44.

Sewell, Lemuel. "The Negro Wants Birth Control." *Birth Control Review* 17 (May 1933): 131.

Sims, Newell. "Hostages to the White Man." *Birth Control Review* 16 (July–August 1932): 214–15.

Sklar, Kathryn Kish. "Hull House in the 1890s: A Community of Women Reformers." *Signs* 10 (Summer 1985): 658–77.

Smith, Helena Huntington. "Wasting Women's Lives." *New Republic* 78 (28 March 1934): 178–80.

Starr, Paul. *Social Transformation in American Medicine.* New York: Basic Books, 1982.

Stix, Regine. "Effectiveness of Birth Control: A Second Study." *Milbank Memorial Fund Quarterly* 13 (April 1935): 162–78.

——. "A Study of Pregnancy Wastage." *Milbank Memorial Fund Quarterly* 13 (1935): 357.

——, and Frank Notestein. "Effectiveness of Birth Control." *Milbank Memorial Fund Quarterly* 12 (January 1934): 57–68.

Works Cited

Stoddard, Lothrap. *The Rising Tide of Color against World White Supremacy.* New York: Scribner's, 1920.

Stone, Hannah. "Therapeutic Contraception." *Medical Journal and Record,* 21 March 1928, pp. 1–18.

"Summary and Recommendations of Report of Planned Parenthood Clinics by the Committee on Public Health Relations of the New York Academy of Medicine." *Bulletin of the New York Academy of Medicine* 22 (1946): 553–56.

Taussig, Fred. *Abortion: Spontaneous and Induced.* St. Louis: C. Y. Mosby, 1936.

Trimberger, Ellen Kay. "Feminism, Men, and Love: Greenwich Village, 1900–1925." In *Powers of Desire: The Politics of Sexuality,* ed. Ann Snitow et. al, pp. 131–52. New York: Monthly Review Press, 1983.

Tuttle, Florence. "Suffrage and Birth Control." *Birth Control Review* 5 (March 1921): 6.

Valenza, Charles. "Was Margaret Sanger a Racist?" *Family Planning Perspectives* 17 (January–February 1985): 44–46.

Vreeland, Francis. "The Process of Reform with Especial Reference to Reform Groups in the Field of Population." Ph.D. dissertation, University of Michigan, 1929.

Ware, Susan. *Beyond Suffrage: Women in the New Deal.* Cambridge: Harvard University Press, 1981.

Weiss, Nancy. *The National Urban League, 1910–1940.* New York: Oxford University Press, 1974.

"What Women Voters Want." *The Woman Citizen* 8 (May 1924): 10–11.

Wiebe, Robert. *The Search for Order, 1880–1920.* Westport, Conn.: Greenwood Press, 1967.

Wolters, Raymond. *Negroes and the Great Depression.* Westport, Conn.: Greenwood Press, 1970.

Index